BEHOLD
MY
SERVANT

The Servant Songs of Isaiah

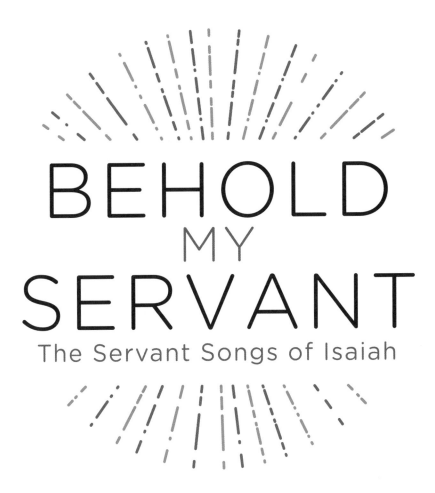

BEHOLD
MY
SERVANT
The Servant Songs of Isaiah

BRIAN A. RUSSELL

CHRISTIAN
FOCUS

To
the elect lady and her children
whom I love in truth

Copyright © Grace Publications Trust 2017

paperback ISBN 978-1-78191-890-6
epub ISBN 978-1-52710-009-1
mobi ISBN 978-1-52710-010-7

Published in 2017
by
Christian Focus Publications Ltd,
Geanies House, Fearn, Ross-shire,
IV20 1TW, Scotland, UK.
www.christianfocus.com

and
Grace Publications Trust
7 Arlington Way
London, EC1R 1XA, England
www.gracepublications.co.uk

Cover design by Daniel van Straaten

Printed and bound by Bell and Bain Ltd, Glasgow

CONTENTS

Acknowledgements

I would like to express my sincere thanks and appreciation to:

Grace Publications Trust for not only publishing five of my books, but also helping to distribute them through Grace Baptist Mission to pastors and Bible College students in Third World countries. It is a ministry very dear to my heart.

Their managing editors, M.J. Adams and D. Crisp, for their valuable assistance in preparing the manuscript for publication.

My wife Muriel, who shares in my ministry by doing all the computer work and helping with the proof-reading. 'He who finds a wife finds a good thing, and obtains favour from the Lord' (Prov. 18:22).

Introduction

The prophecy of Isaiah divides naturally into two main parts. The first part consists of the first thirty-nine chapters and covers the history of the southern kingdom of Judah during the reigns of Uzziah, Jotham, Ahaz and Hezekiah (1:1), from about 739 to 686 BC. Although it contains predictions of the virgin birth of Christ and the Messiah King who shall reign forever on earth (7:14; 9:6-7), the central theme of this section is that of judgment. It predicts the destruction of Babylon, Assyria, Philistia, Moab, Egypt, Tyre and even Judah's captivity in Babylon (14:23-32; 16:1-14; 19:1-17; 23:1-18; 39:1-8).

Part two (chapters 40-66) looks beyond the captivity of God's people to the future plans that God has in store for them, and indeed for the whole earth (40:1-5, 10, 11; 44:21-28; 45:22-25; 51:11; 54:10, 17; 56:8; 65:17-19; 66:22-24). These last twenty-seven chapters are full of the comfort of God's salvation – extended not just to Jews, but also to Gentiles who will enjoy His presence and blessing for ever in a recreated heaven and earth.

Now, one of the most striking characteristics of this second part of the Book of Isaiah is the collection of what are usually called *The Servant Songs*. They are so named because they are poems featuring a fascinating, if shadowy, person simply entitled 'My Servant', with the subject of the pronoun being the 'LORD' (i.e. Jehovah). The term 'servant' occurs twenty times in chapters 40-53 in the singular, where it refers to the prophet once (44:26); to the nation of Israel eleven times outside the Servant Songs (41:8-9; 42:19; 43:10; 44:1, 2, 21; 45:4; 48:20); and eight times to the Person in the Servant Songs (42:1; 49:3, 5, 6, 7; 50:10; 52:13; 53:11). Although there is no evidence that they were ever sung, for over a hundred years these four passages have been designated Servant Songs: 42:1-9; 49:1-7; 50:4-9 and 52:13–53:12.[1]

Biblical scholars have long debated the identity of the Servant, but most are agreed that whatever immediate reference these verses may have had for Isaiah's contemporaries and later generations of Jews after the captivity in Babylon, the perfect fulfilment of them is to be found in Jesus of Nazareth. Not only did our Lord regard Himself as fulfilling the role of the Servant of the LORD, but the accomplishments of the Servant in these songs are and could only be true of the life and work of Jesus Christ recorded in the New Testament.

Jesus saw Himself as the Servant in Isaiah's songs

It was with reference to the character and mission of the Servant that our Lord understood the nature and scope of His Messiahship. He disowned the popular view of His contemporaries who thought that the Messiah would deliver Israel from all her political enemies, particularly the Romans, by military prowess, and rule the world as David's heir from Jerusalem. Instead, He would, as Isaiah foresaw, defeat the enemies of God's people by offering His life as a ransom for theirs; by paying the price to redeem them from the slavery of sin and death and eternal punishment in hell.

It is very significant that this is precisely how our Lord answered James and John, the sons of Zebedee, when, at the urging of their mother, they said to Him, 'Grant us that we may sit, one on Your right hand and the other on Your left, in Your glory.' They wanted authority and power to rule and have others to serve them, and probably did not at this time understand Christ's answer: 'You do not know what you ask. Can you drink the cup that I drink, and be baptized with the baptism that I am baptized with?' The word 'cup' is often a biblical expression for the lot that God apportions us in life, and the word 'baptize' was often used to describe someone submerged in debt. So what Jesus was asking them was: 'Can you bear the suffering that God has allotted to Me if I am to rule the world? Can you face being submerged in hatred, pain, death and damnation, as I must be if I am to be the Saviour of the world?'

---

1. Allan Harman, *Isaiah*, (Christian Focus, 2005), p. 283.

Our Lord saw Himself as the suffering Servant in Isaiah's songs and thus went on to issue this definitive statement to them: 'For even the Son of Man [who, in Daniel 7, is given glory and a kingdom that all peoples should serve Him] did not come to be served, but to serve, and to give His life a ransom for many' (Mark 10:37-39, 45; Matt. 20:20-21; Dan. 7:13-14).

The emphasis is on the words, 'to serve' and 'to give'. The Son of God and the Son of Man came not to be served, but to serve. Although He was Lord of all, whom angels worshipped, He spent His life in service. He said, 'My food is to do the will of Him who sent Me, and to finish His work'; and again, 'I have come down from heaven, not to do My own will, but the will of Him who sent Me' (John 4:34; 6:38). He healed the sick, helped the needy and comforted the sad. In the streets and on the hills of Palestine He preached the good news of the kingdom of God and salvation. But above all, He gave His back to the smiters, His cheeks to those who plucked out the beard, His face to spitting, and His soul as an offering for sin (Isa. 50:6; 53:10; Matt. 26:67; John 19:1). Christ's penal substitutionary death on the cross at Calvary was the price He was willing to pay to ransom 'many' from the slave market of sin.

On the eve of His crucifixion, at the Last Supper, our Lord makes two further statements claiming the role of the Servant as His own. When He gave the cup of wine to His disciples to drink, He said, 'Drink of it, all of you, for this is my blood of the covenant, which is poured out for many for the forgiveness of sins' (Matt. 26:27-28, esv). The 'covenant' our Lord refers to here is not only the 'new covenant' prophesied in Jeremiah 31:31, but also to the 'covenant' of the Servant mentioned in Isaiah 42:6 and 49:8. Moreover, the words 'my blood ... which is poured out for many for the forgiveness of sins' speak of the Servant who 'poured out His soul unto death ... and He bore the sin of many' (53:12).

The second statement alluding to the Servant that Jesus made that night, is recorded in Luke 22:37, 'For I say to you that this which is written must be accomplished in Me: "And He was numbered with the transgressors". For the things concerning Me have an end' [or fulfilment, ESV]. He was quoting from Isaiah 53:12 and claiming its fulfilment in His atoning death on the cross when He would be crucified between two thieves as a criminal bearing the sin of many. As on an earlier occasion, He used the word 'must': 'From that time Jesus began to show to His disciples that He must go to Jerusalem, and suffer many things from the elders and chief priests and scribes, and be killed, and be raised again the third day' (Matt. 16:21; Mark 8:31; Luke 9:22; 17:25). Why did our Lord say 'must'? He told His disciples that it was necessary because 'all things that are written by the prophets concerning the Son of Man will be accomplished' (Luke 18:31). And in Luke 22:37 Jesus pinpoints Isaiah as one of those prophets, and in particular his Fourth Servant Song (53:12).

Clearly, then, Jesus saw Himself as the Servant in Isaiah's songs. To quote Henri Blocher, 'In them our Saviour found the blueprint of His mission. From them Jesus learned that He would have to suffer for us; that He would die for us, as though He were a criminal, under the weight of our sins. How holy the ground we tread when studying the songs! How unspeakably moving it is to imagine Jesus meditating upon those passages, and knowing that this was the Father's will and way for Him; that this Servant was none other than Himself.'[2]

The Apostles confirmed Jesus as the Servant in Isaiah's songs

This is not surprising, as their Master and Teacher had identified Himself as the Servant prophesied in Isaiah's well-known Servant Songs, which were so perplexing to Jewish scholars both before and after Christ. Moreover, as He promised, Jesus sent them the Holy Spirit at Pentecost to 'teach you all things, and bring to your remembrance all things that I said to you' (John 14:26; 16:5-14).

Although Mark and Luke make no reference to the connection between Jesus and Jehovah's Servant in Isaiah (except for the teaching of Jesus that they record), Matthew, in his Gospel, makes two specific references to prophecies in the Servant Songs which were

---

2. Henri Blocher, *Songs of the Servant*, (Regent College Publishing, 2005), pp. 17-18.

fulfilled in our Lord's ministry. The first occurs in Matthew 8:16-17, 'When evening had come, they brought to Him many who were demon-possessed. And He cast out the spirits with a word, and healed all who were sick, that it might be fulfilled which was spoken by Isaiah the prophet, saying: "He Himself took our infirmities and bore our sicknesses."' It is a direct quotation from Isaiah 53:4, 'Surely He has borne our griefs [or pains] and carried our sorrows [or sickness].'

Matthew is saying that Jesus fulfilled this prophecy about the Servant in two ways. He fulfilled it first of all by sympathizing with those He met who were suffering pain and sickness, part of the curse of sin upon the world. Moreover, His sympathy was practical. He healed all who came to Him (Matt. 4:23; 8:16; 9:35; Mark 1:34, and so on). But in the second place, Jesus chiefly 'bore our pains and carried our sickness' by bearing the curse of sin and death through His vicarious suffering for sinners on the cross. William Hendriksen says, 'Our physical afflictions must never be separated from that without which they never would have occurred, namely, our sins. Note how very closely the Isaiah 53:4-5 context connects these two; for verse 4, "Surely our diseases He has borne" ... is immediately followed by: "He was wounded for our transgressions; He was bruised for our iniquities."'[3] Sickness, physical and spiritual, will plague us until it is finally remedied by the return of Jesus Christ at the end of the age, when there 'shall be no more death, nor sorrow, nor crying; and there shall be no more pain' (Rev. 21:4), when the curse itself will have been overthrown (Rev. 22:3).

The second quotation is in Matthew 12:14-21 where the apostle quotes Isaiah 42:1-4 in support of Christ's avoidance of ill-timed publicity or premature confrontation which would only speed up the efforts of the Jewish leaders to destroy Him before His ministry was completed. 'But the Pharisees went out and conspired against Him, how to destroy Him. Jesus, aware of this, withdrew from there. And many followed Him, and He healed them all and ordered them not to make Him known. This was to fulfil what was spoken by

---

3. William Hendriksen, *The Gospel of Matthew*, (Baker, 1992), p. 401.

the prophet Isaiah: "Behold, my servant whom I have chosen, my beloved with whom my soul is well pleased. I will put my Spirit upon him and he will proclaim justice to the Gentiles. He will not quarrel or cry aloud, nor will anyone hear his voice in the streets; a bruised reed he will not break, and a smouldering wick he will not quench, until he brings justice to victory; and in his name the Gentiles will hope'" (ESV).

Luke, indeed, does record the Spirit-inspired testimony of Simeon, a godly old man in Jerusalem who had been 'waiting' for the coming of the Messiah and been given the assurance by God that 'he would not see death before he had seen the Lord's Christ.' When Joseph and Mary brought the baby Jesus to the temple, Simeon identified the Christ Child with Isaiah's Servant when he held Jesus in his arms and said, 'Lord, ... my eyes have seen Your salvation which You have prepared before the face of all peoples, a light to bring revelation to the Gentiles' (Luke 2:25-32). This is the very task Jehovah has commissioned His Servant to do: 'I the LORD ... will keep You and give You ... as a light to the Gentiles'; and again, 'I will also give You as a light to the Gentiles' (Isa. 42:6; 49:6).

The apostle John also bears witness to this truth when he says that Jesus Christ is 'the true Light which gives light to every man who comes into the world', and records our Lord's claim to be 'the light of the world' (John 1:9; 8:12; 12:46). In addition, the apostle records the testimony of John the Baptist, who when he saw Jesus, said, 'Behold! The Lamb of God who takes away the sin of the world', a clear allusion to Isaiah 53:7-8. Another allusion to Jesus as the Servant of Jehovah is found in John 12:37-38, 'But although He had done so many signs before them, they did not believe in Him, that the word of Isaiah the prophet might be fulfilled which he spoke: "Lord, who has believed our report? And to whom has the arm of the LORD been revealed"', quoting the fourth song (53:1).

In the Acts of the Apostles, Peter calls Jesus 'God's Servant' four times (Acts 3:13, 26; 4:27, 30). Later, in his first letter, Peter makes the identification more explicit by declaring God's Son to be the suffering Servant of Isaiah 53. Encouraging Christian servants to be submissive even to harsh masters, the apostle says:

For what credit is it if, when you are beaten for your faults, you take it patiently? But when you do good and suffer for it, if you take it patiently, this is commendable before God. For to this you were called, because Christ also suffered for us, leaving us an example, that you should follow His steps: "Who committed no sin, nor was guile found in His mouth [53:9]; who, when He was reviled, did not revile in return; when He suffered, He did not threaten [53:7], but committed Himself to Him who judges righteously; who Himself bore our sins in His own body on the tree [53:11], that we, having died to sins, might live for righteousness – by whose stripes you were healed [53:5]. For you were like sheep going astray [53:6], but have now returned to the Shepherd and Overseer of your souls" (1 Peter 2:20-25).

The apostle Paul also identifies our Lord Jesus Christ with the Servant in the songs of Isaiah. In Acts 13:46-47, he justifies the preaching of the gospel of salvation through Christ to the Gentiles on the basis of Isaiah 49:6, saying:

It was necessary that the word of God should be spoken to you [Jews] first; but since you reject it, and judge yourselves unworthy of everlasting life, behold, we turn to the Gentiles. For so the Lord has commanded us: 'I have set You [the Servant] to be a light to the Gentiles, that You should be for salvation to the ends of the earth.'

In Romans 10:16, Paul quotes from Isaiah 53:1 to show that the Servant knew that not all who heard the gospel would 'obey the gospel', and that is why He sorrowfully put the question to Jehovah: 'Lord, who has believed our report?' And again in Romans 15:20-21 the apostle vindicates his preaching to the Gentiles by using the words of Jehovah in Isaiah 52:15, 'But as it is written, "Those who have never been told of him will see, and those who have never heard will understand"' (ESV).

Although Luke was not an apostle, he was inspired by the Holy Spirit to write two books of the New Testament: the third Gospel and the Acts of the Apostles. Furthermore, what he wrote in both those books was infallibly true and 'profitable for doctrine' (2 Tim. 3:16). With regard to the doctrine that Jesus of Nazareth is the Messianic Servant in Isaiah 53, Luke records the evangelist Philip's witness to the Ethiopian eunuch on the road from Jerusalem to Gaza. The eunuch was reading from Isaiah 53 the words of verses 7 and 8: 'He was led as a sheep to the slaughter; and like a lamb silent before its shearer, so He opened not His mouth. In His humiliation His justice was taken away. And who will declare His generation? For His life is taken from the earth.' Needing guidance, he said to Philip, '"I ask you, of whom does the prophet say this, of himself or of some other man?" Then Philip opened his mouth, and beginning at this Scripture, preached Jesus to him' (Acts 8:32-35).

Philip's conviction that Jesus is the Servant depicted in Isaiah 53 clearly reflects the belief of the early Christian church. They did not see Cyrus as the Servant of Jehovah, for the simple reason that though God used him to return His people to their homeland, he was not a believer. Of Cyrus, the Lord says, 'I have named you, though you have not known Me' (Isa. 45:4). Nor did the early Christians think that the nation of Israel is the Servant in Isaiah's four songs. Although ethnic Israel is indeed called God's servant eleven times (41:8-9; 42:19; 43:10; 44:1, 2, 21; 45:4; 48:20), she is *not* the Servant in whom God 'delights' (42:1). Israel is a blind and deaf servant (42:18-20); the messianic Servant listens to God every morning and is not rebellious (50:4-5). Israel is a servant who has been justly punished for her disobedience and sin (40:2; 42:21-25); the Servant of Isaiah 53 is sinless, 'and the LORD has laid on Him the iniquity of us all' (vv. 6, 8, 9, 11). There can be no mistaking of the one for the other. To do so would be to misread chapters 40 to 53.

As we have seen, the teaching of Jesus Himself and His apostles clearly identifies our Lord and Saviour, the God-man, with the sinless, suffering Servant of the songs of Isaiah, who dies as an offering for the sins of God's people. Indeed, these four songs or poems of Isaiah are probably the clearest and most complete picture of Messiah/Christ in the Old Testament, especially chapter 53. Jonathan Edwards notes, 'The main business of the prophets was to point out Christ and His redemption ... Some of them are very particular and full in their predictions of these things, and above all the prophet Isaiah, who is therefore deservedly called the evangelical prophet. He seems to teach the glorious doctrines of the gospel almost as plainly as the apostles did ... How plainly and fully does the prophet Isaiah describe the manner and circumstances, the nature and end, of the sufferings and sacrifice of Christ, in the 53rd chapter of his prophecy! There is scarce a chapter in the New Testament itself which is more full of it.'[4]

The context of the Servant Songs

The biblical, historical and theological context of Isaiah's four Servant Songs is universal idol worship as outlined in chapters 40 and 41. All the nations in the world, even Israel, were guilty of idolatry. In 722 BC the ten tribes of the Northern Kingdom of Israel were carried into captivity by the Assyrians, for their worship of the gold calves at Dan and Bethel, as well as worshipping Baal and other gods from the surrounding nations (1 Kings 12:25-33; 2 Kings 17:7-23). One hundred or so years later, between 608 and 586 BC, the Southern Kingdom of Judah went into captivity into Babylon for the same reason (2 Kings 24:17-20; Jer. 2:4-13).

In Isaiah 40 God begins by showing His people, the Jews, the irrationality and absurdity of worshipping idols:

> To whom then will you liken God? Or what likeness will you compare to Him? The workman moulds a graven image, the goldsmith overspreads it with gold, and the silversmith casts silver chains. Whoever is too impoverished for such a contribution chooses a tree that will not rot; he seeks for himself a skilful workman to prepare a carved image that will not totter.
>
> Have you not known? Have you not heard? Has it not been told you from the beginning? Have you not understood from

---

4. Jonathan Edwards, *The Works of Jonathan Edwards* (Banner of Truth, 1974), vol. 1, p. 560.

the foundation of the earth? It is He who sits above the circle of the earth, and its inhabitants are like grasshoppers, who stretches out the heavens like a curtain, and spreads them out like a tent to dwell in. He brings the princes to nothing; He makes the judges of the earth useless [He is the only true God].

Scarcely shall they [the idols] be planted, scarcely shall they be sown, scarcely shall their stock take root in the earth, when He will blow on them, and they will wither, and the whirlwind will take them away like stubble.

'To whom then will you liken Me, or to whom shall I be equal?' says the Holy One. Lift up your eyes on high, and see who has created these things, who brings out their host by number; He calls them all by name, by the greatness of His might and the strength of His power; not one is missing.

Why do you say, O Jacob, and speak, O Israel: 'My way is hidden from the Lord, and my just claim is passed over by my God'? (vv. 18-27).

Isaiah is prophesying to the Jews who will be taken captive to Babylon because of their idolatry. Instead of being humble and repentant, their mood is one of defiant, proud unbelief. They accuse God of failing to deal fairly with them; of disregarding their just rights as His covenant people to be protected and delivered from their oppressors. The verbs are in the present tense. This is what they 'keep saying' and 'keep speaking'. Sin blinds (42:7), and there is no greater sin than idolatry, as we shall see below.

God's answer to the complaint of Israel that He was doing nothing to uphold 'justice' in the world, is to summon all the nations of the world to appear before Him in a court of law to prove who controls the world – Jehovah or the idol gods? Chapter 41 begins:

Be silent before me, you islands [distant lands]! Let the nations renew their strength [muster all their resources]! Let them come forward and speak; let us meet together at the place of judgment (NIV).

As the nations listen in silence, God makes His case first:

> Who stirred up one from the east [Cyrus] whom victory meets at every step? He [God] gives up nations before him, so that he tramples kings underfoot; he makes them like dust with his sword, like driven stubble with his bow. He pursues them and passes on safely by paths his feet have not trod. Who has performed and done this, calling the generations from the beginning [into existence and into doing His will]? I, the LORD, the first, and with the last; I am he (41:2-4, ESV).

God answers the two questions ('Who stirred up?' and, 'Who has performed and done this?') by claiming, 'I am He.' Things do not happen in the world by chance. God is behind everything. History is not a cyclical recurrence of events, but a progression of events which God is directing toward a final and perfect consummation. Cyrus, the future founder of the great Persian empire, is the example God gives of His sovereign control of what happens on earth, for God is predicting here the 'stirring up' of Cyrus to do His bidding, at least 150 years beforehand. Although Cyrus is not named in this passage, he is named in chapter 44:28, 'Who says of Cyrus, "He is My shepherd, and he shall perform all My pleasure, even saying to Jerusalem, 'You shall be built,' and to the temple, 'Your foundation shall be laid"' (see also 45:1-7). Most modern commentators agree that 'the one from the east' is Cyrus (v. 2).

Prophecy, which is the prediction of events well before they happen, is proof positive of God's sovereignty over this world. Only God can predict the future, because He alone knows the future. And He alone knows the future, because every detail of it has been predetermined by Him. As the *Westminster Confession of Faith* says, 'God from all eternity did, by the most wise and holy counsel of His own will, feely and unchangeably ordain whatsoever comes to pass' (III.1). In eternity past nothing forced God into making any of His plans, and all of them will be carried out to the end as He has willed (Isa. 46:10;

Eph. 1:11). This is what God means when He says, 'I, the LORD, am the first; and with the last; I am He' (v. 4). God is 'the first', since, as Creator, He was there before He brought anything into being. He was the first cause. Moreover, God will remain in control of everything that happens until the 'last' event of history transpires.

What, then, will happen when God stirs up Cyrus to conquer the world? In chapter 41:5-7, Isaiah describes the reaction of the idol-worshipping nations. Although they will be reduced to fear and trembling, they will not seek after the true and living God. Instead, they will draw near to each other and their idols for support. God's people, Israel, on the other hand, can be assured of His help: 'Fear not, for I am with you; be not dismayed for I am your God. I will strengthen you, yes, I will help you. I will uphold you with My righteous right hand. Behold, all those who were incensed against you shall be ashamed and disgraced; they shall be as nothing, and those who strive with you shall perish ...' (vv. 8-16).

But God will not only protect Israel from her enemies, He will provide for all her physical needs. He says, in figurative language, 'When the poor and needy seek water, and there is none ... I will make the wilderness a pool of water, and the dry land springs of water. I will plant in the wilderness the cedar and the acacia tree, the myrtle and the oil tree ...' (41:17-19). And what is the purpose of this outpouring of blessing upon His covenant people? It is to glorify God by showing the world that the Sovereign Creator of the universe is the only true God, who is to be trusted and loved: 'That they may see and know, and consider and understand together, that the hand of the LORD has done this, and the Holy One of Israel has created it' (v. 20). In other words, that all may know that God has stirred up Cyrus to 'thresh the mountains' (vv. 15-16), so that the 'worm Jacob' can return home.

The enquiry continues in verses 21-29. The argument here is that the idol-gods cannot predict the future or do anything to determine its course. It is directed at all idol-worshippers, including the idol-aters in Israel.

> 'Present your case,' the LORD says. 'Bring forward your strong arguments,' the King of Jacob says. Let them bring forth and

declare to us [God and His people] what is going to take place; as for the former events [past predictions made in the name of the idol-gods], declare what they were, that we may consider them, and know their outcome [whether they came true or not]; or announce to us what is coming. Declare the things that are going to come afterward, that we may know that you are gods; indeed, do good or evil [do anything to show you have life and power], that we may anxiously look about us and fear together. *Behold*, you are of no account, and your work amounts to nothing; he who chooses you is an abomination (vv. 21-24, NASB, italics added).

The argument now switches from what the idols cannot do to what the LORD can do.

I stirred up one from the north [Cyrus], and he has come, from the rising of the sun ['from the east', v. 2], and he shall call on my name [by restoring the worship of Israel's God at Jerusalem]; he shall trample on rulers as on mortar, as the potter treads clay. Who [among the idols] declared it from the beginning, that we might know, and beforehand, that we might say, 'He is right'?

There was none who declared it ... I was the first to say to Zion, 'Behold, here they are [the predictions about Cyrus]!' and I give to Jerusalem a herald of good news [Cyrus' decree to rebuild the city]. But when I look [for anyone who could accurately predict as God has done], there is no one ... *Behold*, they are all a delusion; their works are nothing [they cannot accomplish anything]; their metal images are empty wind (vv. 25-29, ESV, italics added).

That is the context in Isaiah for chapters 42–66, and in particular the Servant Songs. It is the context of universal idolatry from the beginning of time, which is still true even now, bearing in mind that an idol does not have to be an actual image of wood, stone or metal. Anything can become an idol when our devotion and service to it takes the place of the devotion and service we owe to God. We can make idols of money, pleasure, fame, power, family, career, possessions, a political party, and a host of other things; which is why John Calvin said that 'the human mind is, so to speak, a perpetual forge of idols.'[5]

It is the *worst* of sins because it breaks 'the first and great commandment' which Jesus said was: 'You shall love the LORD your God with all your heart, with all your soul, and with all your mind' (Matt. 22:35-38; Deut. 6:5). Moreover, it is the *mother* of all sins, for the apostle Paul says, 'Claiming to be wise, they [humankind] became fools, and exchanged the glory of the immortal God for images resembling mortal man and birds and animals and creeping things. Therefore God gave them up in the lusts of their hearts to impurity ...' (Rom. 1:22-24, ESV). It is also what he means when he says, 'For the love of money [making money an idol] is a root of all kinds of evil' (1 Tim. 6:10).

It is important to understand that idolatry, deeply ingrained in fallen human nature, is the context of the Servant Songs in Isaiah. Indeed, the *condemnation* of idols in chapter 41:24 and 29, 'Behold, you are nothing ... Behold, they are all a delusion', prepares us for the *exclamation* in chapter 42:1, 'Behold! My Servant.' God's remedy for humanity's idolatry is His Servant; not His servant Israel, who were 'deaf' to God's voice and 'blind' to His truth (41:8; 42:19; 44:21), but His messianic Servant, the 'Elect One in whom [His] soul delights' (42:1); who will 'establish justice in the earth' [i.e. justice for God who has been wronged (42:4)]; and be 'a light to the Gentiles' and God's 'salvation to the ends of the earth' (49:6); and 'shall justify many, for He will bear their iniquities' (53:11).

The name of God and its meaning

In the Old Testament section of the English Bible, 'Lord' always has a capital 'L' when used of God to translate the Hebrew word *adonay*, meaning, lord or master. It occurs 1,300 times. The proper name for God occurs 6,700 times in the Old Testament and is translated

---

5. John Calvin, *Institutes of the Christian Religion* (James Clarke, 1957), I.xi.8.

in the Authorised Version as 'Lᴏʀᴅ' (capital letters), except in four places (Exod. 6:3; Ps. 83:18; Isa. 12:2; 26:4) where God's name is rendered in the Authorised Version as JEHOVAH (Lᴏʀᴅ in the ɴᴋᴊᴠ), which remained the traditional version which the church has used since the 17ᵗʰ century. Throughout the four Servant Songs, the word 'Lᴏʀᴅ' in capitals is the only form of the divine name used, so a word of explanation is needed.

The Hebrew word is actually unpronounceable, being made up of only four consonants: *yhwh*. In all the existing Hebrew manuscripts the word has no vowel pointings, because after the exile in Babylon, the scribes believed that the divine name was too sacred to be pronounced. Technically, these four consonants are known as the 'tetragrammaton' (tetra, meaning 'four', and grammata, meaning 'letters'). Modern scholars believe that the missing vowels are 'A' and 'E', and therefore pronounce the word as *YAHWEH*.

The pronunciation of the sacred name as 'Jehovah' came about through a misunderstanding of the pointings found in the Massoretic text (the traditional Hebrew text with vowel pointings). 'The vowels of *adonay (a-o-a)* were placed under the tetragrammaton to remind the reader that he was not to pronounce *yhwh*, but instead was to read the word *adonay*. Christians who were unaware of this substitution read the vowels as if they actually belonged to *yhwh*, which resulted in the English form 'YeHoWaH' or 'JeHoVaH' (the *a* of *adonay* having been reduced to *e* under the *y* of *yhwh*)'.[6] Regardless of the editorial decision of substituting Lᴏʀᴅ for *yhwh* or of using Jehovah or Yahweh, the reader must keep in mind that although the name of God in the Old Testament is unpronounceable, a blessing is lost when no attention is paid to the difference between the use of a title (Lᴏʀᴅ) and the actual name of the God of Israel. Personally, it is the preference of the author of this book to use the time-honoured version of the divine name: 'Jehovah'.

Now Jehovah, as a label for God, was known to Abraham (Gen. 15:2) and was indeed used in worship before the flood: 'And as for Seth, to him also a son was born; and he named him Enosh. Then

6. W.A. Van Gemeren, *Evangelical Dictionary of Theology*, Walter A. Elwell, editor (Baker, 1989), p. 1080.

men began to call on the name of the LORD' (Jehovah, Gen 4:26, cf. 9:26). It was not till Exodus 3, however, that the meaning of the divine name was made plain. Having received God's commission, at the burning bush, to lead His people out of Egypt, Moses asks God, 'When I come to the children of Israel and say to them, "The God of your fathers has sent me to you", and they say to me, "What is His name?" what shall I say to them?' The meaning of the divine name given to Moses was, 'I AM WHO I AM ... thus you shall say to the children of Israel, "I AM [for short] has sent me to you"' (vv. 13, 14).

As J.I. Packer explains, 'God's phrase-name is thus a proclamation of God's gracious sovereign self-sufficiency and self-consistency: He is free and independent; He acts as He pleases; He does what He wills; what He purposes and promises, that He also performs. Therefore Israel, to whom He extended this staggering promise of redemption, could rely on Him absolutely to do as He had said. Because the God of the promise is almighty to fulfil His word, He is also utterly trustworthy, for He is absolutely invincible ... The meaning of "Yahweh" [Jehovah] is that which was symbolised by the flame in the bush which did not need to feed on the wood of the bush. "Yahweh" [Jehovah] signifies an inexhaustible ruler – God of limitless life and power – a God, therefore, whom it is safe to trust at all times and in all places.'[7]

This exposition of the Servant Songs has been written primarily for devotional, rather than academic purposes. It does not spend much time on problematic issues, but seeks to go to the basic meaning of the text, and then make a suitable application of its truth to the reader. By God's grace and the ministry of the Holy Spirit, may something of the beauty and splendour of our Lord Jesus Christ, the Servant of Jehovah, be manifested to the reader; especially the wonder of His penal substitutionary death on the cross for sinners, and the glory of His exaltation to the right hand of God, 'till He has established justice/righteousness in the earth' (42:4). It is a lofty desire, but Jesus, the Christ, is worthy of everyone's wholehearted faith and adoration forever.

---

7. J.I. Packer, *God's Words* (IVP, 1981), pp. 46, 47.

1

The First Servant Song:
Jehovah introduces His messianic Servant

42:1 Behold my servant, whom I uphold,
  my chosen, in whom my soul delights;
I have put my Spirit upon him;
  he will bring forth justice to the nations.
² He will not cry aloud or lift up his voice,
  or make it heard in the street;
³ a bruised reed he will not break,
  and a faintly burning wick he will not quench;
  he will faithfully [according to truth] bring forth justice.
⁴ He will not grow faint or be discouraged
  till he has established justice in the earth;
  and the coastlands wait for his law.

⁵ Thus says God, the LORD,
  who created the heavens and stretched them out,
  who spread out the earth and what comes from it,
who gives breath to the people on it
  and spirit to those who walk in it;
⁶ 'I am the LORD, I have called you in righteousness;
  I will take you by the hand and keep you;
I will give you as a covenant for the people,
  a light for the nations,
  ⁷ to open the eyes that are blind,

to bring out the prisoners from the dungeon,
   from the prison those who sit in darkness.
⁸ I am the Lord; that is my name;
   my glory I will give to no other,
nor my praise to carved idols.
⁹ Behold, the former things have come to pass,
   and new things I now declare;
before they spring forth
   I tell you of them
                  (Isa. 42:1-9, esv).

The last twenty-seven chapters of Isaiah are bound together by the theme of comfort. It is a book within a book, and is sometimes known as 'the Book of Consolation', because it begins with the command: '"Comfort, yes, comfort My people!" says your God. "Speak comfort to Jerusalem, and cry out to her, that her warfare [or hard service] is ended, that her iniquity is pardoned; for she has received from the Lord's hand double [a suitable match or duplicate] for all her sins"' (40:1-2).

How encouraging these succeeding chapters must have been to their Jewish readers in exile in Babylon! They were sorely in need of divine comfort, for their holy city Jerusalem and its beautiful temple had been destroyed by the Babylonians, and they themselves had been languishing in the land of their captors for nearly seventy long and hard years. They have no king and no place of worship. They are defeated and disillusioned, feeling that God has not dealt justly with them; that He has been over-harsh in His treatment of them. That is how human beings typically react. But God is full of grace; and here, as in every case, He comes with a promise of help which does not depend on us, but only on Himself. And as we believe His promise of salvation, we are strengthened to face what is ahead while we wait for His perfect time.

There is an end to the discipline of God, our Father. We do sin, as His children, and like a good Father, He disciplines us in love (Heb. 12:5-6). But when His discipline has done its work, He comforts us with promises of help. As Matthew Henry observes:

'Before God sent His people into captivity, He furnished them with precious promises for their support and comfort in their trouble; and we may well imagine of what great use to them the glorious, gracious light of this prophecy was in that cloudy and dark day, and how much it helped to dry up their tears by the rivers of Babylon.'[1]

To this people, then, suffering physical and political bondage under their Babylonian captors, God, through Isaiah's prophecy, has an immediate and temporal message of comfort to give. Jehovah is the only true God and sovereign of the universe, and He is about to do 'new things' for His people Israel (v. 9). He is going to use Cyrus, a Persian king and an idol worshipper, to conquer Babylon, free the Jews, and send them back to Jerusalem to rebuild their city and the temple (Isa. 44:21–45:7). This will happen, as foretold by Jeremiah, when they have completed their sentence of seventy years of captivity in Babylon (Jer. 25:11-12; 29:10; Dan. 9:1-2). So it is coming soon, but like all physical and earthly comfort it will be temporal. They would lose it all again in 600 years' time, when the Romans would destroy Jerusalem and the temple in AD 70, and scatter the survivors throughout the empire.

God, however, has a greater and more enduring promise of comfort to offer His chosen people. It will be a spiritual and eternal deliverance from the bondage of sin's curse upon their lives and all of creation. It will come through another Deliverer, who unlike Cyrus, is not named in these remaining chapters of Isaiah. Jehovah calls Him simply, 'My Servant', and in the First Servant Song we are introduced to Him: His mission, His empowerment, His manner, His perseverance, His reward, and our need to seriously consider Him.

The commission of Jehovah's Servant

The Hebrew word for *servant* means a person at the disposal of another; to carry out his will, do his work, and represent his interests. What is God's will for His Servant? It is that He should 'bring forth justice to the nations' and 'establish justice in the earth'. This mission is so important that it is repeated three times in the first

---

1. Matthew Henry, *Matthew Henry's Commentary* (Revell Publishing Co., 1708), vol. IV, p. 211.

four verses (vv. 1, 3, 4). The word 'justice' is a very common one in the Old Testament, and it means much more than God's judgment or punishment of wrongdoing. The 'justice' which the Servant is to 'bring forth' and 'establish' in the earth is justice for God. And justice for God means the restoration of His plan for a just and righteous order on earth which sin disrupted. Indeed, the word translated 'justice' here is translated as 'plan' in Exodus 26:30, speaking of God's 'plan' for the tabernacle, which was the blueprint revealed by God to Moses on Mount Sinai. Verse 3 in the song confirms this meaning, for the Servant 'will *faithfully* bring forth justice'. A literal translation would read, 'He will bring forth justice for truth' (NKJV) or 'according to truth' (namely, His original plan).

Sin destroyed the just order that God planned from the beginning for His glory and mankind's good. God is now profaned by idolatry, and humanity has been reduced to abject misery in this life and ever-lasting hell hereafter. The Servant's commission, then, is to 'establish' on earth what is right in God's judgment, what is 'according to truth' or the divine plan. He is to establish God's kingdom on earth, in order that God's will may be done on earth as it is in heaven (Matt. 6:9-10). Of course, justice in our courts of law cannot do that. It can sentence a murderer to death, but it cannot restore the murdered victim to his or her loved ones. To repair the ruin sin has caused is utterly beyond our power, but not His: 'He will bring forth justice to the nations ... He will faithfully bring forth justice ... till He has established justice in the earth.' This is what Jesus came to do. He inaugurated the kingdom of God on earth and proclaimed it as a kingdom of righteousness, to enter which men and women must 'repent and believe in the gospel' (the good news of forgiveness and eternal life through Him, Mark 1:14-15; 2:1-11; Luke 24:46-48; John 3:13-18).

J.I. Packer amplifies this truth when commenting on the greatest commandment, 'Love the LORD your God with all your heart and with all your soul and with all your strength' (Deut. 6:5, NIV):

> When God made us, His purpose was that we should love and honour Him, praising Him for the wonderfully ordered

complexity and variety of His world, using it according to His will, and so enjoying both it and Him. And though we have fallen, God has not abandoned His first purpose. Still He plans that a great host of humankind should come to love and honour Him. His ultimate objective is to bring them to a state in which they please Him entirely and praise Him adequately, a state in which He is all in all to them and He and they rejoice continually in the knowledge of each other's love – people rejoicing in the saving love of God, set upon them from all eternity, and God rejoicing in the responsive love of people, drawn out of them by grace through the gospel. This is God's glory, our glory too, in every sense that that weighty word can bear.[2]

The empowerment of Jehovah's Servant

How will the Servant accomplish His task? God answers, 'I have put My Spirit upon Him'; and again, 'I will take You by the hand and keep You' (vv. 1, 6). The Servant of the LORD will be equipped by the Spirit of the LORD to fulfil the commission of the LORD from His conception to His crucifixion. The Gospel writers tell us that the Holy Spirit was personally and uniquely active at the conception of Jesus. It was by the Spirit's creative activity that the virgin Mary conceived with no human father involved in the procreative act (Luke 1:35; Matt. 1:20). His humanity was taken from Mary, but creatively enlivened by God's Spirit. 'Mary had her part in the procreation or generation of the human nature of our Lord. She did not merely incubate a *separately* produced foetus.'[3]

The Holy Spirit was also at work in the human development of Jesus. There was no area of the human nature of Jehovah's Servant which was not developed and conditioned by the Spirit of Jehovah. Even His understanding of His mission did not take place in a vacuum, but came with prayer and much reflection on the Old Testament Scriptures as the Holy Spirit unfolded to His young mind a growing awareness of His identity and destiny (Luke 2:39-50). Jesus

---

2. J.I. Packer, *Knowing God Devotional Journal* (IVP, 2009), p. 120.
3. Peter Lewis, *The Glory of Christ* (Moody, 1997), p. 54.

was no doubt filled with the Holy Spirit from birth, since as much is said of His forerunner, John the Baptist, who was not as great as He (Luke 1:15; 3:15, 16). Moreover, God did not give His Spirit to Him 'by measure' (John 3:34, NIV). So at His baptism in the river Jordan all four Gospels refer to the unique descent of the Spirit on Jesus like a dove (Matt. 3:13-17; Mark 1:9-11; Luke 3:21-22; John 1:32).

The importance of this event was twofold. In the first place, it proclaimed to those who heard the voice from heaven that Jesus was not only the Servant of God, but also the Son of God: 'This is My beloved Son, in whom I am well pleased' (Matt. 3:17; cf. Mark 1:11; Luke 3:22). In the second place, it inaugurated and empowered the Servant–Son's public ministry. According to Luke, Jesus went up from the river Jordan 'being filled with the Holy Spirit', and after resisting the temptations of the devil in the wilderness, He 'returned in the power of the Spirit to Galilee'. There, in the synagogue at Nazareth, He announced: 'The Spirit of the LORD is upon Me, because He has anointed Me to preach the gospel to the poor. He has sent Me to heal the brokenhearted, to preach deliverance to the captives and recovery of sight to the blind, to set at liberty those who are oppressed, to preach the acceptable year of the Lord' (Luke 4:1, 14, 16-19; Isa. 61:1, 2). Looking back on our Lord's ministry, the apostle Peter could testify of 'how God anointed Jesus of Nazareth with the Holy Spirit and with power, who went about doing good and healing all who were oppressed by the devil, for God was with Him' (Acts 10:38). The Servant of Jehovah was equipped by the Spirit of Jehovah from His conception in the womb of the virgin Mary to His exaltation to the right hand of God on high.

The manner of Jehovah's Servant

Verses 2 and 3 of this song describe the *manner* in which the Servant of the LORD will carry out His work on earth. They are very remarkable verses, because they stand out in such stark contrast with the way the world does things. The power-hungry and kingdom-builders in the world have never shied away from the blasts of noisy propaganda and high-pressure advertising techniques to gain attention and win followers. The Servant–Son will have an altogether different manner and method. It is most striking to observe in these verses how quietly and gently the Servant of Jehovah will pursue His task.

The Servant of Jehovah is *quiet:* 'He will not cry aloud or lift up His voice, or make it heard in the street.' How is this statement to be understood? Clearly it is not a biblical prohibition of preaching out in the open-air! Still less are we here forbidden to spread the good news publicly. Jesus preached in streets and fields, and commanded all His followers to be 'witnesses to [Him] in Jerusalem, and in all Judea and Samaria, and to the end of the earth' (Acts 1:8). Moreover, when preaching to the crowds, He surely needed to raise His voice. These words, therefore, do not mean that we are only to preach the gospel in a soft voice, in our homes.

The words are figurative, and mean that the Servant will not shout or carry on to draw attention to Himself. He will not advertise or promote Himself. Instead, He will focus on the work Jehovah has sent Him to do in a quiet and unostentatious manner. Thus, the Apostle Matthew applied the words of this first song to the fact that Jesus told the people not to broadcast the news if they had been healed (12:15-21). This was because He wanted to avoid the wrong kind of publicity. He did not want to be known as a wonder worker or an aspiring king, but rather as a lowly Saviour, who had come to suffer and die. So Jesus shunned publicity. He served God and men quietly. He used no bombast or bluster. He wanted His kingdom to spread inconspicuously. Is there not a lesson here for us? Christians are called to be servants of the Servant of the LORD, but I think that the church seems to be steadily moving away from the quiet and humble ministry of our supreme example. Let us examine ourselves. Are we prone to promote ourselves? Do we hanker after publicity? Are we eager for quick and showy results? Is it the limelight we are after? The Servant of Jehovah works quietly.

More importantly, however, He is *gentle:* 'A bruised reed He will not break, and a faintly burning wick He will not quench' (v. 3). The gentleness of the Servant is illustrated by these two metaphors which are now proverbial. What is weaker than a bruised reed? Let anything brush against it, and it will break. Again, nothing has a more precarious existence than a dimly burning wick. In a few moments it will die out. These are weak and needy things, and yet Jehovah says that His Servant will neither break the bruised reed nor quench the smoking flax. If He finds the reed bent and damaged by the wind or an animal, He will not trample it callously under foot, but take care of it and make it strong again. And if He finds a lamp which is burning low and on the point of going out, He will not smother the flickering wick. Rather, He will blow gently upon it until it starts burning brightly again.

In sharp contrast, we tend to be harsh in our impatience with the weaknesses of others. 'Of what use is a reed that cannot stand upright on its own?' we ask, and cast it aside. 'And what good is a lamp whose wick is nearly exhausted?' We quickly snuff out flickering wicks. But Jesus was as gentle as He was quiet. He was no more guilty of bullying than of bombast. To those weighed down by the burden of sin, He said: 'Come to Me all you who labour and are heavy laden, and I will give you rest. Take My yoke upon you and learn from Me, for I am gentle and lowly in heart, and you will find rest for your souls. For My yoke is easy and My burden is light' (Matt. 11:28-30).

These are the people Jesus came 'to serve and to give His life a ransom for' (Mark 10:45). When He was criticized by the Pharisees for dining with sinners, He replied: 'Those who are well do not need a physician, but those who are sick; I have not come to call the righteous, but sinners, to repentance' (Luke 5:31-32). How tender He was with the Samaritan woman whom the villagers avoided because of her promiscuity (John 4:3-30; 39-42)! How patient He was with His obtuse disciples (Matt. 16:5-12; Mark 10:35-45; Luke 24:13-35)! How gracious was His refusal to condemn the woman caught in the act of adultery, and His forgiveness of the woman whom the Pharisees dubbed 'a sinner' (John 8:1-12; Luke 7:36-50)! There is only one word for this – *grace*, the undeserved mercy and favour of God to sinners. When the apostle Paul wrote to Timothy, saying, 'A servant of the Lord must not quarrel but be gentle to all, able to teach, patient, in humility correcting those who are in opposition ...' was he thinking of *the* Servant of Jehovah? Jesus Christ is our example *par excellence* in everything. Christians must be humble and gentle like Him. It is easy to ride roughshod over the delicate feelings of others and to disregard their conscientious scruples. It is easy to look with disdain upon their folly, and condemn their failures and weaknesses. Let us emulate our great role model and be unostentatious and gentle in our Christian service.

The perseverance of Jehovah's Servant

The Servant will not give up the mission God has assigned to Him until He has successfully completed it. His perseverance in this regard will require two things. The first requirement is perseverance in the *righteousness* in which He has been called (v. 6a). The phrase in verse 4a, 'He will not fail or be discouraged' (RSV) is translated in the margin, 'He will not burn dimly or be bruised.' The words are the same as those in the previous verse. So what God is saying, is this: although His Servant will not despise the frailty of others, He will not become frail Himself in any moral sense at all. He will not be corrupted by the weakness of those around Him. They may burn dimly and be bruised by sin, but not He.

So, when Jesus came to earth, He mixed with sinners, but never sinned (Luke 15:1, 2; John 8:46; Heb. 4:15). He was surrounded by unbelief, but His faith never failed (Matt. 8:26; 14:22-33). He was betrayed and denied, but never Himself swerved from the path of suffering (Matt. 26:14-16, 30-56, 68-75). It is so easy for us to lower our standards to the level of those among whom we live; to let our spirits be cowed by the scornful threats of our enemies; and to lose our zeal through the insidious influence of a compromising world. The Servant of Jehovah, however, 'will not burn dimly or be bruised'.

The second requirement which the Servant of the LORD met, was perseverance in His *mission*. That is the theme of verses 5-9: 'He will not grow faint or be discouraged till He has established justice [a just or righteous order] in the earth; and the coastlands [distant lands] wait for His law' (v. 4). The 'law' which all the lands wait for is the *moral* law of Jehovah given to Moses on Mount Sinai, for there is only one moral law. But now it is called the Servant's 'law', because when He comes, He will give it its true and fullest meaning. It will be the law of the Ten Commandments, without the additional *civic* and *ceremonial* laws which were also given to Moses, but will no longer apply after the atoning death of the Servant on the cross of Calvary and the destruction of Jerusalem in AD 70. To avoid any misunderstanding, Jesus clearly said, 'Do not think that I came to destroy the Law or the Prophets. I did not come to destroy, but to fulfil' (Matt. 5:17).

Because this will be such a daunting task – the task of establishing a just world order in which everyone will obey God's moral law perfectly – divine assurance is once again given to the Servant. 'Thus says God, the LORD, who created the heavens and stretched them out, who spread out the earth and what comes from it, who gives breath to the people on it and spirit to those who walk in it: I am the LORD; I have called you in righteousness [for a righteous purpose, just as God would call Cyrus, 45:13]; I will take You by the hand and keep You' (v. 5). A God with enough power to create the universe, and everything in it, is well able to empower His Servant to bring righteousness to the earth.

The divine mission is further elaborated on in verses 6-7, 'I will give You as a covenant for the people, a light for the nations, to open eyes that are blind, to bring out the prisoners from the dungeon, from the prison those who sit in darkness.' Jehovah had already made a covenant with Abraham, Isaac and Jacob, as well as their descendants. The essence of that covenant was: 'I will be your God, and you shall be My people' (Exod. 6:2-7; Jer. 11:1-4). But now God promises to make a 'new covenant' with His people through His Servant, who 'will put [God's] law in their minds, and write it' on their hearts (Jer. 31:31-34; 24:7; Ezek. 36:22-28). The essence of the new covenant, however, will remain the same as the old: 'I will be your God, and you shall be My people' (2 Cor. 6:16; Rev. 21:3).

So it is going to be a more *intensive* covenant than the old one, because its spiritual effects will be more radical. He is going to open the eyes of the 'blind' to the truth of the gospel, and release idolaters from the 'darkness' of their self-created dungeons. These are all descriptions of spiritual deliverance from sin (cf. 61:1 and Jesus' application of it in Luke 4:16-21). What is more, the new covenant mediated by the Servant of Jehovah will be more *extensive*.

His mission will be a mission to the whole world, and not just to ethnic Israel. This is made clear by the fact that the Servant is to be 'a light for the nations'; He is to 'establish justice in the earth', and 'His law' will go to 'the coastlands'. Indeed, the apostle Paul appealed to Isaiah 42:6 and 49:6 to vindicate his mission to take the 'light' of salvation to the Gentiles (Acts 13:46-48).

Held and kept by the Almighty Creator's hand, the Servant 'will not grow faint or be discouraged' in the fulfilment of His task. Or as Henri Blocher puts it, 'Because the Servant will be obedient to the end, even to the point of death for sins not His own, His light will never grow dim. He will endure incomprehensible agonies in God's service and will not be beaten down by them. He will not yield to the pressures to which we constantly, sinfully, yield: He will not. He will patiently go on without fainting.'[4]

The reward of Jehovah's Servant

By and large, Jesus was not honoured by men. The official leaders of Judaism repudiated Him. He was condemned by the supreme council of the Jews, the Sanhedrin, and then handed over to the secular authority of Rome and crucified (Matt. 26:57-68; 27:1, 2). But, although He was despised and rejected by men, His reward was to have the unqualified approval of Jehovah, who addresses Him as 'My chosen [elect], in whom My soul delights' (v. 1). John L. Mackay says, 'My soul (cf. 1:14) is not to be construed as providing insight into the being of God, but as a Hebrew idiom for intense involvement of an individual with the sense of "I personally" or "I deeply".'[5]

All through His ministry the Servant walked with God, and on three occasions the Heavenly Voice broke the silence of the unseen world and gave a public, audible assurance of His favour toward Jesus. The first occurred at His baptism, where the onlookers heard 'a voice from heaven, saying, "This is My beloved Son, with whom I am well pleased"' (Matt. 3:16, 17). The second occasion was probably a year or so later when, on a high mountain, Jesus was transfigured before

---

4. Henri Blocher, *Songs of the Servant*, p. 32.

5. John L. Mackay, *Isaiah* (E.P. Books, 2009), vol. 2, p. 84.

Peter, James and John. A bright cloud overshadowed them, and a voice from the cloud said, 'This is My beloved Son, in whom I am well pleased. Hear Him!' (Matt. 17:5). The third occasion occurred a few days before His crucifixion. Our Lord prayed to His Father, saying, 'Now My soul is troubled, and what shall I say? "Father, save Me from this hour"? But for this purpose I came to this hour. "Father, glorify Your name." Then a voice came from heaven, saying, "I have both glorified it and will glorify it again." Therefore, the people who stood by and heard it said that it had thundered. Others said, "An angel has spoken to Him"' (John 12:27-29).

Never before, and never since, has any human being been so honoured. The Servant alone is the only one who will fulfil and satisfy all Jehovah's desires for humanity. All Jehovah's other servants, with the best of intentions, have failed and will fail Him, but in the Servant He will have one in whom He can fully delight. That will be reward enough for all Christ's trials and sufferings. If we are servants of the Lord, we too must aspire to this, however flawed our efforts may be. There can surely be no greater reward than this. We may not receive the plaudits of men; perhaps not even a pat on the back. But we will feel no need of the glory or praise of men, when, like Paul, 'we make it our aim ... to be well pleasing to Him' (2 Cor. 5:9).

The contemplation of Jehovah's Servant

We are summoned by a strong imperative, right at the beginning of the song to 'Behold My Servant'. 'Here is my servant' (NIV) is a weak translation. What we have here is a call for the strongest exercise of our cognitive powers to contemplate and give our fullest attention to the highest of all objects. We are to be engaged in a thorough consideration of Jesus Christ, the Servant, because all our spiritual well-being depends on our beholding His glory (2 Cor. 3:12-18). When Jesus began His public ministry, John the Baptist pointed Him out to the crowds, saying, 'Behold! The Lamb of God who takes away the sin of the world ... and I have seen and testified that this is the Son of God' (John 1:29, 34). At the end of His earthly life, when Pilate saw that the Jews were determined to put an innocent man to death, he brought Jesus out to the crowd, 'wearing the crown

of thorns and the purple robe, and said to them, "Behold the Man!'"
(John 19:4, 5).

Beholding the Servant–Son is the duty of all men and women
in every age from His first coming to His return 'with power and
great glory' (Matt. 24:30, 31; Rev. 1:7). This is what God the Father
Himself does with love and delight, and He commands us to do
what He does. In God's sight there is no greater sin than to have no
regard and delight in His only begotten and beloved Servant–Son,
Jesus Christ. No one goes to hell solely because they have broken the
Ten Commandments, but because they have rejected Jesus Christ
as the Saviour of the world (John 3:16-19, 35, 36; 4:42). As long as
we close our eyes to the truth and remain unbelieving, we will think
nothing of Christ. But once our eyes have been opened to behold
Him, we will exclaim with Charles Wesley, 'Thou, O Christ, art all
I want; more than all in Thee I find ... Plenteous grace with Thee is
found, grace to cover all my sin.'

Moreover, and on this note the first song fittingly ends, we are to
behold God's Servant, because nothing is to be gained from looking at
anything else in an idolatrous world: 'Behold, they are all a delusion;
their works are nothing, their metal images are empty wind' (41:29).
No idol, tangible or intangible, could match the redemptive work
that Jehovah is going to achieve through His Servant when He
brings a just or righteous order to the world. Jehovah will ultimately
triumph, for, as He says, 'I am Jehovah [the name of the gracious
redeeming God of the covenant], that is My name; My glory I give
to no other, nor My praise to carved idols' (v. 8).

We should believe this, the divine argument continues, because
Jehovah proves His deity by declaring these 'new things' which will
be accomplished by His Servant: 'Behold, the former things have
come to pass, and new things I now declare; before they spring
forth I tell you of them' (v. 9). The 'former things' refers to prophecies which have already been fulfilled; namely, Israel's exodus from
Egypt, and then, 900 years later, their liberation from Babylon. In
other words, God is saying, 'If I kept My word about delivering you
through Moses and Cyrus, which I did, then you can believe that
I will keep My word about My Servant. He is going to bring a new

"covenant", new "light", a new "just order", and a "new song" of praise to Jehovah "from the ends of the earth'" (v. 10).

As Jesus says at the end of the Bible, 'Behold, I make all things new' (Rev. 21:5). Yes, He is going to make 'new things' even out of bruised reeds and faintly burning wicks. 'Hallelujah! What a Saviour!' That is Jehovah's introduction of His chosen Servant in whom He delights, who serves Him with perfect obedience and complete success. By the power of Jehovah's Spirit 'put ... upon Him', He will indeed create a new glorified humanity out of a ruined humanity, and 'a new earth in which righteousness dwells' out of a sin-cursed earth (Isa. 42:1; 2 Pet. 3:13). Why would anyone in their right mind not trust God's Servant to do this for them and the world?

I like the way C.S. Lewis puts it in the first of his *Narnia* books for children, *The Lion, the Witch and the Wardrobe.* Narnia is an imaginary country ruled by a usurper queen called the White Witch, for in the words of one of the characters: 'She has made an enchantment [cast a spell] over the whole country so that it is always winter here and never Christmas.' But Aslan, the great Lion, the true King of Narnia (who represents Jesus), comes to the rescue and fulfils 'an old rhyme' in that winter-land:

> Wrong will be right, when Aslan comes in sight,
> At the sound of his roar, sorrows will be no more,
> When he bares his teeth, winter meets its death
> And when he shakes his mane, we shall have spring again.[6]

---

6. C.S. Lewis, *The Lion, the Witch and the Wardrobe* (Collins, 1968), pp. 59, 77.

2

The Second Servant Song:
The Servant's calling and work

49:1 Listen to Me, O coastlands,
  and give attention, you peoples from afar.
The Lord called me from the womb,
  from the body of my mother he named my name.
² He made my mouth like a sharp sword;
  in the shadow of his hand he hid me;
he made me a polished arrow;
  in his quiver he hid me away.
³ And he said to me, 'You are my servant,
  Israel, in whom I will be glorified.'
⁴ But I said, 'I have laboured in vain;
  I have spent my strength for nothing and vanity;
yet surely my right is with the Lord,
  and my recompense with my God.'

⁵ And now the Lord says,
  he who formed me from the womb to be his servant,
to bring Jacob back to him;
  and that Israel might be gathered to him –
for I am honoured in the eyes of the Lord,
  and my God has become my strength –
⁶ he says:
  'It is too light a thing that you should be my servant,

to raise up the tribes of Jacob
and to bring back the preserved of Israel;
I will make you as a light for the nations,
that my salvation may reach to the end of the earth.'

[7] Thus says the LORD, the Redeemer of Israel and his Holy One,
to one deeply despised, abhorred by the nation,
the servant of rulers:
'Kings shall see and arise;
princes, and they shall prostrate themselves;
because of the LORD, who is faithful,
the Holy One of Israel, who has chosen you.'
(Isa. 49:1-7, ESV).

This is the second of Isaiah's four Servant Songs which foretell the coming of Messiah/Christ as the Saviour of the world, of Jews and Gentiles. The human race in its entirety is doomed to everlasting destruction in hell, because it has turned from the living and true God to serve idols, substitute false gods, both material and immaterial. The only hope, and humanity's great need, is to be spiritually liberated by a God-sent Redeemer. Isaiah's good news is that God in an unsolicited act of free grace has provided such a Deliverer for humankind.

In the first song we are told a little about His character and mission. He is being sent by Jehovah to establish a just or righteous order on the earth, and He will do so in a quiet, gentle and unostentatious way that will be well-pleasing to Jehovah. The message of the Second Servant Song expands on the promise that Jehovah will 'give [Him] as a covenant to the people, as a light to the Gentiles, to open blind eyes, to bring out prisoners from the prison, those who sit in darkness from the prison house' (42:6, 7). It promises not only the 'light' of truth, but supremely God's salvation: 'I will make You as a light for the nations, that My salvation may reach to the end of the earth' (49:6). The Servant will not only expose the utter and heinous folly of worshipping idols, but rescue men and women from its deadly consequences.

The most important new revelation in the Second Servant Song, however, is the intimation that to all outward appearance His mission will seem to have failed, because He will be 'despised' and 'abhorred' by men (49:7). It is the first hint given in Isaiah of the suffering and rejection that the messianic Servant will experience before He successfully completes His divine mission.

The Third Servant Song will reveal even more graphic details of His suffering, while the fourth song will explain the necessity of His sufferings: they are vicarious sufferings offered as an atonement for the sins of His many people (50:5-7; 53:2-8). The supreme note in these four poems, therefore, is triumph. The Servant is a victor, who against all human expectations, snatches victory out of the jaws of defeat (42:3, 4; 49:3-7; 50:5-7; 52:13-15; 53:10-12).

One more feature needs to be pointed out before we expound the second song: it is autobiographical. Although God is the speaker in the first and fourth songs, the Servant is the speaker in the second and third songs which are written in the first person singular. The Servant speaks and then reports Jehovah's response. Henri Bolcher writes:

> This is exceptional. Apart from the Third Servant Song, and the kindred prophecy of Isaiah 61, this kind of I-discourse is found nowhere else in the entire book of Isaiah. When the prophet tells us about events in his own life (for instance, when he recounts his call to the prophetic office in chapter 6, or his dramatic encounter with King Ahaz in chapter 7) the style, mood and situation are altogether different. The kind of I-discourse which we have in the second song is found only when God is the speaker. God – and the Servant. Is this striking detail a hint of what Peter was to unfold centuries later (in 1 Peter 1:10-12); that the Spirit who revealed God's plan to the prophets was not only the Spirit of God, but the Spirit of Christ? If Isaiah is inspired by the divine Spirit of the Servant, then the Servant may speak in the first person when His future sufferings and the glory which is to follow are revealed.[1]

1. Henri Blocher, *Songs of the Servant*, pp. 35-36.

Thus 'the Servant speaks with absolute authority, commanding the world to listen.'[2] He demands attention and obedience: 'Listen to Me, O coastlands, and give attention, you peoples from afar!' (v. 1). He speaks with a divine voice, addressing the world as only Jehovah could address them. 'Listen to Me', in this sense, is not used by any prophet, but only of the LORD. The Servant is God and man. He is the Servant–Son of Isaiah 42 in whom God the Father 'delights', because His life is without sin in every respect, and His obedience absolutely perfect. Here in chapter 49:1, He speaks not just as a prophet of flesh and blood, but as the divine Spirit of Christ (Rom. 8:9; 1 Pet. 1:11), exercising worldwide authority over the distant shores of the Mediterranean Sea ('coastlands') and all 'peoples from afar'. All the remote areas of the world owe their allegiance to the LORD's Servant.

That, chiefly, is how the Servant saw Himself. He is the Messiah/Christ whom Scripture says is the 'Companion' or equal of God (Ps. 45:7; Zech. 13:7). As for His life's work or calling, the servant of Jehovah saw several things of note, which our study will follow in order.

He has been predestined for His divine mission

'The LORD has called Me from the womb; from the body of My mother He has named My name' (v. 1). The Servant announces to the world His prenatal call by Jehovah. He will enter the world by a normal birth. Isaiah has already said that Messiah/Christ will have a mother, but not a father: 'Behold, the virgin shall conceive and bear a Son, and shall call His name Immanuel' (margin: God with us, 7:14). His miraculous conception in His virgin mother's womb was predetermined, because He is Jehovah's 'Elect' or chosen One to save the world (42:1; John 4:42).

The Servant's election, however, was not just prenatal, but before creation itself. God's choices and callings are not made on the spur of the moment, because they are not contingent on anything outside Himself. God's choices and callings were determined before the world was made, and are carried out on His timetable. Thus the

2. E.J. Young, *The Book of Isaiah* (Eerdmans, 1972), vol. 3, p. 268.

apostle John can write of 'the Lamb [Jesus] slain from the foundation of the world' and of those whose names are 'written in the Book of Life from the foundation of the world' (Rev. 13:8; 17:8). The phrase 'from the womb' is simply a Hebrew idiom for emphasising that God's grace precedes and antedates any possible human merit. God's electing and predestinating grace is sovereign, independent of human factors, and therefore absolutely supreme.

Indeed, it even included the naming of the Servant: 'From the body of My mother He named My name.' Literally this means, 'to bring to/put into people's minds, to announce.'[3] What that predetermined name was, is revealed in the fuller light of the New Testament. The LORD kept His name secret within the Godhead until the right moment came to announce it to Joseph, His legal guardian. Matthew records, 'Behold, an angel of the Lord appeared to him in a dream, saying, "Joseph, son of David, do not fear to take Mary as your wife, for that which is conceived in her is from the Holy Spirit. She will bear a son, and you shall call his name Jesus, for he will save his people from their sins"' (1:20-21, ESV). Luke records, 'And at the end of eight days, when He was circumcised, he was called Jesus, the name given by the angel before he was conceived in the womb' (2:21, ESV). Our English word 'Jesus' is really the Latin version of the Hebrew *Jehoshua*, the basic meaning of which is 'Jehovah will save'. But whereas Joshua, 'Moses' assistant', and 'Joshua the high priest', who had the same name (Josh. 1:1; Zech. 3:1), would testify by their names to the LORD's salvation, the One who would be born to Mary, as the angel explained, will Himself actually 'save His people from their sins.' In the fullest sense of its meaning it is uniquely *His* proper Name.

He will be prepared for His work in obscurity

'He made My mouth like a sharp sword; in the shadow of His hand He hid Me; He made Me a polished arrow; in His quiver He hid Me away' (v. 2). The Servant is to be God's instrument to bring righteousness and salvation to the ends of the earth, and His preparation will focus on His message ('My mouth'). He is to be the

---

3. J. Alec Motyer, *The Prophecy of Isaiah* (IVP, 1993), p.385.

mouthpiece of Jehovah spreading afar the gospel of salvation from sin through Him, saying, 'the time is fulfilled, and the kingdom of God is at hand. Repent, and believe in the gospel'; and again, 'For God so loved the world that He gave His only begotten Son, that whoever believes in Him should not perish but have everlasting life' (Mark 1:15; John 3:16).

In Revelation, the apostle John depicts the Lord Jesus with a sharp sword coming out of His mouth (1:16; 19:15, 21). The sword is a favourite symbol in the New Testament for God's word (Eph. 6:17). The word of God is a two-edged sword that is able to penetrate the deepest recesses of our being, and able to discern the thoughts and intentions of the heart (Heb. 4:12). Motyer says, 'The sharpness of a *sword* is its effectiveness; a *polished arrow* is rubbed free from roughness or unevenness which might deflect it in flight, hence its accuracy. The *sword* wins victories close at hand (v. 6a); the *arrow* hits distant targets (v. 6b; cf. 57:19; Eph. 2:17).'[4] The Servant's task will be difficult, but He tells us in verse 2 that Jehovah will not send Him to it until He has been properly prepared for it; not with the weapons of military warfare, but with spiritual weapons which are 'mighty in God for pulling down strongholds, casting down arguments and every high thing that exalts itself against the knowledge of God, bringing every thought into captivity to the obedience of Christ' (2 Cor. 10:3-5).

The strange thing, however, is that the sword and the arrow are hidden from sight: 'In the shadow of His hand [i.e. along the inside of His hand and arm] He hid Me ... in His quiver He hid Me away.' Except for a very small number of people, God concealed the presence, the identity and the mission of the Servant from the nation of Israel for thirty years. For all that long time Jesus, the Messiah/Christ, grew up in the obscurity of a peasant home in Nazareth, a city generally dismissed as of no importance (John 1:45-46). What is the significance of this concealment? It was partly for protection from authorities who would seek to harm Him, and partly to give Him time to be fully prepared – physically, intellectually, emotionally and spiritually. But when the sword was

---

4. J. Alec Motyer, *The Prophecy of Isaiah* (IVP, 1993), p. 386.

sharp and the arrow polished to God's satisfaction, it was time for His Servant to go public.

He will fulfil Israel's calling to glorify God

In verse 3 the Servant continues His report to 'peoples from afar' (v. 1). He rehearses something highly significant that Jehovah had said to Him: 'And He said to Me, "You are My Servant, Israel, in whom I will be glorified."' Some scholars think that the Israel being spoken of here is the nation itself, but if that were the case, how would we explain what is said in verses 5 and 6, in which the Servant's task is to bring back Jacob to the Lord, because the nation had failed to glorify the Lord and be His obedient servant (48:1-8)? No! The One in whom, God says, 'I will display my splendour' (NIV) is the messianic Servant who truly deserves the name 'Israel' (literally 'Prince with God'). Moreover, in becoming 'Israel', the Servant will become the 'Head' of a new community which He is to redeem, who will be called 'the Israel of God' and 'children of the promise' (Gal. 6:16; 3:26-29; Rom. 9:6-8).

Raymond Ortlund sums it up well:

> So the Israel of verse 3 is Messiah, the Servant who embodies all that historic Israel should have been. He is the Israel *in whom God will be glorified.* We can't make sense of the Old Testament without Christ. He's the One on whom all lines converge. All the persons, events, and institutions of the Old Testament, including the nation of Israel itself, find their truest meaning in Christ. The Old Testament has obsolescence built into it. It points beyond itself, both because of the human failure its story tells and also because, even at their best, the figures moving through the pages of the Old Testament were only meant to prepare for something greater. The incompleteness of the Old Testament demands resolution, a breakthrough. On every page it cries out for Christ. So we shouldn't be surprised when the Old Testament uses the name Israel for the Messiah. We should expect it, because *the whole Bible is all about Christ.* If we understand

the signals the Old Testament itself is sending us, we'll read it that way. Why shouldn't we? The apostles did, and they were good theologians. Better than we are.[5]

In spite of apparent failure, God will vindicate Him

'But I said, "I have laboured in vain; I have spent My strength for nothing and vanity; yet surely My right is with the LORD, and My recompense with My God"' (v. 4). This is another difficult verse to interpret if we try to do so by taking the verse in isolation, which is always a bad policy in interpreting Scripture. The problem raised when interpreting verse 4 on its own is this: Is it possible that Jesus, the Servant–Son, could ever have said to God or anyone else, 'I have laboured in vain; I have spent My strength for nothing and vanity'? We can readily imagine ourselves as fallen, sinful creatures, doing so! But surely not Jesus; not the Servant in whom Jehovah 'delights'; not God's beloved Son of whom He can say, 'I am well pleased'; not Jesus of Nazareth who said, 'The Father has not left Me alone, for I always do those things that please Him' (42:1; Matt. 3:17; 17:5; John 8:29)?

It is true that as perfect man, Jesus 'was in all points tempted as we are', but the writer of Hebrews is also careful to add, 'yet without sin' (4:15). It would not be a sin to be tempted to doubt God's promise to crown His labours with success, but to give in to that temptation and harbour doubt, would be sin. Elijah was tempted in a similar way and gave in to doubt and discouragement. After three years of fighting the idolatry of Baalism without success, he ran for his life and prayed: 'It is enough! Now, Lord, take my life, for I am no better than my fathers!' (1 Kings 19:1-4).

Our Lord, however, was born sinless and remained sinless right to His last breath on the cross. He could say to the Pharisees who sought to kill Him, 'Which one of you convicts Me of sin?' And the writer of Hebrews says, 'For it was indeed fitting that we should have such a high priest, holy, innocent, unstained, separated from sinners, and exalted above the heavens' (John 8:46; Heb. 7:26). That is the wider context of the New Testament in which verse 4 must

5. Raymond C. Ortlund, Jr., *Isaiah* (Crossway, 2005), p. 325.

be interpreted. Jesus was tempted to doubt God's promise of a successful mission, but He never gave in to that temptation, strong as it was. Well into His public ministry we read: 'From that time many of His disciples went back and walked with Him no more' (John 6:66). When it came to His death on the cross, Judas betrayed Him, and the eleven 'forsook Him and fled' (Matt. 26:47-56). But through it all He trusted God for success.

Verse 4 must also be interpreted in the light of its immediate context, particularly verse 1. In this entire song, the Servant is not talking to Himself, but to all 'peoples from afar' (v. 1). It is not a personal confession of failure and of giving in, even if momentarily, to doubt and pessimism and discouragement. Rather, it is a declaration to the entire world that although His mission will be difficult and seemingly unsuccessful, He will not lose faith in God. 'Yet surely', He avows, 'my right [the final verdict upon My labours] is with the LORD, and My recompense with My God'. The New Testament comment on this confession of faith by the Servant is: 'Let us run with endurance the race [or course] that is set before us, looking unto Jesus, the author and finisher of our faith, who for the joy that was set before Him endured the cross, despising the shame, and has sat down at the right hand of the throne of God' (Heb. 12:1-2).

He will bring salvation to Jews and Gentiles

'And now the LORD says, He who formed Me from the womb to be His Servant, to bring back Jacob to Him; and that Israel might be gathered to Him – for I am honoured in the eyes of the LORD, and My God has become My strength –' (v. 5). The Servant is still testifying to the nations, calling upon them to acknowledge and accept the divine 'work' which God has given Him, and which God will 'reward' with success (v. 4). He tells them that the LORD 'formed Me from the womb' for this divine purpose, and He will be 'My strength' to complete it. He has not only 'called Me from the womb' (v. 1), but 'formed Me from the womb to be His Servant' (v. 5). Thus our Lord Jesus Christ was miraculously conceived in the womb of the virgin Mary (Matt. 1:20; Luke 1:34, 35). The Servant is repeating the claim He has just made in verse 1, because He does not want any doubt or confusion in the minds of His hearers about His divine calling and origin.

What, then, is the 'work' for which the Servant has been divinely 'called' and supernaturally 'formed'? F. Duane Lindsey answers, 'The purpose of the Servant's mission as stated in this verse is *spiritual:* to bring Israel back to God Himself (cf. Isa. 55:7; Jer. 4:1), not to bring them back from Babylon.'[6] It is therefore significant that immediately after His resurrection, Jesus brought back to God the eleven apostles who had deserted Him (Matt. 26:56; 28:10; Mark 16:9-14). Then the eleven became one hundred and twenty (Acts 1:15). At Pentecost three thousand more were 'gathered' to God, Jewish people from many nations who were visiting Jerusalem for the feast of Pentecost (Acts 2:5, 41). A little later about five thousand Jewish men believed the gospel of Christ (Acts 4:4).

Indeed, this is a repeated refrain of Luke's: 'And believers were increasingly added to the Lord, multitudes of both men and women'; again, 'And the word of God spread, and the number of disciples multiplied greatly in Jerusalem, and a great many of the priests were obedient to the faith' (Acts 5:14; 6:7). When the apostle Paul visited Jerusalem some twenty or so years after Pentecost and gave a report on his missionary endeavours, the elders 'glorified the Lord, and said to him, "You see, brother, how many thousands there are among the Jews of those who have believed"' (Acts 21:20). It started in that first generation of Christians, and down through all church history there has been a remnant of Jewish men and women whom the Servant has brought back to God in faith. And it will continue until the 'fullness' (the full number) of elect Jews is 'gathered to Him' (Rom. 11:1-5, 12, 25-27).

Now, for the successful completion of this work, the Servant will be 'honoured' (esv). So He says (nkjv), 'I shall be glorious in the eyes of the Lord'. Not only will God be glorified in the world by the work of the Servant (v. 3), but the Servant will be glorified by God for His work. In fact, the glory of the one is dependent on the glory of the other. This is how our Lord Jesus understood this promise when He prayed for Himself the night before He died on the cross

---

6. F. Duane Lindsey, *The Servant Songs* (Moody Press, 1985), p. 69.

for the sins of His people. The apostle John records, 'Jesus spoke these words, lifted up His eyes to heaven, and said: "Father, the hour has come. Glorify Your Son, that Your Son may glorify You"' (John 17:1; see also 13:31). In other words, make Me successful in the task You have given Me, and I will make You glorious in the eyes of the people You have sent Me to redeem. Failure will result only in shame, not glory. The glory of Jehovah and the glory of His Servant are inseparable. So the outcome is not in doubt. 'My God', He says, 'shall be My strength' (NKJV).

Indeed, far from failing 'to restore the preserved ones of Israel' (those kept by God through the centuries for salvation), the Servant has been given an even greater task. Jehovah has designated Him to be the Saviour of the world, saying, 'It is too light [or small] a thing that You should be My Servant to raise up the tribes of Jacob and to bring back the preserved of Israel; I will make You as a light for the nations, that My salvation may reach to the end of the earth' (v. 6). The LORD is not dismissing the salvation of Jews as insignificant, rather, He is saying that, important as that aspect of the Servant's work is, an even greater task awaits Him which will bring further glory to God; namely, the salvation of Gentiles from all over the world.

The apostles clearly understood this. Thus Paul could say, 'For I am not ashamed of the gospel of Christ, for it is the power of God to salvation for everyone who believes, for the Jew first and also for the Greek' (or Gentiles, Rom. 1:16). The priority of the Jews as recipients of the gospel stems from the fact that God chose them to be the custodians of His truth and made a covenant with them to be their God, but it was never meant to exclude Gentiles (Gen. 12:1-3; 22:18).

Though our Lord ministered mainly to Jews while He was on earth, His final commission to His disciples was to 'make disciples of all the nations', and to 'Go into all the world and preach the gospel to every creature' (Matt. 28:19; Mark 16:15). Prior to the great commission, Jesus commended the faith of a Roman centurion and a Canaanite woman; predicted that 'many will come from east and west, and sit down with Abraham, Isaac, and Jacob in the kingdom of heaven'; and also clearly stated: 'Other sheep I have which are not of this fold [His Jewish disciples]; them also I must bring, and they will hear My voice; and there will be one flock and one shepherd' (Matt. 8:5-13; 15:21-28; John 10:16).

What was hinted at in the first song, is now more fully stated in the second (42:6; 49:6). The Servant, and He alone, is to be the Saviour of the world. The 'light' which He will bring 'to the Gentiles' will not only be the light of truth, but also the light of 'salvation' (Ps. 27:1). Every religion that is not 'in accordance with the truth that is in Jesus' (Eph. 4:21, NIV) keeps men and women in the deepest spiritual darkness, unable to see or feel their need of salvation. But Jehovah's Servant lights the way of salvation for all men. As our Lord Himself said, 'I am the way, the truth, and the life. No one comes to the Father except through Me'; and again, 'I am the light of the world. He who follows Me shall not walk in darkness, but have the light of life' (John 14:6; 8:12). This is good news indeed! The Servant's God-appointed mission to bring the light of salvation into our natural darkness, will succeed with worldwide conversions.

His humiliation will result in His exaltation

'Thus says the LORD, the Redeemer of Israel and his Holy One, to one deeply despised, abhorred by the nation, the Servant of rulers: "Kings shall see and arise; princes, and they shall prostrate themselves; because of the LORD, who is faithful, the Holy One of Israel, who has chosen You"' (v. 7). Though the Servant will be the Saviour of Jews and Gentiles 'to the end of the earth', this does not mean that everyone will receive Him as such. He will be 'deeply despised' in general, and 'abhorred by the nation' of Israel in particular as they collectively turn away from Him in revulsion. This new revelation of what Jehovah's Servant will experience on earth is repeated in the third and Fourth Servant Songs: 'I did not hide My face from shame and spitting', and 'When we see Him, there is no beauty that we should desire Him. He is despised and rejected by men, a man of sorrows and acquainted with grief. And we hid, as it were, our faces from Him; He was despised, and we did not esteem Him' (50:6; 53:2, 3).

The New Testament chronicle of the fulfilment of these prophecies in the life of Jesus Christ makes for sad reading:

> He was in the world, and the world was made through Him, and the world did not know Him. He came to His own [the Jews], and His own did not receive Him. But as many as received Him, to them He gave the right to become children of God, even to those who believe in His name (John 1:10:12).

> Then the chief priests, the scribes, and the elders of the people assembled at the palace of the high priest, who was called Caiaphas, and plotted to take Jesus by trickery and kill Him (Matt. 26:3, 4).

> And when they had come to the place called Calvary, there they crucified Him ... and the people stood looking on. But even the rulers sneered, saying, 'He saved others; let Him save Himself if He is the Christ, the chosen of God' (Luke 23:33, 35).

Rulers like Caiaphas, Herod and Pilate treated Him like a 'servant' or slave whom they thought they could dispose of as they saw fit (cf. John 19:10). Judas Iscariot actually sold Jesus to the 'chief priests' for thirty pieces of silver which was the price of a slave (Matt. 26:14-16; Exod. 21:32). But this was the danger the Servant was exposed to when He accepted the mission Jehovah assigned Him. Accepting servanthood made it easy for people to dismiss Him with contempt. The meekness of Jesus was so real that He could be ill-treated and rejected. But in the wisdom and sovereignty of God, the humiliation of the Servant would ultimately result in His supreme exaltation.

Although Jehovah does not explain how this will come about, He does assure His servant that the day will come when He will be recognised and worshipped worldwide, even by its great ones: 'Kings shall see [the achievements of the Servant] and arise [stand up to honour Him], princes, and they shall prostrate themselves.' The mention of 'kings' and 'princes' asserts that worldwide glory will be given to Him, and it is repeated in the Fourth Servant Song:

'Behold, My Servant shall deal prudently, He shall be exalted and extolled and be very high ... Kings shall shut their mouths at Him; for what had not been told them they shall see, and what they had not heard they shall consider' (52:13, 15).

The reversal of the Servant's status from humiliation to exaltation is due solely to 'the LORD, who is faithful, the Holy One of Israel, who has chosen You' (v. 7), and has never dealt falsely with His Servant or gone back on His choice of Him to be the Saviour of the world. It is a prophecy, therefore, that will be fully and perfectly fulfilled when Jehovah's Servant has brought His 'salvation to the end of the earth' (v.6). And the fullest commentary on verse 7 is surely that which the apostle Paul was inspired to write:

> Let this mind be in you which was also in Christ Jesus, who, being in the form of God, did not consider it robbery to be equal with God, but made Himself of no reputation, taking the form of a servant, and coming in the likeness of men. And being found in appearance as a man, He humbled Himself and became obedient to the point of death, even the death of the cross. Therefore God also has highly exalted Him and given Him the name which is above every name, that at the name of Jesus every knee should bow, of those in heaven, and of those on earth, and of those under the earth, and that every tongue should confess that Jesus Christ is Lord, to the glory of God the Father (Phil. 2:5-11).

When the Servant of Jehovah humbled Himself to the death of the cross and thereby made atonement for the sins of His believing people, God 'raised Him from the dead and seated Him at His right hand in the heavenly places, far above all rule and authority and power and dominion, and above every name that is named, not only in this age but also in the one to come. And He put all things under His feet' (Eph. 1:20-21). So in a sermon on Philippians 2:5-11, D. Martyn Lloyd-Jones says:

> He is now in the place at which every knee should bow and every tongue should confess, but alas, that is not being done.

There are men who, in their foolishness, stand arrogantly in defiance of Him. They laugh and ridicule Him; they refuse to bow the knee; they will not confess with the lip and the tongue that Jesus Christ is Lord. They deny Him, yes, but it says in the New Testament that He who has been exalted will appear, not in the form of a servant this time ... He will come on the clouds as King of kings, and Lord of lords. He will come attended by the heavenly hosts and will finally rout His every enemy. At that time every knee *shall* bow to Him, while those who pierced Him will see Him, and the sight of Him in glory, and the sight of His holiness, will subdue them, and He will consign them to their punishment. Then reluctantly and with shame, but nevertheless with awe, they will have to confess that Jesus Christ is Lord; that the lowly, despised Jesus was none other than the Son of God; that the death on the cross at which they laughed, and which they regarded as a sign of weakness, was the work of the Messiah, the anointed One who has removed the guilt of sin from those who believe on Him. They will have to confess that He is the eternal Son of God. He is there in the position of authority and power. He has already had His victory, and He will finally manifest Himself beyond any doubt or question in the sight of the whole world.[7]

This is the Servant whom God sent 'to give His life as a ransom for many' (Mark 10:45). We must all ask ourselves, have we put our trust in Him for the forgiveness of our sins, and have we submitted to Him as our Lord? If we refuse to do it voluntarily now, we will be made to do it when we stand before Him on the Day of Judgment.

---

7. D. Martyn Lloyd-Jones, *The Life of Joy* (Baker, 1989), pp. 157-158.

3

The Third Servant Song:
His suffering for righteousness' sake

50:4 The Lord GOD has given me the tongue of those who
   are taught,
that I may know how to sustain with a word him who is
   weary.
Morning by morning he awakens;
   he awakens my ear to hear as those who are taught.
⁵ The Lord GOD has opened my ear,
   and I was not rebellious; I turned not backward.
⁶ I gave my back to those who strike,
   and my cheeks to those who pull out the beard;
I hid not my face from disgrace and spitting.

⁷ But the Lord GOD helps me;
   therefore I have not been disgraced;
therefore I have set my face like a flint,
   and I know that I shall not be put to shame.
   ⁸ He who vindicates me is near.
Who will contend with me?
   Let us stand up together.
Who is my adversary?
   Let him come near to me.
⁹ Behold, the Lord GOD helps me;
   who will declare me guilty?

Behold, all of them will wear out like a garment;
the moth will eat them up.

¹⁰ Who among you fears the Lord
and obeys the voice of His Servant?
Let him who walks in darkness and has no light
trust in the name of the Lord and rely on his God.
¹¹ Behold, all you who kindle a fire,
who equip yourselves with burning torches!
Walk by the light of your fire,
and by the torches that you have kindled!
This you have from my hand:
you shall lie down in torment.
(Isa. 50:4-11, esv).

The Third Servant Song (50:4-11), like the second (49:1-7), is autobiographical. The Servant Himself is the speaker, and it is the most personal of all the Servant Songs, describing His daily communion with God throughout His life, His ill-treatment at the hands of men as a result, and God's help in vindicating Him before the world. Although the identity of the speaker is not revealed in verses 4-9, He is identified as Jehovah's Servant in verse 10.

Several distinctive features stand out, which connect the third song to the previous two. In the first song, Jehovah introduces His Servant as the One He will give as a 'light for the nations' to establish 'justice [a just order] in the earth' (42:1, 4, 6). In the second song, the Servant recalls the promise of Jehovah, saying, 'I will make you as a light for the nations, that my salvation may reach to the end of the earth' (49:6, esv). In the third song, the Servant reveals that the 'light' He will bring to the nations will be His teaching, and that God's salvation will deliver him who 'obeys the voice of His Servant' from the 'torment' that those who reject His light will suffer (50:4, 10, 11).

There is also further revelation given on the difficulties which Jehovah's Servant will experience in the fulfilment of His divine mission. In the first song the Servant 'will not faint nor be discouraged' because of the opposition He will have to face (42:4). In the second song the Servant will be 'despised' and 'abhorred' by those He comes to save (49:7). And in the third song the opposition is described as being not just verbal, but physical (50:5-6).

Another recurring theme is the success which will accompany the Servant's labours. In the first song, it is because Jehovah puts His 'Spirit upon Him' and holds His 'hand', that the Servant 'will not fail nor be discouraged, till He has established justice in the earth' (42:1, 4, 6). In the second song, though it may seem as if He has 'laboured in vain', the Servant can say: 'Yet surely My right is with the LORD, and My recompense with My God ... kings shall see and arise; princes, and they shall prostrate themselves; because of the LORD who is faithful' (49:4, 7). And in the third song, the Servant can confidently say that because 'the Lord GOD will help Me, therefore I will not be disgraced ... I know that I will not be ashamed. He is near who justifies Me' (50:7-8).

One more common feature is the repeated affirmation of the Servant's divinity. In the first song, the Servant is described as One in whom Jehovah 'delights', who will be 'as a light to the Gentiles, to open blind eyes' (42:1, 6, 7). God can only delight in His perfect Son who became a man and lived a sinless life on earth (Matt. 3:13-17; John 8:46). Moreover, 'God is light' and He alone can be a light to sinful men who walk in darkness (1 John 1:5; John 8:12). So the Servant is both God and man in one Person. In the second song, the Servant speaks with the authority of God and receives worship which is due only to God (49:1, 2, 7). And in the third song, to fear the LORD and to obey the voice of His Servant are equivalents, for the Servant's word is to be obeyed as God's word (50:10).

Now, if Jehovah is divine and His Servant whom He calls 'My beloved Son' is divine, what is the relation between the two? J.I. Packer, one of the leading evangelical theologians of our time, explains it in this way:

> The Son appears in the Gospels not as an independent divine
> Person, but as a dependent one, who thinks and acts only
> and wholly as the Father [Jehovah] directs. 'The Son can

do nothing of His own accord' (John 5:19, RSV). 'I have come down from heaven, not to do My own will, but the will of Him who sent Me' (John 6:38, RSV). 'I do nothing on My own authority ... I always do what is pleasing to Him' (John 8:28-29, RSV).

It is the nature of the Second Person of the Trinity to acknowledge the authority and submit to the good pleasure of the First. That is why He declares Himself to be the Son, and the First Person to be His Father. Though co-equal with the Father in eternity, power and glory, it is natural to Him to play the Son's part and find all His joy in doing His Father's will, just as it is natural to the First Person of the Trinity to plan and initiate the works of the Godhead and natural to the Third Person to proceed from the Father and the Son to do Their joint bidding.

Thus the obedience of the God–man to the Father while He was on earth was not a new relationship occasioned by the incarnation, but the continuation in time of the eternal relationship between the Son and the Father in heaven. Both in heaven and on earth, the Son was utterly dependent upon the Father's will. He only did what the Father willed Him to do and knew what the Father willed Him to know.[1]

These major truths, as we shall see in the following chapters, appear with even greater clarity in the Fourth Servant Song. Together, the songs demonstrate the divinely inspired consistency of Old Testament prophecy and its supernatural fulfilment in the Person and work of the Lord Jesus Christ, our Saviour. The Servant of Jehovah is without doubt a prophetic revelation of Jesus Christ, whom the apostles in the book of Acts called 'God's Servant' (3:26; 4:27). At the same time, in a secondary sense, these verses apply to us, for every Christian is a 'servant of the LORD'. By God's grace and for His glory, those who belong to Christ have been called

---

1. J.I. Packer, *Your Father Loves You* (Harold Shaw, 1986), Jan. 19.

and commissioned to serve God as our Lord did. There is indeed much to learn from the portrait of the messianic Servant in this third song, concerning the kind of men and women we should be, and how we should fulfil our role as the Lord's servants.

Jehovah's Servant will have an instructed tongue

'The Lord GOD has given me the tongue of those who are taught [an instructed tongue, NIV], that I may know how to sustain with a word him who is weary' (v. 4). Before He explains how He has been taught by Jehovah, the Servant asserts the results of that process. He has been instructed in the things of God and is now able to support and encourage those who are spiritually weary, and need the word of God. As a learner (NKJV), the 'word' of the Servant is not His own. It is a word which He has 'learned' from God. Moreover, it is not just intellectual but experiential knowledge of divine wisdom which enables the Servant to give strength and hope to weary Jews and Gentiles.

This prophecy was wonderfully fulfilled in the life and ministry of our Lord Jesus Christ. When Nicodemus came to Jesus by night, he opened the conversation with the words: 'Rabbi, we know that You are a teacher come from God' (John 3:2). History has echoed his verdict, for the teaching of Jesus has had a power and an effect with which the influence of no other teacher can ever for a moment be compared. People flocked to hear Him. Mark says, 'The common people heard Him gladly' (Mark 12:37). Luke says, 'All bore witness to him, and marvelled at the gracious words which proceeded out of his mouth'; and again, 'for all the people were hanging on his words' (Luke 4:22; 19:48, ESV). Clearly, our Lord's words touched the core of their being, as His recorded words still do to this day.

Take His words to Nicodemus, a prominent Pharisee and member of the Sanhedrin ('a ruler of the Jews', John 3:1). The Pharisees represented the orthodox core of Judaism and were highly zealous for ritual and religious purity according to the law of Moses and their own traditions which they had added to Mosaic legislation. But by coming to seek counsel from Jesus, whom his fellow-Pharisees opposed and dismissed as a fraud, Nicodemus gave evidence of a deeply felt spiritual need. He did not come out of curiosity, but because he was weary of the emptiness of a religion of human works. No matter how hard he tried to please God, he had no personal relationship with God. God was always a distant reality whose presence, power, peace and love he had never felt. But before Nicodemus could even ask for the answer to his weary search, our Lord read his heart and gave him the answer He had learned from God. Nicodemus needed to be spiritually regenerated before he could 'see the kingdom of God' and 'enter the kingdom of God', and be given 'the right to become [a child] of God, born not of blood ... but of God' (John 3:1-8; 1:12, 13).

In John chapter 4, Jesus meets a Samaritan woman at Jacob's well. She has come to draw water at noon, in the full heat of the day, to avoid being shunned by the other women of the town who would come in groups earlier or later in the day. She had had five husbands and was now living conjugally with another man who was not her husband. She was weary of trying to find happiness and satisfaction in life. Jesus knew this without an inkling from her, and so He said to her: 'Everyone who drinks of this water [from Jacob's well] will be thirsty again, but whoever drinks of the water that I will give him will never thirst again. The water that I will give him will become in him a spring of water welling up to eternal life'. This word, and the further words He went on to give her, inspired her to believe in Him as the Christ and to give her testimony to others in the town. As a result, John says, 'He stayed there two days. And many more believed because of his word' (4:1-54, ESV).

It is all in the Gospels: we see Jesus speaking to a leper, a Roman centurion, a demon-possessed man, a paralytic, a tax collector, a woman with an issue of blood, John the Baptist, a prostitute who anointed His feet with expensive ointment, to Peter before he betrayed Him, and the penitent thief on the cross, just to cite some examples (Matt. 8:1-4; 5-13; 8:28-34; 9:1-8, 9-13, 18-26; 11:2-6; Luke 7:36-50; 22:31-34; 23:39-43). He had a word to sustain all of them in their weariness through guilt, emptiness, despair and sadness. It is an extraordinary thing that a young man of thirty years knew 'how to sustain with a word him [or her] who is weary.'

The tongue is a Christian's chief natural asset. The ministry to which every believer is called is a teaching/witnessing ministry of communicating the gospel, and it would be virtually impossible to exercise it without the tongue. It is by the tongue that a direct and precise message is conveyed, and the particular power of the tongue which is being singled out here is that of bringing counsel and hope to the weary. So many men and women are weary, weighed down with the burdens of life; weary with the sorrow and guilt and power of sin. Such people can be comforted; the weary can be reinvigorated; sinners can be saved, and all this by words.

What tremendous power there is in the human tongue! Our words sometimes cut, wound and cause irreparable harm, but they can also comfort and heal. Many a person bowed down with sin and despair has been given new hope by appropriate words of encouragement and guidance from Scripture. We always need to bear in mind the words of Proverbs 12:18, 'There is one whose rash words are like sword thrusts, but the tongue of the wise brings healing' (ESV). It is Jehovah who can give us 'the tongue of those who are taught, that [we] may know how to sustain with a word him who is weary.' Let us ask Him to teach us.

Jehovah's Servant will have an open ear

There is certainly a close connection between the ear and the tongue. There can be no instructed tongue without an open ear. So the messianic Servant goes on to say, 'The Lord GOD has given Me the tongue of those who are taught … Morning by morning He awakens; He awakens my ear to hear as those who are taught' (vv. 1, 4). Our Lord's great learning at the young age of thirty was a mystery that really baffled His contemporary hearers. There was a combination of profundity of thought and lucid expression in His preaching and teaching, especially in His homely parables, which to this day have impressed everybody who has truly studied the recorded words of Jesus in the Gospels.

So at the beginning of His public ministry, after Jesus had preached in the synagogue of Nazareth, His home town, Mark records the response of the congregation: 'And many hearing Him were astonished, saying, "Where did this Man get these things? And what wisdom is this which is given to Him? ... Is not this the carpenter, the Son of Mary, and brother of James, Joses, Judas, and Simon? And are not His sisters here with us?'" (Mark 6:2, 3). In other words, He is just a carpenter from a humble home who never went to Jerusalem to study. So where did He get this wisdom from?

Much later in His ministry, our Lord visited Jerusalem during the Feast of Tabernacles and taught in the temple. And the Jews marvelled, saying, 'How is it that this Man has learning, when He has never studied? So Jesus answered them, "My teaching is not mine, but his who sent me. If anyone's will is to do God's will, he will know whether the teaching is from God or whether I am speaking on my own authority'" (John 7:15-17, ESV). Of course, Jesus had studied in a sense. Like the other children in Nazareth, He would have attended the elementary school attached to the local synagogue, where, as He grew up, He would also have had the opportunity to read and meditate upon the Old Testament scrolls for Himself. But what these Jews meant was that Jesus had received no formal education. He had not received the higher education which the scribes or Pharisees received. He had never sat at the feet of a master Rabbi like Gamaliel (Acts 5:34; 22:3).

We read some similar words on yet another occasion after Jesus preached in the synagogue of Capernaum: 'And they were astonished at His teaching, for He taught them as one having authority, and not as the scribes' (Mark 1:22). The scribes were very respected members of the Jewish community. They were well-educated, and as such they were the custodians and teachers of the law. But in their teaching they were essentially traditionalists. In all their discussions on the law of God the scribes would quote from their ancient authorities. They would quote this Rabbi and that Rabbi as an authority for what they were teaching. They never dared to speak in their own name.

With Jesus, however, it was different. He never quoted any other Rabbi from the past or the present, like the scribes. He spoke with a quiet, sure authority of His own. Our Lord was completely self-possessed and self-assured in His teaching. There was no guesswork, or speculation, or fumbling, or faltering in His discourses. Expressions like: It may be so, or perhaps, or I think so, were not part of His vocabulary. Jesus knew what He wanted to say, and He said it with a calm dogmatism which astonished those who heard Him.

Again, the teaching of the world's great teachers developed and improved over the years. But it is a very remarkable thing that Jesus never contradicted Himself. He never withdrew or even modified anything that He had said previously. Moreover, as a teacher, our Lord expected men and women to believe His teaching and obey it. Indeed, He dared even to assert that on the last day His hearers would be judged by their acceptance or rejection of His teaching. In John 12 we read, 'The one who rejects me and does not receive my words has a judge; the word that I have spoken will judge him on the last day' (John 12:48, ESV).

So where did Jesus, the messianic Servant, get His teaching from? His answer in the third song is: 'Morning by morning He [Jehovah] awakens; He awakens My ear to hear as those who are taught' (v. 4). It came through daily communication initiated by Jehovah God early in the morning all through the Servant's life (Mark 1:35). Nothing took priority over this. The Father did the teaching, while His Servant–Son did the listening and the learning. As the Scripture says, 'Jesus increased in wisdom and stature' (Luke 2:52). As God incarnate, His infinite divine nature did not take over His finite human nature. Rather, the characteristics of each nature are preserved in His one Person, and so it was necessary for Jesus as a man to be taught and to learn. The mechanics of this we are not told, but it must have involved both direct communication from the Father and disciplined meditation upon and memorization of the Old Testament Scriptures, which were available to Him in the synagogue at Nazareth (Luke 4:16).

There were times, certainly, when the Father spoke directly to the Son. When Jesus said, 'I have not spoken on My own authority; but the Father who sent Me gave Me a command, what I should say and what I should speak ... Therefore, whatever I speak, just as the Father has told Me, so I speak' (John 12:49-50), He was clearly referring to direct communion between Himself and God, such as the prophets had known. After all, He was *the* Prophet God predicted when He said to Moses, 'I will raise up for them a Prophet like you from among their brethren, and will put My words in His mouth, and He shall speak to them all that I command Him' (Deut. 18:18; Acts 3:22; 7:37).

It is also clear, I believe, that Jesus learned the understanding of His own calling as the messianic Servant of God through reading the Old Testament Scriptures and allowing God to speak to Him through them. He was absolutely saturated in the word of God. To give but one example, when Jesus was taken into the wilderness to be tempted by the devil, we read of Him, as it were, throwing the Book at him. Three times He quoted Scripture in rejecting the devil's evil suggestions, and thereby asserted that He was committed to do God's will and live by Scripture which He had learned since a child (Matt. 4:1-11; Luke 2:46-47).

To be sure, our Lord was not born all-knowing. He appeared on earth as a helpless human baby, needing to be fed and changed and taught to talk and gain knowledge like any other child. And there was no illusion or deception in this. The babyhood of the Son of God was a reality. To quote J.I. Packer again, 'The baby born at Bethlehem was God made man. He had not ceased to be God; He was no less God than before; but He had begun to be man. He was not now God *minus* some elements of His deity but God *plus* all that He had made His own by taking manhood to Himself. He who made man was now learning what it felt like to be man.'[2]

There is surely an important lesson here for us to learn. We too need 'the tongue of those who are taught'. We dare not presume to teach others until we have first been taught ourselves. We need God to give us the tongue of the taught and deliver us from the tongue of the untaught! Before we speak, we must listen; before we open our lips to utter God's message, we need to open our ears to hear His word. Indeed, it has been said that since God has given us two ears and only one mouth, He means us to listen twice as much as we speak.

One of the commonest hindrances to effective teaching and witnessing, whether to a group or an individual, is that we have no

---

2. J.I. Packer, *Knowing God Devotional Journal*, p. 29.

understanding of God's truth to impart. No Sunday school teacher should face his or her class if they have not set aside time to be quiet before God and prepare the lesson. And no Christian can expect to win a friend to Christ, if they have never taken the time to grasp the truth of the gospel. Many, I am sure, are dumb because they are deaf. Their mouth is shut because their mind is empty and their ear is closed. The remedy lies in verse 4, 'Morning by morning He awakens; He awakens My ear to hear as those who are taught.' It is obvious that if God wakens my ear to hear, it is because He has something to say to me. He is willing to do this wakening and speaking 'morning by morning', but I must be willing to read His word and listen.

Jehovah's Servant will be afflicted in body

'The Lord GOD has opened My ear, and I was not rebellious; I turned not backward. I gave My back to those who strike, and My cheeks to those who pull out the beard; I hid not My face from disgrace [insults or mocking] and spitting' (vv. 5-6). The Servant in these verses is not speaking of the sufferings of damnation and hell which He will undergo 'for the transgressions of [His] people'. Those sufferings, unique to Him alone, will be described in the Fourth Servant Song (53:5-11). Here, in the third song, He is portraying the sufferings He will endure for righteousness' sake; for doing the will of God. Thus He introduces the subject of His persecutions with the statement: 'The Lord GOD has opened My ear, and I was not rebellious; I turned not backward.' Into the Servant's open ear God speaks, and His message is to be both obeyed and communicated. But the communication of divine truth invariably involves suffering. There is something in the teaching of repentance and faith that rouses anger and hatred in the hearts of men and women against the messenger.

This opposition was hinted at in the first song, where, in spite of it, Jehovah says that His Servant 'will not grow faint or be discouraged till he has established justice in the earth' (42:4, ESV). That clearly suggests that the Servant in His mission on earth is going to experience difficulties that could reasonably 'discourage' Him, and make Him 'turn back' from His assignment. In the second song the opposition is now personal, and not just circumstantial. It has intensified into verbal and psychological abuse of God's Servant, who is described as 'One deeply despised, abhorred by the nation' (49:7, ESV). But it is still presented in general terms. But now, in the third song, the opposition intensifies into the most appalling physical suffering.

There are three elements to it in verse 6. First, the Servant will be treated as a criminal and sentenced to be *judicially flogged:* 'I gave My back to those who strike.' The fulfilment of this persecution on an innocent man is recorded in John 19:1, 'So then Pilate took Jesus and scourged Him' (see also verse 4, and Matt. 27:26). Scourging under Roman law was the most brutal punishment imaginable. According to William Hendriksen, 'The Roman scourge consisted of a short wooden handle to which several thongs were attached, the ends equipped with pieces of lead or brass and with sharply pointed bits of bone. The stripes were laid especially (not always exclusively) on the victim's back, bared and bent. The body was at times torn and lacerated to such an extent that deep-seated veins and arteries – sometimes even entrails and inner organs – were exposed. Such flogging, from which Roman citizens were exempt, often resulted in death.'[3]

The second element in the unjust suffering of the Servant for righteousness' sake is what J.A. Motyer calls '*gratuitous torture*'[4]: 'I gave ... My cheeks to those who pull out the beard.' This was ill-treatment which went beyond punishment by a court of law. No court of law would sentence a man to have his beard pulled out. This is simply sadistic cruelty inflicted by brutal men as a sign of contempt for the Person of God's Servant and all He stood for (2 Sam. 10:4; Neh. 13:25). Although this part of the Servant's ill-treatment is not recorded in the Gospels, it must have been endured by Christ, perhaps during His mockery by the soldiers, after Pilate condemned Him. No prophecy concerning His sufferings could go unfulfilled (Luke 24:25-27).

---

3. William Hendriksen, *John* (Banner of Truth, 1973), p. 414.

4. J. Alec Motyer, *The Prophecy of Isaiah*, p. 400.

The third element in the Servant's suffering for righteousness' sake is *public humiliation*. The Servant–Son in whom God the Father delights is going to be subjected to 'mocking and spitting' (NIV).

> Then they [the chief priests and the whole Council] spat in His face and beat Him with their fists; and others slapped Him, and said, 'Prophesy to us, You Christ, who is the one who hit You?' (Matt. 26:67, 68, NASB).

> Then the soldiers of the governor [Pilate] took Jesus into the Praetorium and gathered the whole Roman cohort around Him. And they stripped Him, and put a scarlet robe on Him. And after weaving a crown of thorns, they put it on His head, and a reed in His right hand; and they kneeled down before Him and mocked Him, saying, 'Hail, King of the Jews!' And they spat on Him, and took the reed and began to beat Him on the head (Matt. 27:27-30, NASB).

> At that time two robbers were crucified with Him, one on the right and one on the left. And those who were passing by were hurling abuse at Him, wagging their heads, and saying, 'You who destroy the temple and rebuild it in three days [words said by Jesus concerning His bodily resurrection], save Yourself! If You are the Son of God, come down from the cross.' In the same way the chief priests, along with the scribes and elders, were mocking Him, and saying, 'He saved others, He cannot save Himself. He is the King of Israel; let Him come down from the cross, and we shall believe in Him. He trusts in God; let Him deliver Him now, if He takes pleasure in Him; for He said, "I am the Son of God."' And the robbers also who had been crucified with Him were casting the same insults at Him (Matt. 27:38-44, NASB).

The judicial flogging, the gratuitous torture and public humiliation were all the more shocking, not only because they were unjust, inhumane and blatantly false, but brazenly inflicted upon the very person of God incarnate. The messianic Servant, if He had wished, could have destroyed His enemies and vindicated Himself with a mere word, but that would have nullified the purpose for which He had been sent to the earth; namely, to be the Saviour of the world (Matt. 26:50-54). So, instead of being 'rebellious' and 'turning away' from the will of Jehovah, the Servant 'gave' His back and His cheeks to His persecutors (vv. 5, 6). His obedience was an active and voluntary acceptance, rather than a helpless resignation to His fate. He was willing to go through all this in order to do Jehovah's will.

In every successive chapter of the history of God's people, there are illustrations of lesser servants of God who obeyed God's will at personal cost. Elijah had to flee for his life from the wrath of Queen Jezebel (1 Kings 19:1-4). Jeremiah was jailed several times and then forced to go to Egypt against his will (Jer. 37:15; 38:6; 43:5, 6). John the Baptist was beheaded in prison; the apostle Paul was beaten five times by the Jews, three times by the Romans and imprisoned twice for more than four years (Mark 6:22-27; 2 Cor. 11:24, 25; Acts 24:27; 28:30; 2 Tim. 2:9). These men, as well as many others ever since, had done nothing to deserve their afflictions, but teach and preach the word of God. But like Paul, they could say, 'Now I rejoice in my sufferings for your sake, and in my flesh I am filling up what is lacking in Christ's afflictions for the sake of His body, that is, the church' (Col. 1:24). Christians cannot suffer without Christ also suffering (Acts 9:4), and so as they suffer for righteousness' sake, He continues to suffer with His people at the hands of ungodly men. It is part of the bitter cup ordained for Him which will only be filled up on the last day (Matt. 20:22; 26:39, 42).

The Lord Jesus, God's chief Servant, is the supreme example of undeserved suffering. He never spoke anything but the words that the Father taught Him, yet His teaching aroused the bitterest opposition, and His enemies showed no respect for His sacred Person and His miraculous works of mercy. Neither can Christians, as servants of the Servant, expect to escape suffering. Our Lord plainly warned us: 'If the world hates you, you know that it hated Me before it hated you. If you were of the world, the world would love its own. Yet because you are not of the world, but I chose you out of the world, therefore the world hates you. Remember the word that I said to you, "A servant is not greater than his master." If they persecuted Me, they will also persecute you' (John 15:18-20).

Moreover, His apostles echoed His teaching. Paul says, 'For to you it has been granted on behalf of Christ, not only to believe in Him, but also to suffer for His sake'; and again, 'All who desire to live godly in Christ Jesus will suffer persecution' (Phil. 1:29; 2 Tim. 3:12). Likewise, Peter says, 'For to this you were called, because Christ also suffered for us, leaving us an example, that you should follow in His steps: "Who committed no sin, nor was guile found in His mouth", who, when He was reviled, did not revile in return; when He suffered, He did not threaten, but committed Himself to Him who judges righteously' (1 Pet. 2:21-23).

To live for Christ and serve Him, even in civilized countries where there is little or no physical persecution, still brings humiliation, criticism and ostracism from men and women. Of course, we must not court or provoke abuse from unbelievers, but we must be prepared for it. The visitor may not have the door slammed in his face, but his spirit may be intimidated by a hostile reception. The Christian who seeks to win a friend must be prepared to be snubbed and laughed at, or called a fanatic. It hurts to be thus treated, but it is the inevitable lot of God's servants who must remember the words of their Master: 'Blessed are those who are persecuted for righteousness' sake, for theirs is the kingdom of heaven. Blessed are you when they revile and persecute you, and say all kinds of evil against you falsely for My sake. Rejoice and be exceedingly glad, for great is your reward in heaven, for so they persecuted the prophets who were before you' (Matt. 5:10-12).

Jehovah's Servant will have a flint face

The Servant of Jehovah, who knows that His face is going to be fouled by the spittle of His enemies, will set His face like a flint to accomplish His divine mission, no matter what the cost. He sets His face like a flint against the cruellest opposition of men: 'But the Lord GOD helps Me; therefore I have not been disgraced; therefore I have set My face like a flint, and I know that I shall not be put to shame' (v. 7). Flint is hard stone of nearly pure silica which is synonymous with anything hard and unyielding. Luke captures this spirit in the life of Jesus when he says, 'Now it came to pass, when the time had come for Him to be received up [to die and ascend to heaven], that He steadfastly set His face to go to Jerusalem' (Luke 9:51). He hardened His resolve to go to Jerusalem, knowing full well all the suffering He would have to endure there. He did not allow His determination to be weakened by His own human distaste for suffering.

The Servant's courage, however, was not based on false reliance on human fortitude. The Servant is courageous because His confidence is in God who will not fail Him: 'The Lord GOD helps Me; therefore I have not been disgraced [publicly let down] ... and I know that I shall not be put to shame' (v. 7). The Servant endured all the buffetings of Satan with the assurance that Jehovah would 'vindicate' Him (v. 8). God promised to give courage to Jeremiah and Ezekiel who were called to preach the truth in the midst of almost universal apostasy (Jer. 1:18; Ezek. 3:8, 9). We too are called to show the same resolute determination to serve God in our own day, but so many today do not seem to have the grit and endurance of former generations. We so easily give up when the going is hard and we are not sustained by the applause of men. We do not find it easy to persevere in the face of opposition and ridicule. So often we have faces of clay and putty, rather than faces of flint and iron.

We cannot transform ourselves from men of *flesh* to men of *flint* by our own strength of will and forbearance. The secret is to know that 'the Lord GOD helps Me'; and that 'He who vindicates Me is near' (vv. 7-8). To vindicate means to 'declare righteous', free from all censure. And Jehovah's vindication of His Servant was demonstrated in Christ's resurrection and exaltation to 'the right hand of the throne of God' (Heb. 12:2). Speaking of our Lord's vindication, Paul says, 'Beyond all question, the mystery of godliness is great: "He appeared in a body, was vindicated by the Spirit, was seen by angels, was preached among the nations, was believed on in the world, was taken up in glory"' (1 Tim. 3:16, NIV). Men condemned and killed Him, but God justified Him and raised Him from the dead. Men debased and tortured Him as if He were a criminal, but 'God has highly exalted Him and given Him the name which is above every name, that at the name of Jesus every knee should bow, of those in heaven, and of those on earth, and of those under the earth, and that every tongue should confess that Jesus Christ is Lord, to the glory of God the Father' (Phil. 2:9-11).

The resurrection and exaltation, however, were just the beginning of Jehovah God's vindication of His beloved Son, Jesus Christ, His chosen messianic Servant in whom He delights (42:1; Matt. 3:16, 17; 12:15-21; 17:1-8). God's vindication of Him will continue throughout the ages, as men, women and children from every nation are brought to Him in faith and His divine mission is successfully completed. Then on the last day, the final Day of Judgment, the whole human race will stand on trial at the judgment seat of Christ, and He will arraign those who condemned Him for blasphemy and fraud on earth. This will be a just tribunal with God as the righteous Judge and His Servant as His invincible Prosecutor. And He will say, 'He who vindicates me is near. Who then will bring charges against me? Let us face each other! Who is my accuser? Let him confront me! It is the Sovereign Lord who helps me. Who is he that will condemn me? They will all wear out like a garment; the moths will eat them up' (vv. 8, 9, NIV).

No power, human or demonic, will be able to successfully challenge the verdict of Jehovah God when He 'justifies' His Servant (v. 8, NKJV). Jesus Christ finally will be publicly and universally acknowledged as God's representative on earth, whose enemies are the enemies of God. Their destruction may be gradual, but it is certain. John Mackay writes: 'The imagery of the moth (cf. 51:8) adds a note of impotence. The garment cannot defend itself against the predatory moth; no more can the Servant's opponents win their case in the court of heaven. No matter how plausible His enemies might seem now, they and their arguments will be swept aside by the divine verdict.'[5]

Moreover, if we are Christ's servants; if we 'obey the voice of [Jehovah's] Servant' (v. 10), then we are in the same position as He is. Thus the apostle Paul can echo these words of the Servant, not

---

5. John L. Mackay, *Isaiah*, vol. 2, p. 283.

only as a declaration of His assurance, but also that of His people. And so we too can confidently say: 'If God is for us, who can be against us? ... Who shall bring a charge against God's elect? It is God who justifies. Who is he who condemns? It is Christ who died, and furthermore is also risen, who is even at the right hand of God, who also makes intercession for us' (Rom. 8:31-34). Every Christian can have this assurance. We have nothing to fear, for God, the righteous Judge, 'justifies' us. Our standing of righteousness and that of the Servant are joined together.

Jehovah's Servant will determine everybody's destiny

Verses 10-11 form a fitting conclusion and application to the Third Servant Song. The Servant is still the speaker who now invites those who obey His word to emulate His example and put their trust in the name of the Lord. To depend on their own wits and resources will only incur the fire of divine condemnation: 'Who among you fears the Lord and obeys the voice of His Servant? Let him who walks in darkness and has no light trust in the name of the Lord and rely on His God. Behold, all you who kindle a fire, who equip yourselves with burning torches! Walk by the light of your fire, and by the torches that you have kindled! This you will have from My hand: you shall lie down in torment.'

The darkness being spoken of here is obviously spiritual darkness which blots out the face of God and makes Him seem to be far removed. Both those who fear God and those who don't, experience spiritual darkness. But there is a significant difference. Whereas believers experience only *temporary* darkness during times when God is testing the genuineness of their faith, or sometimes when they walk in disobedience, unbelievers live in a *permanent* darkness of ignorance concerning the one true living God. They have no belief in His existence, or any knowledge of how they may come to know Him. Accordingly, because humankind must have some god, they worship god substitutes of their own imagination.

The Servant is therefore informing His followers that there will be seasons when they will 'walk in darkness and have no light'. God will seem strangely silent and distant. They will feel all alone and unable to cope with their circumstances. But they must not think it strange, for the Servant Himself will go through such difficult and hard-to-understand situations. Those who obey His voice, then, must follow His example of quiet and patient trust. For the Servant it is going to be the darkness of persecution, rejection and apparent failure. But He will not stop trusting in or relying on His God, even when there is not even a glimmer of light on His pathway. As the Servant Songs predict: 'He will not grow faint or be discouraged'; 'surely my right is with the LORD, and my recompense with my God'; and 'I was not rebellious; I turned not backward ... the Lord GOD helps me' (42:4; 49:4; 50:5, 7, ESV).

To those who 'fear the LORD and obey the voice of His Servant', there will come, sooner or later, similar times of temporary darkness. True, Jesus promised, 'He who follows Me shall not walk in darkness, but have the light of life' (John 8:12). But at the same time, He did not promise that life would be a bed of roses. Faith in God cannot be strengthened, nor Christian character refined, without being tried in the fires of affliction, whatever they be: a tragic accident, bankruptcy, the betrayal of a spouse, a crippling illness, or martyrdom.

It is a spiritual state so normal to the Christian life that those godly men who drafted the Westminster Confession included it in their Confession of Faith: 'True believers may have the assurance of their salvation divers ways shaken, diminished and intermitted ... by falling into some special sin which woundeth the conscience and grieveth the Spirit; by sudden or vehement temptation; by God's withdrawing the light of His countenance, and suffering even such as fear Him to walk in darkness and to have no light ...'[6]

Besides the Servant, other biblical characters went through times of temporary spiritual darkness, and continued to believe in the goodness of God and rely on His help. When Job lost all his children and property, he still held on to God with reverence and faith, saying, 'The LORD gave, and the LORD has taken away; blessed be the name of the LORD' (Job 1:21). And then when his body was covered with the most painful sores, neither Satan nor his wife could persuade Job to curse God. While he could not understand why all this was

---

6. *The Westminster Confession*, ch. 18.

happening to him, and at times misspoke, he could still say, 'Though He slay me, yet will I trust Him' (Job 13:15).

The prophet Habakkuk is another example. He could not understand how, in spite of his ministry in Judah, violence and iniquity were just getting worse. When he asked God to intervene, he was shocked to hear that God was going to send the Chaldeans, a nation more violent and wicked than Judah, to punish them. This was grievous news, which tested Habakkuk's faith severely. Yet, notwithstanding his perplexity at the devastation that was coming to Judah, he could still conclude his prophecy with a hymn of faith: 'Though the fig tree may not blossom, nor fruit be on the vines; though the labour of the olive may fail, and the fields yield no food; though the flock be cut off from the fold, and there be no herd in the stalls – yet I will rejoice in the LORD, I will joy in the God of my salvation. The LORD God is my strength ...' (Hab. 3:17-19).

The third song ends with a warning to those who do not fear Jehovah or obey the voice of His Servant. There is no distinction between fearing Jehovah and obeying His Servant's voice. Indeed, to disobey His voice will determine a man or woman's eternal destiny (v. 11). To 'lie down' or sleep is a euphemism for death (1 Kings 2:10, ESV), and 'to lie down in torment' designates a place of suffering after death that is the result of God's judgment (cf. 66:24; Luke 16:19-31). This group are also walking (or living) in spiritual darkness (permanent, not temporary darkness), and have resorted to generating their own light or wisdom to guide them in life. So the prophet warns them of their folly: 'Behold, all you who kindle a fire, who equip yourselves with burning torches! Walk by the light of your fire, and by the torches that you have kindled!' Human sources of light cannot illumine spiritual darkness. Only the Servant, whom Jehovah is sending as 'a light for the nations' can dispel spiritual darkness.

Commenting on this, Raymond Ortlund says, 'People light their own fires, to use Isaiah's metaphor. They have their own ideas to live by. Why listen to Christ when there are plausible, and certainly easier, ways to live? Some people sit through sermons, but are they listening? Their lives are not set apart from the convenient soft ways of the world. Why? They don't feel in their hearts that Christ can be counted on when it matters. They are making their own way. But remember the drawback to that approach to life: "There is a way that seems right to a man, but its end is the way to death" (Prov. 16:25, ESV).[7] The Servant will determine everybody's destiny by whether or not they obey His voice: 'This you shall have from My hand; you shall lie down in torment.'

A life of torment after death is not the desire of Jehovah or His Servant for anyone:

> I have stretched out My hands all day long to a rebellious people, who walk in a way that is not good, according to their own thoughts; a people who provoke Me to anger continually to My face (Isa. 65:2, 3).

> 'As I live', says the Lord GOD, 'I have no pleasure in the death of the wicked, but that the wicked turn from his way and live. Turn, turn from your evil ways! For why should you die, O house of Israel?' (Ezek. 33:11).

> 'O Jerusalem, Jerusalem, the one who kills the prophets and stones those who are sent to her! How often I wanted to gather your children together, as a hen gathers her chicks under her wings, but you were not willing! See! Your house is left to you desolate' (Matt. 23:37, 38).

> 'As many as I love, I rebuke and chasten. Therefore be zealous and repent [turn away from your sin]. Behold, I stand at the door and knock. If anyone hears My voice and opens the door, I will come in to him and dine with him, and he with Me. To him who overcomes [sin or dark trials] I will grant to sit with Me on My throne, as I also overcame and sat down with My Father on His throne' (Rev. 3:19-21).

The wisest action for us all is to 'trust in the name [revealed character] of the LORD and rely upon his God', by obeying 'the voice of His Servant' whom He has sent to show us the 'way' (John 14:16).

---

7. Raymond C. Ortlund, Jr., *Isaiah*, p. 338.

4

The Fourth Servant Song I:
His path to glory will be extreme suffering

52:13 Behold, my servant shall act wisely;
  he shall be high and lifted up,
and shall be exalted.
[14] As many were astonished at you –
  his appearance was so marred, beyond human semblance,
  and his form beyond that of the children of mankind –
[15] so shall he sprinkle many nations;
  kings shall shut their mouths because of him;
for that which has not been told them they see,
  and that which they have not heard they understand.

53:1 Who has believed what he has heard from us?
  And to whom has the arm of the LORD been revealed?
[2] For He grew up before him like a young plant,
  and like a root out of dry ground;
he had no form or majesty that we should look at him,
  and no beauty that we should desire him.
[3] He was despised and rejected by men;
  a man of sorrows, and acquainted with grief;
and as one from whom men hide their faces
  he was despised, and we esteemed him not.

[4] Surely he has borne our griefs
  and carried our sorrows;

yet we esteemed him stricken,
  smitten by God, and afflicted.
⁵ But he was wounded for our transgressions;
  he was crushed for our iniquities;
upon him was the chastisement that brought us peace,
  and with his stripes we are healed.
⁶ All we like sheep have gone astray;
  we have turned – every one – to his own way;
and the Lord has laid on him
  the iniquity of us all.

⁷ He was oppressed, and He was afflicted,
  yet He opened not his mouth;
like a lamb that is led to the slaughter,
  and like a sheep that before its shearers is silent,
  so he opened not his mouth.
⁸ By oppression and judgment he was taken away;
  and as for his generation, who considered
that he was cut off out of the land of the living,
  stricken for the transgression of my people?
⁹ And they made his grave with the wicked
  and with a rich man in his death,
although he had done no violence,
  and there was no deceit in his mouth.

¹⁰ Yet it was the will of the Lord to crush him;
he has put him to grief;
  when his soul makes an offering for guilt,
he shall see his offspring; he shall prolong his days;
  the will of the Lord shall prosper in his hand.
¹¹ Out of the anguish of his soul he shall see and be satisfied;
by his knowledge shall the righteous one, my servant,
  make many to be accounted righteous,
  and he shall bear their iniquities.
¹² Therefore I will divide him a portion with the many,
  and he shall divide the spoil with the strong,
because he poured out his soul to death

and was numbered with the transgressors;
yet he bore the sin of many,
and makes intercession for the transgressors.
(Isa. 52:13–53:12, ESV).

The Fourth Servant Song is the longest and most important of the four songs. Indeed, it may, in my opinion, be called the most important passage of the Old Testament, because it is more frequently quoted in the New Testament than any other Old Testament passage (Luke 22:37; John 12:38; Acts 8:26-35; Rom. 10:16; 15:21; 1 Pet. 2:21-25). Not surprisingly, Robert F. Pfeiffer has said, 'The extant [Jewish and Christian] literature on the monumental fifty-third chapter of Isaiah is so vast that, perhaps, no person could read it in a lifetime.'[1]

E.J. Young, in his book, *Old Testament Prophecy*, calls it 'a capstone of all Old Testament prophecies'.[2] J. Gresham Machen (1881-1937), a great biblical scholar, agrees: 'If there is any one passage in the Old Testament which seems to the Christian heart to be a prophecy of the redeeming work of Christ, it is that matchless fifty-third chapter of Isaiah. We read it today, often even in preference to New Testament passages, as setting forth the atonement which our Lord made for the sins of others upon the cross. Never, says the simple Christian, was there a prophecy more gloriously plain.'[3]

In this famous passage we also have both the culmination and resolution of the partial predictions of the Servant's life and work already given in the first three Songs; namely His commission to establish a just and righteous order on earth, and the glory that will accrue to Him (42:4; 49:5c,7c). The Servant's task, however, will be fraught with rejection and suffering (49:7b; 50:6). In the fourth song, Isaiah tells us that this opposition will culminate in the Servant's death and burial (53:7-9). And because this will be in accordance with the will of God (53:10) it will not impede Messiah/Christ's success, but facilitate it (53:10-12), for His suffering and death will

---

1. Quoted by F. Duane Lindsey, *The Servant Songs*, p. 98.
2. E.J. Young, *Old Testament Prophecy* (Britannia Printers, 1990), p. 106.
3. Quoted from E.J. Young, *Isaiah Fifty-Three* (Eerdmans, 1957), p. 5.

be endured on behalf of the 'many' for whom Jehovah has sent Him to secure peace, healing and justification (53:5, 11).

Not only that, the messianic Servant's success in bringing God's salvation to the end of the earth (49:6) will result in the greatest exaltation ever conferred upon a servant of God. He will not only be the object of God's delight (42:1), and receive obeisance from kings and princes (49:5c,7c), and be vindicated before His enemies (50:8, 9), but 'He will be raised and lifted up and highly exalted' (52:13, NIV). The fourth song, therefore, is not simply a poem about the suffering of the Servant; it is about the redemption which the Servant will accomplish when through His penal, substitutionary death, He will 'make many to be accounted righteous' (53:11), and be greatly exalted as a result.

Regarding its structure, the fourth song is a hymn of five stanzas, each consisting of three verses which are clearly demarcated in our modern English versions by a paragraph division between the stanzas. The first and fifth stanzas outline the parameter of the message of this lyrical prophecy, both providing in summary form, different aspects of the messianic Servant's sufferings and resultant glory (52:13-15; 53:10-12). The second stanza (53:1-3) reveals the difficulty of faith without divine intervention, for the natural tendency of human beings is to reject Jehovah's Servant with contempt.

In the third stanza, Isaiah puts himself in the position of God's believing people, both Jews and Gentiles (53:4-6). The stanza is full of first person plural pronouns like 'our', 'we' and 'us'. 'He was wounded for *our* transgressions'; 'with His stripes *we* are healed'; 'the LORD has laid on Him the iniquity of *us* all.' The fourth stanza (53:7-9) emphasises the voluntary and silent submission of Jehovah's Servant to those who so unjustly put Him to death.

Something else of note is the tenses of the verbs that are used. In the first and last stanzas the verbs are mainly future tense, because Isaiah is predicting the first coming of Jesus Christ which will not take place for another 700 years. Thus we read in the first stanza: 'My Servant shall act wisely ... and shall be exalted ... so shall He sprinkle many nations.' And in the last stanza, Isaiah says, 'He shall see His offspring ... He shall bear their iniquities ... and He shall divide the spoil with the many.' But when we come to the central portion of the song, all the verbs are past tense: 'He was despised and rejected by men ... and we esteemed Him not ... He has borne our griefs and carried our sorrows ... He was wounded for our transgressions ... He was oppressed and He was afflicted, yet He opened not His mouth ... they made His grave with the wicked.' When the prophet puts the main body of the fourth song in the past tense, it is not because he is referring to some figure in the past. Rather, he is using a prophetic perfect tense to proclaim with certainty that the Servant will come. All the predictions in this fourth song about His life and work are so sure that they are as good as done.

Previously, we have made the case in our introduction to the Servant Songs that the New Testament writers declare, under the inspiration of the Holy Spirit, that Jesus of Nazareth is the Servant of Jehovah and the promised Messiah of whom God said, 'I will make you as a light for the nations, that My salvation may reach to the end of the earth' (49:6). And of all the songs, the fourth is most clearly identified in the New Testament as messianic (Luke 22:37; Acts 8:26-35; Rom. 15:21; 1 Pet. 2:21-35). Indeed, before our Lord Jesus Christ came into the world, most of the Jewish scribes and rabbis said that it was a prophecy about the coming Messiah.

How, then, are we to account for the different interpretations of the Servant's identity held by Jewish and some Christian scholars today? John L. Mackay gives the correct explanation: 'The messianic interpretation was indeed the earliest one among the Jews, being witnessed to by the Targum *Jonathan*, a paraphrase of the Old Testament Scripture which identifies the Servant in 52:13 as the Messiah. It was the early church's successful apologetic use of the passage to prove that Jesus was the prophesied Messiah that led Jewish commentators to develop alternative interpretations of the passage, and it was only under the influence of Enlightenment philosophy [liberalism] that these became commonly adopted in Western Christianity.'[4]

With that necessary introduction to the Fourth Servant Song, we can begin our exposition of the first stanza:

---

4. John L. Mackay, *Isaiah*, vol. 2, p. 331.

> ^{13} Behold, my servant shall act wisely;
>   he shall be high and lifted up,
> and shall be exalted.
> ^{14} As many were astonished at you –
>   his appearance was so marred, beyond human semblance,
>   and his form beyond that of the children of mankind –
> ^{15} so shall he sprinkle many nations;
>   kings shall shut their mouths because of him;
> for that which has not been told them they see,
>   and that which they have not heard they understand.
>   (Isa. 52:13-15, ESV).

The chapter divisions in the Bible are not inspired; they are man-made for the sake of easy reference. The Fourth Servant Song, therefore, begins at verse 13 of chapter 52 and not at verse one of chapter 53. Thus, just as the First Servant Song begins with God's command to all men to 'Behold, My Servant', so the beginning of the last song reiterates the command and thereby provides a rounded finish.

Behold, My Servant

The first stanza is really an introductory summary of the fourth song, and contains in brief the amazing story of Messiah/Christ's sufferings and the glory which He will enter when Jehovah vindicates Him (as anticipated in 50:8-9). The little word 'Behold' is often used in Scripture when God wants to draw the attention of men and women to something very important. In several places it is used to introduce Messiah/Christ to Old Testament readers. In Zechariah 6:12 we read, 'Behold, the Man whose name is the BRANCH' (a name for Messiah, cf. Zech. 3:8); and in Zechariah 9:9 we read, 'Rejoice greatly, O daughter of Zion! Behold, your King is coming to you; He is just and having salvation, lowly and riding on a donkey, a colt, the foal of a donkey.'

But here in the Servant Songs, He is introduced as Jehovah's Servant who has a mission to fulfil: 'Behold, My Servant' (42:1; 52:13). Unlike Israel who had been a 'blind' servant and a 'deaf' messenger (42:18ff), Jehovah's messianic Servant could say: 'Behold, I come; in the scroll of the Book it is written of me. I delight to do Your will,

O my God, and Your law is within my heart' (Ps. 40:7, 8). When He came, He could also say, 'My food is to do the will of Him who sent Me, and to finish His work'; 'I do not seek My own will but the will of the Father who sent Me'; 'For I have come down from heaven, not to do My own will, but the will of Him who sent Me' (John 4:34; 5:30; 6:38). Even on the eve of His death, in the garden of Gethsemane, when He had to choose between dying the death of the cross or being spared that suffering, He prayed, 'Oh My Father, if this cup [of suffering] cannot pass away from Me unless I drink it, Your will be done' (Matt. 26:42).

In another garden, at least 4000 years before Christ (if not quite a bit more), another choice was made. Adam and Eve, our fore-fathers, disobeyed the will of God and brought the curse of sin upon the world and all their posterity. But God the Father had a pre-determined plan to save a people for Himself; to deliver them from the penalty (death), power, and ultimately from the very presence of sin. His only begotten Son voluntarily became His Servant in order to carry out His plan, and Jesus did it by a life of perfect obedience right to the end. Thus we speak of the *active obedience* of Christ. In His everyday life He actively obeyed all the commandments of God, so that He might be able to impute (credit) that sinless life to all who trust Him for salvation. But we also speak of Christ's *passive* obedience by which He voluntarily assumed the guilt and penalty of His people's sins, in obedience to His Father's will.

My Servant will endure appalling suffering

The second half of verse 13 will be treated under the next sub-heading, for it is important, at this point, to see that the context of the Servant's amazing success is the appalling suffering He will have to undergo. Isaiah says, 'As many were astonished at you – His appearance was so marred, beyond human semblance, and His form beyond that of the children of mankind –.' Verse 14 in the Hebrew is quite difficult to translate, and scholars have differed as to how it should be understood. It is generally agreed among commentators, however, that the main body of the verse should be regarded as a parenthesis which explains the reason why so many are 'astonished' at the Servant. Thus after the opening statement, the English Standard Version and the New International Version use a *dash* to introduce the explanation, as well as a *dash* to conclude it.

The difficulty stems from the fact that there are no punctuation marks in the Hebrew script. There are no commas, or full-stops (periods), or parentheses, *etc.* They have to be supplied by the translator. So by supplying the *dash* after the first clause, and then again after the last clause, the meaning of verse 14 becomes quite clear. The reason for the astonishment of men and women is to be found in the disfigured appearance of the Sufferer. Some take the words 'at you' (masculine singular) as referring to Israel and the astonishment of the surrounding nations at Jehovah's appalling punishment of the Jews in destroying their city and temple, and sending them into captivity in Babylon. The New American Standard Bible follows this line: 'Just as many were astonished at you, My people.' In other words, the suffering of Israel will be paralleled by the suffering that the Servant of Jehovah will have to go through.

It is better, however, to take 'You' as a reference to the Servant Himself. God is still speaking, as in verse 13, to all who will hear, but the Servant is now in His presence, exalted and glorified. Why, then, will the many be astonished at Him? God's answer is given in parenthesis: 'His [the Servant's] appearance was so marred, beyond human semblance, and His form beyond that of the children of mankind.' The change from the second person singular ('You') to the third person singular ('His') is common to Isaiah (cf. 31:6; 42:20). The word 'astonished' in the context could be better translated as 'shocked' or 'appalled' (NIV). The word is frequently used to describe human reaction to God's punishment of the wicked: 'I will bring the land to desolation, and your enemies who dwell in it shall be astonished at it' (Lev. 26:32; see also Jer. 18:16; 19:8; Ezek. 27:35). The word 'astonished' has the same meaning here. 'Many', in Israel and in the world, will look on the severity of the Servant's sufferings and conclude that He is being punished by God for some great wickedness. It is a picture of unimaginable suffering; of suffering that marred His appearance so much that the Servant of Jehovah no longer resembled a human being.

But we must be cautious here. The prophet Isaiah, surely, is not just thinking of the Servant's physical sufferings, great though they were at the end of His earthly life. These were predicted in the Third Servant Song (50:6), and as F.B. Meyer so aptly says, 'There is only one brow which this crown of thorns will fit.'[5] Nonetheless, when Jesus was brought out to the mob, having been scourged, wearing the crown of thorns and the purple robe, Pilate said to them, 'Behold the Man!' (John 19:5). It was a factual statement, not mockery or sarcasm. He was clearly recognisable! Moreover, when His mother and John stood by the cross of Jesus just before He gave up His spirit and heard Him say to them, 'Woman, behold your son! ... Behold your mother', they were not repulsed by His physical appearance.

What, then, is Isaiah saying in verse 14? I believe he is speaking metaphorically of the cumulative effect of both the physical and spiritual suffering of the Servant at His death. The death He had to die in order to 'give His life as a ransom for many' (Mark 10:45) would necessitate both physical and spiritual death; the death of the body and the death of the soul, which is the torment of hell, or what Scripture calls the 'second death' (Rev. 20:11-15). The suffering of the soul, of course, is infinitely worse than mere physical death, whatever its form. Indeed, this baptism or immersion in incomprehensible spiritual suffering was constantly on the mind of the Saviour, and in the garden of Gethsemane, on the eve of His death, He was so 'distressed' that 'His sweat became like great drops of blood falling down to the ground' (Luke 12:50; 22:39-46). In the following verses, Isaiah will predict that the messianic Servant will 'bear' the iniquities of many (53:11, 12), and to bear iniquity is an Old Testament expression for bearing its punishment (Exod. 28:43; Lev. 19:8; 21:9; Num. 18:22). So to bear the punishment our sins deserve, Jesus had to endure the same spiritual agony that we would have had to suffer if God had sent us to hell.

Now, it is not everyone who considers the sufferings of Jesus upon the cross, who sees the true nature and extent of the agony He endured. Only those who, by the grace of God, are given eyes to see what happened on the cross of Calvary, will understand

5. F.B. Meyer, *Christ in Isaiah* (Marshall, Morgan and Scott, 1957), p. 125.

in some small measure that during those three hours from noon to 3 pm when God forsook Him and total darkness fell on the land, Jesus endured unimaginable suffering. For He bore not just the punishment of one of His people's sins, but of all of them. By divine intervention, darkness fell over the land so that no human eye should see how the terrible torment of hell He endured in our stead, would mar His 'appearance ... beyond human semblance'. 'Behold, My Servant', says Jehovah. Keep thinking of what it cost Him, physically and spiritually, to die for our sins, and be appalled at what it did to Him personally.

My Servant will act wisely

The New King James Version has 'prudently', and the New American Standard Version has 'will prosper' (v. 13). Both translations are correct, for the Hebrew verb combines the notion of using the best means to accomplish the highest end. The thought is not so much that the Servant Himself will become prosperous, but that His mission will be brought to a successful conclusion. Indeed, the penal, substitutionary death of God's Servant on the cross for the sins of His people, will be the most profitable and successful accomplishment ever in the history of the world. This assurance is repeated in chapter 53:10, 'the will of the LORD shall prosper in His hand'.

What a comfort this is to the 'many' who will believe in Him and are shocked at the enormity and severity of the Servant's suffering on their behalf. Their Messiah/Christ did not die as a helpless victim, but as the victor of sin and death. He voluntarily submitted to death, but death could not keep its hold on Him. Hell's torment was swallowed up in full. His suffering was not in vain. It bore fruit. His mission was successful: 'When His soul makes an offering for guilt, He shall see His offspring ... out of the anguish of His soul He shall see and be satisfied; by His knowledge shall the righteous One, My Servant, make many to be accounted righteous, and He shall bear their iniquities' (vv. 10-11).

True, at the time of His crucifixion it did not seem so. The world looked at Him and said: 'He has failed. He saved others by His miraculous powers, but He could not save Himself.' Even His original disciples thought Jesus had failed. Luke records two of them saying, 'We were hoping that it was He who was going to redeem Israel.' But on the third day He rose from the dead and showed Himself to His disciples to prove that His mission to save a people for Himself was successful. He had carried out to the letter the mission on which the Father had sent Him. 'Behold, My Servant shall act wisely', or 'shall prosper'. The question, then, is: 'In what way is the Servant's mission to be judged a success? How is it to be measured?'

The answer is given in verse 15: 'So shall He sprinkle many nations.' The 'so' in verse 15 goes back to the 'As' or 'just as' in verse 14: 'As many were appalled at Him … so shall He sprinkle many nations.' The many who are appalled at His sufferings, are the many among the nations whom He will 'sprinkle.' The Revised Standard Version and its New edition (1989) follow the old Greek translation of the Old Testament (the Septuagint) and translate the verb as 'startle'. The Hebrew verb, however, appears several times in the Old Testament, and in every case it means 'to sprinkle'. It indicates the priestly activity of sprinkling either with blood for expiation (expunging guilt), or to sprinkle with water for purification (Lev. 4:6; 16:14, 19; Num. 19:18, 21). The measure of the Servant's success is in direct proportion to the measure of His extreme suffering. That suffering culminated in His death and the shedding of His blood, the sprinkling of which shall be powerful enough and plentiful enough to cleanse 'many nations' (see Lev. 17:11 and Heb. 9:22).

Isaiah goes on to say that the Servant's work will be so successful that 'kings shall shut their mouths because of Him.' The Servant's priestly work of purifying the lives of so many of their subjects will be so effective that when they see its completion on the Day of Judgment, the kings (human rulers and authorities) will be speechless. In the early days of Job's greatness, he met with a similar reaction: 'The princes refrained from talking, and put their hand on their mouth; the voice of nobles was hushed, and their tongue stuck to the roof of their mouth' (Job 29:9, 10). This will be the reaction of the rulers of the world when on the last day they stand before 'the judgment seat of Christ' (Rom. 14:10). They will see what the apostle John predicts in Revelation 7:9-10, 'a great multitude which no one could number, of all nations, tribes, peoples and tongues, standing before the throne and before the Lamb, clothed with white robes, with palm branches in their hands, and crying out with a loud voice, saying, "Salvation belongs to our God who sits on the throne, and to the Lamb."' No wonder the great men and women of the world will be speechless on that Day, 'for that which has not been told them they see, and that which they have not heard they understand' (v. 15).

By nature, sinful men and women cannot see the truth nor understand the wisdom of God's plan of salvation, unless God by grace gives them eyes to see, ears to hear and minds to understand. Isaiah speaks to this hiddenness of the gospel, the good news of a God who saves sinners in chapter 64:4, 'From of old no one has heard or perceived by the ear, no eye has seen a God besides you, who acts for those who wait for him' (esv). Thus the apostle Paul applies this verse in Isaiah to affirm our need for God the Holy Spirit to enable us to understand the gospel. He says to the Corinthians, 'For I decided to know nothing among you except Jesus Christ and Him crucified … and my speech and my message were not in plausible words of wisdom, but in demonstration of the Spirit and of power, that your faith might not rest in the wisdom of men but in the power of God … But we impart a secret and hidden wisdom of God, which God decreed before the ages for our glory. None of the rulers of this age understood this, for if they had, they would not have crucified the Lord of glory. But, as it is written [in Isaiah 64:4], "What no eye has seen, nor ear heard, nor the heart of man imagined, what God has prepared for those who love him" – these things God has revealed to us through the Spirit' (1 Cor. 2:2-10, esv).

These words from Isaiah 64 can be applied to the glories that await the believer in heaven, but Paul's primary application of them is to the truths of salvation in the gospel which are hidden to the natural, unregenerate mind. That is why the kings of this world, generally speaking, have no interest in the gospel and no understanding of it. On the last day of history, however, they will see and understand the glory and triumph of the Servant's mission to redeem a people for Himself and establish righteousness on earth, and they will be speechless. They will have no excuse for their rejection of Him. There is no substitute for the gospel. It alone is 'the power of God for salvation to everyone who believes' (Rom. 1:16).

Accordingly, Raymond Ortlund says, 'This is something new. All the world's top experts never thought of removing our guilt this way. That the Servant of the LORD would judge our evil by bearing it Himself in His own sufferings … Here is the wisdom of God – the undeserved sufferings of Jesus Christ outperforming the best of this world's "sweet oblivious antidotes" [from Shakespeare's *Macbeth*]. And the mission of the church is not to offer the world a Christianized version of their own false salvations but to communicate a good news they've never seen or heard before. If people do not sense that the gospel is saying something unheard of in the usual remedies for human misery, are we speaking clearly?'[6]

My Servant will be exalted very high

The success of Jehovah's Servant is now described, not just in terms of His purification of sinners from all nations, but in terms of His relationship with God Himself: 'He will be raised and lifted up and highly exalted' (v. 13b, NIV). The humiliation of the extreme physical and spiritual suffering for sinners that the Servant will have to undergo (v. 14) will result in His super-exaltation which is unfolded here in three verbs which are sequential and respectively describe its beginning ('raised'), continuation ('and lifted up') and climax ('and highly exalted'). These verbs are used elsewhere in Isaiah of divine status (cf. 6:1; 33:10; 57:15). This, then, is a prediction that the messianic Servant will be given a status comparable to that of God Himself. The suffering Servant of the LORD is not to be pitied, but worshipped.

It is impossible to read this prophecy in verse 13b and not see its fulfilment in the resurrection, ascension into heaven, and the sitting down of Jesus Christ at the right hand of God. The third verb is literally 'He will be very high' and is intended to be taken as

6. Raymond C. Ortlund, Jr., *Isaiah*, p. 355.

the culmination. The verb is stative (speaking of a static condition). It does not imply motion. 'The addition of the third verb, "be very high" shows very clearly that it is intended to be taken as the final result; the Servant of Jehovah, rising from stage to stage, reaches at last an immeasurable height that towers above everything besides.'[7] The glorious fulfilment of this amazing, unexpected prophecy in the person of our Lord Jesus Christ, is attested to throughout the New Testament:

> The patriarch David, [who] is both dead and buried … knowing that God had sworn with an oath to him that of the fruit of his body, according to the flesh, He would raise up the Christ to sit on his throne, he foreseeing this, spoke concerning the resurrection of the Christ, that His soul was not left in Hades, nor did His flesh see corruption. This Jesus God raised up, of which we are all witnesses. Therefore being exalted to the right hand of God, and having received from the Father the promise of the Holy Spirit, He poured out this which you now see and hear [the disciples praising God in foreign languages they had never learnt]. For David did not ascend into the heavens, but he says himself: 'Jehovah said to my Lord, "Sit at My right hand, till I make Your enemies Your footstool"' [Ps. 110:1]. Therefore let all the house of Israel know assuredly that God has made this Jesus, whom you crucified, both Lord and Christ (Acts 2:29-36).

> For to this end Christ died and rose and lived again, that He might be Lord of both the dead and the living (Rom. 14:9).

> That you may know … what is the exceeding greatness of His power … which He worked in Christ when He raised Him from the dead and seated Him at His right hand in the heavenly places, far above all principality and power and might and dominion, and every name that is named, not only in this age but also in that which is to come. And He put

---

7. Franz J. Delitzsch, *Isaiah* (Eerdmans, 1973), vol. 2, p. 305.

all things under His feet, and gave Him to be head over all things to the church (Eph. 1:18-22).

Christ Jesus ... made Himself of no reputation, taking the form of a servant, and coming in the likeness of men ... He humbled Himself and became obedient to the point of death, even the death of the cross. Therefore God also has highly exalted Him and given Him the name which is above every name, that at the name of Jesus every knee should bow, of those in heaven, and of those on earth, and of those under the earth; and that every tongue should confess that Jesus Christ is Lord, to the glory of God the Father (Phil. 2:5-11).

Seeing then that we have a great High Priest who has passed through the heavens, Jesus the Son of God ... therefore He is able to save to the uttermost those who come to God through Him, seeing He ever lives to make intercession for them (Heb. 4:14; 7:25).

'Behold, My Servant,' says God the Father. Behold His dreadful, incomprehensible sufferings, the sprinkling of His blood for the cleansing of many nations. Behold His exaltation to the throne of God in heaven from which He is able to save to the uttermost those who come to God through Him. Keep looking at Jesus until your heart is melted at the greatness of His love and power to save you. And in responsive, grateful love put your trust in Him to cleanse you from all sin and be His devoted servant for the rest of your days (1 John 1:7; Rom. 12:1).

5

The Fourth Servant Song II:
His good news will encounter unbelief

53:1 Who has believed what he has heard from us?
  And to whom has the arm of the LORD been revealed?
    (Isa. 53:1, ESV).

In the first stanza of the Fourth Servant Song (52:13-15), the prophet, under the Spirit of God, has given us the very heart of God's revelation of the life and work of the Servant Jehovah has chosen to 'be [His] salvation to the ends of the earth' (49:6). He has portrayed the Servant as One who endures unimaginable suffering and death so that He might 'sprinkle many nations'. It is a picture taken from the Day of Atonement when the High Priest of Israel would enter the Most Holy Place with innocent blood and sprinkle it upon the Mercy Seat to cleanse the nation of its sins (Lev. 16:15-16). So vast and so great is the salvation that the Servant will win by His appalling suffering for sinners, that 'kings shall shut their mouths at Him' in astonishment.

Now, if God is the speaker in the first stanza ('Behold, My Servant', v. 13), who is the speaker or speakers in the second stanza? In general, two main answers have been given. The first answer, which is held by many modern scholars, ascribes the rhetorical question of verse 1 to the Gentile kings in chapter 52:15. This interpretation is unlikely, however, because until Judgment Day the kings will not have heard about the Servant's suffering and exaltation; whereas the speakers in verse 1 have now heard the good news. Again, after hearing the good news, the kings shut their mouths in shock and amazement; whereas the speakers in verse 1 are expressing sadness over the unbelief that their 'report' (KJV) of the good news is meeting.

The second answer, and the more natural interpretation, is that Isaiah himself is speaking as the representative of all the heralds of the messianic Servant who will follow, to the end of the age. The English Standard Version, following other modern versions, has correctly translated all the verbs in verses 1-9 in the past tense, because the speakers are pictured as looking backward to the Servant's rejection by the Jewish nation and His ensuing sufferings and death.

The meaning of the Hebrew text

To understand verse 1 correctly, is to recognise that it is written in the form of Hebrew poetry known as *parallelism*. E. J. Young explains it this way:

> Parallelism simply means that a thought is stated once, and then stated the second time in slightly different terms. By way of example, 'The earth is the LORD's and the fullness thereof.' There is the truth, and that is all we need. But David goes on to say, 'the world, and they that dwell therein' (Ps. 24:1). 'The world' corresponds to 'the earth', and 'they that dwell therein' corresponds to 'the fullness thereof'... Hebrew poetry is characterized [not by rhyme, but] by parallelism, and that is because it is didactic poetry. The form helps us to remember it; it impresses the truth upon our mind and is employed for that reason. Sometimes the second member is not a mere repetition of the first, but a consequence of the first. For example, 'The Lord is my Shepherd', and then we have the consequence, 'I shall not want'.[1]

The use of parallelism in verse 1 is therefore an aid to understanding the truth that the prophet Isaiah is conveying. The first half of the couplet asks the question, 'Who has believed what he has heard from

---

1. E. J. Young, *Old Testament Prophecy*, p. 121.

us?' This is a literal translation of the Hebrew text, which is then followed by a second question: 'And to whom has the arm of the LORD been revealed?' The first question is answered by the second. Believing what we hear from the messengers of the Christ is equivalent to receiving the revelation of 'the arm of the LORD'. God's 'arm' is a common biblical metaphor for His power and strength exercised in the salvation of His people. We first meet with it when God says to Moses, 'Say to the children of Israel: "I am the LORD; I will bring you out from under the burdens of the Egyptians, I will rescue you from their bondage, and I will redeem you with an outstretched arm and with great judgments"' (Exod. 6:6; see also Deut. 5:15; Ps. 77:15 and 98:1 for some other prominent references).

In Isaiah 51:9 we have the faithful in Israel appealing to God: 'Awake, awake, put on strength, O arm of the LORD! Awake as in the ancient days, in generations of old.' In chapter 52:10 we read, 'The LORD has made bare His holy arm in the eyes of all the nations; and all the ends of the earth shall see the salvation of our God.' The verbs are in the past tense because, although the baring of Jehovah's arm of salvation before all nations is still future, from Isaiah's perspective it is as good as done; God has decreed it. The point of chapter 53:1, therefore, is that there can be no belief without prior revelation from God.

The preposition in the second question is better translated 'upon whom', rather than 'to whom', and here is how E.J. Young very simply sums it up:

> The revelation of the arm of the LORD upon a person, in other words, is a revelation of power, and since this question is parallel in meaning with the first, it therefore follows that to believe the 'report' which has been proclaimed is evidence that God's power has been revealed. If one believes the message concerning the Servant, he does so only because God has given him the strength to do so. Every believer is a manifestation of the fact that the arm of the LORD has been revealed upon him.[2]

---

2. E.J. Young, *Isaiah Fifty-Three*, p. 29.

The success of the gospel of Christ is all important

If Jehovah's holy arm is going to be made bare in the eyes of all the nations, and all the ends of the earth are going to see the salvation of our God (52:10), then the servants of the Servant must be diligent in giving a full report of His life and saving work to all humankind, as He has commanded them. Indeed, His faithful messengers are described in picturesque terms in chapter 52:7 as those who have 'beautiful feet', because in Isaiah's day anyone who had an important message to deliver, carried it on foot. 'How beautiful upon the mountains are the feet of him who brings good news, who proclaims peace, who brings glad tidings of good things, who proclaims salvation, who says to Zion, "Your God reigns!"' Because God rules the world, His messengers know that His will is always accomplished. His plans are always carried out successfully. But that success is not always apparent to the heralds of the gospel. From their vantage point as they travel the highways and byways of the world, it often seems as if only a few are willing to believe the 'good news' of 'salvation' won by the Christ, the Servant of Jehovah, through His atoning sufferings for sinners.

So when Isaiah, as their representative, asks: 'Who has believed what he has heard from us?' it is not because he thinks that no one has believed, but because so many of its hearers do not believe the good news. These words are the lament of those who preach the gospel of Jesus Christ. The message of Christ is so clear and convincing; His sinless life so beautiful, and His penal, substitutionary death on the cross so wonderful, that the preachers are amazed that anyone could reject it. Or, as the seventeenth-century Presbyterian preacher, James Durham, puts it in his book of seventy-two sermons on Isaiah 53:

> The most part of men and women think not much of the preached gospel. Yet, if it were considered what is the Lord's end in it, it would be the most refreshful news that ever people heard, to hear the report of a Saviour: that is, and should be, great and glad tidings of great joy to all nations ... It is a wonder that God had sent such a report to people, and in it has laid Christ so near them ... even at their feet

as it were; and as great a wonder that when the LORD has condescended to give such a Saviour and brought Him so near ... that all He calls for is faith, to believe the report, or rather faith in Him of whom the report is.[3]

It is a lament expressed by preachers of the gospel throughout the age, when so few of their hearers are converted; a sadness every parent expresses over unconverted children; a sorrow every Christian knows who witnesses about Christ to friends who are unmoved. 'Who has believed our report? And to whom has the arm of the LORD been revealed?' These are not just the words of a seventh-century BC prophet who happened to be feeling depressed at the time. They are a fitting sentiment for any true believer who is concerned for the glory of God. So, both the apostle John and the apostle Paul quoted this verse when they witnessed the stubborn unbelief of the Jews to the message of the gospel (John 12:37-38; Rom. 10:16).

It is true that there are some Christians who believe it is unspiritual to think or even pray about numbers, or the lack thereof, when it comes to the fewness of converts observed. To question why so few respond to the good news of Christ, to their mind, is to question the wisdom and power and sovereignty of God in sending His Son to be the Saviour of the world (John 4:42; 1 John 4:14). But God the Father does not rebuke the prophet Isaiah for questioning this seeming anomaly. He does not say: 'It is not for you to question what I am doing. Your business is to preach the good news to everyone you meet, and leave the results to Me. My plan of salvation will be fulfilled as I have purposed.' True as that is, it is not a sufficient answer to the apparent problem for two reasons.

The first reason is the *glory of God*. God is not glorified by small accomplishments, either in size or nature. Numbers are important, if God's kingdom is truly going to be the greatest kingdom ever set up on earth, consisting of 'a great multitude which no one [can] number, of all nations, tribes, peoples, and tongues' (Dan. 2:44-45; Rev. 7:9). When visitors come to church on a Sunday and find only a

---

3. James Durham, *Christ Crucified: or, the Marrow of the Gospel* (Naphtali Press, 2007), p. 86.

handful of worshippers present, God is not glorified. God is glorified by the success of His gospel, as repeatedly evidenced in the early church (Acts 2:47; 4:4; 5:14; 6:7; 9:31; 11:21, 24; 12:24; 13:49; 17:4, 12; 19:20).

Christ did not die for a few, but, as promised to Abraham, the father of the faithful, for a people as many 'as the stars of the heaven and as the sand which is on the seashore' (Gen. 22:15-18; Matt. 1:21; 8:11; Rom. 4:16; Gal. 3:7-9, 29). All the above references support the prophecy at the end of Isaiah 52, 'So shall He [the Servant] sprinkle many nations', cleansing them through His atoning blood from the defilement of all their sin. Numbers do matter! The success of the gospel, the good news that Christ died for the ungodly, is very important to the messengers who proclaim it. They are rightly saddened when people fail to respond to it in faith, and they ask why. They are jealous with a godly jealousy for the glory of God (Exod. 20:4-6; 34:14; 1 Kings 19:10).

The second reason why the heralds of Jesus, the messianic Servant, are concerned about the success of the gospel, is *compassion for the lost He came to save*. 'Without Christ', sinners are without 'hope and without God in the world' (Eph. 2:12). Our Lord Himself said, 'I am the way, the truth, and the life. No one comes to the Father except through Me' (John 14:6). The apostle Peter is equally emphatic: 'This Jesus ... was rejected by you ... And there is salvation in no one else, for there is no other name under heaven given among men by which we must be saved' (Acts 4:11-12, esv).

In the face of man's utter helplessness, God mercifully intervened. Paul says, 'At just the right time, when we were still powerless, Christ died for the ungodly. Very rarely will anyone die for a righteous man ... But God demonstrates His own love for us in this: While we were still sinners, Christ died for us' (Rom. 5:6-8, niv). The same divine love motivated God's Servant when He was on earth. We are often told of Jesus, that 'when He saw the multitudes, He was moved with compassion for them, because they were weary and scattered, like sheep having no shepherd' (Matt. 9:36; 14:14; 15:32). A few days before His crucifixion our Lord uttered this lament, 'O Jerusalem, Jerusalem, the one who kills the prophets and stones those who are sent to her! How often I wanted to gather your children together, as a hen gathers her chicks under her wings, but you were not willing!' (Matt. 23:37; Isa. 65:2; Rom. 10:21). He was also moved with compassion on individuals (Luke 7:34; Mark 1:41; Matt. 20:34). He had eyes to see and a heart to feel the suffering of sinners, and their rejection of God's salvation also evoked deep sorrow. Indeed, on Palm Sunday, Luke says, 'As He drew near, He saw the city [Jerusalem] and wept over it' (Luke 19:41-44).

This is true not only of the public ministry of Jesus, but above all of His atoning sacrifice for the sins of men and women on the cross. He so loved us that He gave Himself for us. Unworthy and undeserving though we are, Jehovah's Servant–Son saw us in our deep spiritual need, had compassion on us, died in our place on the cross, and at enormous cost to Himself, bore the penalty for our sin. If Jesus Christ showed such compassion for sinners, should we not show similar compassion and entreat them to believe in Him who is mighty to save? He has made us His 'ambassadors' to implore sinners on His behalf to 'be reconciled to God' (2 Cor. 5:20).

Let these words of Richard Baxter, the Puritan divine who wrote *The Reformed Pastor* (1656), apply this truth to us:

> O then, let us hear these arguments of Christ, whenever we feel ourselves grow dull and careless: 'Did I die for them, and wilt not thou look after them? Were they worth My blood, and are they not worth thy labour? Did I come down from heaven to earth, to seek and to save that which was lost; and wilt thou not go to the next door or street, or village to seek them? How small is thy labour and condescension as to Mine? I debased Myself to this, but it is thy honour to be so employed. Have I done and suffered so much for their salvation; and was I willing to make thee a co-worker with Me, and wilt thou refuse that little that lies upon thy hands?'[4]

Similarly, the apostle Paul, constrained by the love of Christ (2 Cor. 5:14), was deeply grieved by the continued unbelief of his

---

4. Richard Baxter, *The Reformed Pastor* (Epworth Press, 1961), pp. 121-122.

fellow Jews; so much so that he could say, 'I tell you the truth in Christ, I am not lying, my conscience also bearing me witness in the Holy Spirit, that I have great sorrow and continual grief in my heart. For I could wish that I myself were accursed from Christ for my brethren, my kinsmen according to the flesh, who are Israelites ...' (Rom. 9:1-4). The Apostle is not literally expressing a wish to be damned, in order that unbelieving Israelites could be saved. That would not be possible! He is simply saying that his sorrow at their unbelief is so great that he could express such a wish, if it could achieve its objective. Moses felt the same way (Exod. 32:32). The Servant of Jehovah needs more messengers of this spiritual calibre.

Success is not achieved by human compromises

All through the ages, God's servants have struggled with the indifference of unbelieving men and women to God and the things of God. We are jealous for the promotion of the work of God and the glory it brings to His name. We long to see God's kingdom grow, as sinners turn to Him in repentance and faith for salvation. But we have to learn to balance our desire for the success of God's work with the recognition that God's way of reaching out to sinners may not always coincide with what we think is best. The godly longing in our hearts to see multitudes following Christ, must never lead us to try and make Him more acceptable in the eyes of the world.

Verse two makes it clear that, at first sight, the Lord Jesus Christ never appears attractive to sinners. The Saviour has a spiritual beauty which initially puts sinners off. He has a purity and goodness that makes all of us in our natural, fallen state feel ashamed and uncomfortable when we first encounter Him. Moreover, whipped and nailed to a cross like a criminal, made the Saviour not only spiritually unattractive, but physically as well ('and we hid as it were our faces from Him', v. 3). So, Isaiah says, the reason why so few seem to believe our message is because 'He had no form or majesty that we should look at Him' (v. 2, ESV). The word translated 'form' means a person whose physique is handsome. It is used of David and Rachel (1 Sam. 16:12; Gen. 29:17). The word translated 'majesty' signifies the outward splendour or impressiveness normally associated with any important person (Ps. 96:6; Isa. 2:10, ESV). Next, follows Isaiah's statement that 'there is no beauty that we should desire Him.' Verse two therefore teaches that the Servant, when He comes, will not be strikingly well-built or majestic and handsome to His contemporaries. There will be nothing in His appearance in life or death to meet their expectation of what 'the Saviour of the world' should look like. And that has been the natural reaction of humankind ever since.

Moreover, what is very significant, is that when the Son of God came to earth as the Servant of Jehovah, He did not try to win the admiration of His hearers with eloquent speech, or fine clothes, or liberation theology, or accommodating ethics. He kept a low profile, even discouraging those He healed from advertising Him as a wonder-worker (Luke 5:14). If Jesus had used worldly means to attract more people to Himself, it would only have diverted attention away from who He really was and what He had come to do. No amount of admirers could make the Servant more than He was; 'God ... manifested in the flesh' (1 Tim. 3:16). And no amount of admirers could help Him do what He came to do, 'to seek and to save that which was lost' (Luke 19:10).

Here is another lesson we need to learn from Isaiah 53:1. The success of the gospel is all-important if the Servant's mission is to be completed and an innumerable company of people from all races and every age are to be gathered into the kingdom of heaven (Matt. 8:11; 13:31-32; 47-50). It is something every follower of Christ earnestly desires, but not at the cost of bringing the proclamation of our Saviour down to the carnal level of worldly expectations. He is 'the Alpha and the Omega, the Beginning and the End'; 'the First and the Last', who has 'the keys of Hades and of Death'; the 'King of kings and Lord of lords' (Rev. 1:8, 17, 18, 19:16). All the efforts of some preachers to make Jesus the patron saint of sports stars, or political leaders or generals, is sinfully misguided. It will not work, because God will have nothing to do with it! That challenges us as to how we are to witness. If sinners want a Saviour of their own fancy and Jesus Christ will not accommodate them, what can be done to resolve the situation?

Only the arm of the Lord can reveal Christ to sinners

The gospel can sometimes be presented in a way that is contrary to Scripture. Misguided preachers or counsellors have been known to say from the pulpit or in personal conversation: 'God has done everything He can to save you. He gave His Son, Jesus Christ, to die on the cross for the forgiveness of your sins. It is now up to you to accept or reject Him as your Saviour.' That is a very dangerous and unbiblical way to share the gospel. God is never a helpless onlooker at any point in the process of salvation. There are, of course, many decisions that men and women are free to make in accordance with their fallen human nature. But because our basic human nature is sinful and anti-God, we cannot in our own strength and volition decide that we are going to do God's will and surrender our lives to Jesus Christ as our Lord and Saviour. A change in our essential nature has to take place first, and only God the Holy Spirit can make that change. Whenever a sinner comes to faith in Christ, God is at work. No sinner can be saved apart from sovereign grace.

The apostle Paul brings this out very clearly in 2 Corinthians 4:1-6 (ESV):

> Therefore, having this ministry by the mercy of God, we do not lose heart. But we have renounced disgraceful, under-handed ways. We refuse to practise cunning or to tamper with God's word, but by the open statement of the truth we would commend ourselves to everyone's conscience in the sight of God. And even if our gospel is veiled, it is veiled only to those who are perishing. In their case the god of this world has blinded the minds of unbelievers, to keep them from seeing the light of the gospel of the glory of Christ, who is the image of God. For what we proclaim is not ourselves, but Jesus Christ as Lord, with ourselves as your servants for Jesus' sake. For God, who said, 'Let light shine out of darkness', has shone in our hearts to give the light of the knowledge of the glory of God in the face of Jesus Christ.

Some elaboration on these verses is necessary to better understand what the apostle is saying. In the face of the tremendous difficulties of winning unbelievers to Christ, Paul confidently states twice, 'we do not lose heart' (vv. 1, 16). We do not grow weary and give way to despair. We do not underestimate the spiritual blindness of the lost, but we know from our own experience that it can be divinely healed. Moreover, because of the Spirit's power to open blind eyes, 'we have renounced disgraceful, underhanded ways' (v. 2) or methods of evangelism. We shun the use of psychological pressure and sales techniques to try to persuade people to believe in Christ. Also, 'we refuse to practise cunning or to tamper with God's word' (v. 2). We do not reason that if sinners will not accept the gospel as it is, then we must adjust its message to make it easier to accept.

This is the strategy of liberal churchmen as well as some misguided evangelical Christians, but it is something we should shun like the plague. To drop the demand of the gospel to repent of sin (easy-believism); or to portray Christ's death as essentially an example of sacrificial love (liberalism), rather than a penal, substitutionary sacrifice to atone for sin; or to exchange self-reformation (salvation by human works) for divine regeneration, is to 'tamper with the word of God.' Our Lord Jesus Christ compared the communication of God's word to sowing good seed like 'wheat' (Matt. 13:1-9, 18-23). You reap what you sow. So if you sow bad seed like 'tares' or 'darnel' (a counterfeit wheat-like weed), you will reap a bad harvest (Matt. 13:24-30, 36-43). Peter, therefore, can say to his Christian readers, 'You have been born again, not of perishable seed but of imperishable, through the living and abiding word of God ... And this word is the good news that was preached to you' (1 Pet. 1:23, 25, ESV).

What, then, do we do? Our great concern, says Paul, is that 'by the open statement of the truth we would commend ourselves to everyone's conscience in the sight of God' (v. 2). Our presentation of the truth must be so faithful and transparent that no one in good conscience can deny the genuineness and sincerity of our motives, for it is conducted 'in the sight of God' before whom 'everything is uncovered and laid bare' (Heb. 4:13, NIV). There is a higher scrutiny than that of the human conscience. It is to God that every messenger of the gospel is ultimately and eternally answerable.

This, however, exposes another problem; this time not with us, the messengers, but with our hearers. For if this is the biblical way to do evangelism, to make an 'open statement of the truth' of the gospel, why is it that people do not receive it? Paul's reply is, 'And even if our gospel is veiled, it is veiled only to those who are perishing' (v. 3). And in such a case, it is not we who put a veil over the gospel. We unveil the gospel. We make an open statement of it. So if unbelievers cannot see the truth, it is not because of us. Rather, it is Satan who has impaired their vision: 'In their case the god of this world has blinded the minds of the unbelievers, to keep them from seeing the light of the gospel of the glory of Christ, who is the image of God' (v. 4). Satan cannot rob the gospel of its light and truth. What he can do is blind men by unbelief, so that its light and truth do not shine into their minds and hearts. As a result, unlike those who are physically blind, unbelievers love their spiritual darkness and hate 'the light of the gospel of the glory of Christ, who is the image of God.' Thus, our Saviour said, 'And this is the condemnation, that the light has come into the world, and men loved darkness rather than light, because their deeds were evil. For everyone practising evil hates the light and does not come to the light, lest his deeds should be exposed' (John 3:19, 20).

Now, if unbelievers are spiritually blind, how can they be made to see? Paul's answer is, 'For God, who said, "Let light shine out of darkness", has shone in our hearts to give the light of the knowledge of the glory of God in the face of Jesus Christ' (v. 6). The apostle takes us back to Genesis 1:2-3, 'the earth was without form, and void; and darkness was on the face of the deep … Then God said, "Let there be light"; and there was light.' The condition of the heart of the unregenerate is like the primeval chaos, dark and dead; and so it will remain, until God Himself shines in their hearts. This is what God did for Paul on the road to Damascus. The light of the glorified Christ, 'brighter than the sun', shone down upon him from heaven (Acts 26:12-28). Unbelievers do not see the truth *until* God shines the light of the gospel upon them. It is a spiritual regeneration, nothing short of a 'new creation' by the almighty power of God (2 Cor. 5:17).

This is why, as the messengers of Jesus Christ, 'we do not lose heart'. The god of this world blinds the minds of unbelievers to the light of the gospel, but God enables the gospel to shine in their hearts 'to give the light of the knowledge of the glory of God in the face of Jesus Christ' (v. 6). Preaching or sharing the gospel is the God-appointed means by which the devil is overthrown and God shines gospel light into men's souls. Let us always make sure that what we preach 'is not ourselves, but Jesus Christ as Lord' (v. 5). That is to say, as the One 'who is the image of God' (v. 4), and who by His obedience to 'the death of the cross' has been highly exalted and 'given the name which is above every name', the name Lord or God (Phil. 2:8-11). Moreover, our preaching of Christ must be so wholehearted that we become the 'bondservants' (v. 5) of those we preach to. We are committed to a lifetime of double, lowly servitude. We are both Christ's servants and their servants, and we do it 'for Jesus' sake' who is our sole Master, and came 'not to be served, but to serve' (Mark 10:45).

The arm of the Lord is made bare in answer to prayer

This is what Isaiah is doing in verse one. He is praying. He is not talking to himself, or sharing his grief with the believing remnant in the nation of Israel. He is talking directly to God. Both the apostle John and the apostle Paul quote verse one as a lamentation addressed to the Lord: 'But although He had done so many signs before them, they did not believe in Him, that the word of Isaiah the prophet might be fulfilled, which he spoke: "Lord, who has believed our report? And to whom has the arm of the Lord been revealed?"' (John 12:37-38; Rom. 10:16). A similar prayer is offered in Isaiah 51:9, 'Awake, awake, put on strength, O arm of the Lord! Awake as in the ancient days, in the generations of old.' And in chapter 52:10 the prophet looks down the corridors of time and sees his prayer gloriously answered: 'The Lord has made bare His holy arm in the eyes of all the nations; and all the ends of the earth shall see the salvation of our God.'

Our Lord is our supreme example. Before He began His public ministry, He 'fasted [and prayed] forty days and forty nights', not only for Himself, but also for His disciples. I believe He prayed for the calling of the twelve apostles, and as a result, when the right moment came, the Holy Spirit led Him to the right men who immediately left what they were doing to spend the rest of their lives following Him. Only God could have done that! None of them had yet seen or heard anything to convince them that Jesus was God's long promised Messiah. Their response has no human explanation (Matt. 4:1-2, 17-22).

How, then, did they come to recognise Jesus as Messiah/Christ? Seeing His miracles and hearing His teaching would have been enough to convince them, as it had convinced many others, that He was a prophet (Matt. 21:1-11; 21:46). However, it was only well into His public ministry that the Father answered the prayer of His Servant–Son and revealed His messiahship to the disciples. After the feeding of the four thousand, we read:

> When Jesus came into the region of Caesarea Philippi, He asked His disciples, saying, 'Who do men say that I, the Son of Man, am?' So they said, 'Some say John the Baptist, some Elijah, and others Jeremiah or one of the prophets.' He said to them, 'But who do you say that I am?' And Simon Peter answered and said, 'You are the Christ, the Son of the living God.' Jesus answered and said to him, 'Blessed are you, Simon Bar-Jonah, for flesh and blood has not revealed this to you, but My Father who is in heaven' (Matt. 16:13-17).

Again, when 'the cities in which most of His mighty works had been done ... did not repent', our Lord prayed and said, 'I thank You, Father, Lord of heaven and earth, because You have hidden these things from the wise and prudent and have revealed them to babes. Even so, Father, for so it seemed good in Your sight' (Matt. 11:20, 25-26). It is not to the 'wise and prudent' ('learned', NIV) who are spiritually proud in the sight of God and rely solely on their own understanding, but to spiritual 'babes' who acknowledge their need of divine enlightenment, that God has sovereignly chosen to reveal the truths of the gospel. A baby is totally dependent on its parents to provide what it needs, and sinners are totally dependent on God to understand and accept the spiritual truths of the gospel.

One last example comes from Paul's preaching in Philippi, the gospel's first advance into Europe. He had been especially called by God in a vision to go there. The city, however, had no synagogue, the normal place for the apostle to begin preaching the gospel. So Luke says, 'And on the Sabbath day we went out of the city to the riverside, where prayer was customarily made; and we sat down and spoke to the women who met there. Now a certain woman named Lydia heard us. She was a seller of purple from the city of Thyatira, who worshipped God. The Lord opened her heart to heed the things spoken by Paul' (Acts 16:6-15). She and her household were the first converts of Europe, and it came about because the arm of the Lord was made bare in answer to the prayers of the women who regularly met there.

If we are true believers, we need to be saddened by the smallness of the response of people in general to the truth of the gospel today. We must never be content with seeing or hearing of just a few coming to faith in Jesus Christ. God's promises are clear and encouraging: 'For as the rain comes down and the snow from heaven, and do not return there, but water the earth, and make it bring forth and bud, that it may give seed to the sower and bread to the eater, so shall My word be that goes forth from My mouth; it shall not return to Me void [empty, esv], but it shall accomplish what I please, and it shall prosper in the thing for which I sent it' (Isa. 55:10-11). Paul says, 'For I am not ashamed of the gospel of Christ, for it is the power of God to salvation for everyone who believes, for the Jew first and also for the Greek' (Gentile, niv; Rom. 1:16). God's word is all-sufficient! We certainly do not need to try to improve on the gospel or repackage Christ and the salvation He offers. All we are required to do is to make an open statement of the truth, accompanied by believing prayer for the Holy Spirit to open the eyes of our hearers to see the glory of God in the face of Jesus Christ (2 Cor. 3:12-17).

If any of us does not see any beauty in God's Servant, the Lord Jesus Christ, we should be deeply concerned, for the fault lies with us and not with Him. It means that the eyes of our soul have been blinded by the god of this world. For those with eyes to see, to whom the arm of the LORD has been revealed in enlightenment, conviction and salvation, Jesus is the most beautiful and most desirable Saviour in all the world, and indeed the only Saviour! (John 14:6). 'To you who believe', says Peter, 'He is precious' (1 Pet. 2:7). Again, He is the 'pearl of great price', who is worth giving up everything to possess (Matt. 13:45-46). If any of us have seen members of our family and friends give up the passing pleasures of sin to follow Jesus, and cannot understand what they see in Him, it is because we are spiritually blind. We know neither the beauty of Jesus, nor the repulsiveness of the devil who has inflicted such terrible blindness on our souls.

We need to learn from Bartimaeus in the Gospels. He was physically blind, but the story of his healing has much to teach us. Jesus was leaving Jericho with His disciples and a great multitude. Bartimaeus was sitting by the roadside begging:

> And when he heard that it was Jesus of Nazareth, he began to cry out and say, 'Jesus, Son of David, have mercy on me!' Then many warned him to be quiet; but he cried out all the more, 'Son of David, have mercy on me!' So Jesus stood still and commanded him to be called. Then they called the blind man, saying to him, 'Be of good cheer. Rise, He is calling you.' And throwing aside his garment, he rose and came to Jesus. And Jesus answered and said to him, 'What do you want Me to do for you?' The blind man said to Him, 'Rabboni, that I may receive my sight.' Then Jesus said to him, 'Go your way; your faith has made you well.' And immediately he received his sight and followed Jesus on the road (Mark 10:46-52).

Scripture says, 'The LORD is longsuffering and abundant in mercy, forgiving iniquity and transgression' (Num. 14:18), and there are multiple instances where sinners have asked for God to have mercy upon them and have received it. There are ten such pleas in the book of Psalms alone, and quite a few in the gospels, the most notable being the tax collector in the temple. He 'would not so much as raise his eyes to heaven, but beat his breast, saying, "God be merciful to me a sinner!"' and went home justified (Luke 18:9-14). Though this is a parable, it expresses a precious truth. Sinners can ask God to be merciful to them and heal their spiritual blindness; to make bare His holy arm and reveal the beauty of Jesus to them, and He will. With that captivating sight, faith in Jesus Christ as Lord and Saviour, will surely come.

6

The Fourth Servant Song III:
He will be despised and rejected by men

53:2 For He grew up before him like a young plant,
   and like a root out of dry ground;
he had no form or majesty that we should look at him,
   and no beauty that we should desire him.
³ He was despised and rejected by men;
   a man of sorrows, and acquainted with grief,
And as one from whom men hide their faces
   he was despised and we esteemed him not.
                  (Isa. 53:2-3, ESV).

In chapter five, we studied the effect which the good news of salvation through the Servant will have on everyone who hears it, till the end of time. While some will believe the 'report/message' of the gospel and receive Jesus Christ as their personal Saviour, others will not. Moreover, the response of each person will change their attitude to Christ: 'Therefore, to you who believe, He is precious; but to those who are disobedient, "the stone which the builders rejected has become the chief cornerstone", and "a stone of stumbling and a rock of offence"' (1 Pet. 2:7-8). No one comes to faith in Christ without being captivated by the beauty of His character and person. Of course, our first opinion of the Saviour is that He 'has no beauty that we should desire Him' (v. 3). But the more we, as believers, read and hear the gospel, the more the Holy Spirit reveals the loveliness of Jesus to us (2 Cor. 3:12-17). The more we ponder who He is and what He has done for us, the more we begin to see 'the glory of God in the face of Jesus Christ' and are drawn to Him in faith and love by God (2 Cor. 4:6; John 6:44, 65; 1 John 4:10).

The Gospels are full of such examples. The following are just some of many:

> Now after Jesus was born in Bethlehem of Judea in the days of Herod the king, behold, wise men from the East came to Jerusalem, saying, 'Where is He who has been born King of the Jews? For we have seen His star in the East and have come to worship Him ... And when they had come into the house, they saw the young Child with Mary His mother, and fell down and worshipped Him. And when they had opened their treasures, they presented gifts to Him: gold, frankincense, and myrrh (Matt. 2:1, 11).

> And behold, there was a man in Jerusalem whose name was Simeon ... And it had been revealed to him by the Holy Spirit that he would not see death before he had seen the Lord's Christ. So he came by the Spirit into the temple. And when the parents brought in the Child Jesus, to do for Him according to the custom of the law, he took Him up in his arms and blessed God and said: 'Lord, now You are letting Your servant depart in peace, according to Your word; for my eyes have seen Your salvation which you have prepared before the face of all peoples, a light to bring revelation to the Gentiles and the glory of Your people Israel' (Luke 2:25-32).

> Then one of the Pharisees asked Him to eat with him ... And behold, a woman in the city who was a sinner, when she knew that Jesus sat at table in the Pharisee's house, brought an alabaster flask of fragrant oil, and stood at His feet behind Him weeping; and she began to wash His feet with her tears, and wiped them with the hair of her head; and she kissed His feet and anointed them with fragrant oil. Now when the Pharisee who had invited Him saw this, he spoke to himself,

saying, 'This man, if He were a prophet, would know who and what manner of woman this is who is touching Him, for she is a sinner.' And Jesus answered and said to him, 'Simon, I have something to say to you ... her sins, which are many, are forgiven, for she loved much. But to whom little is forgiven, the same loves little.' And He said to her, 'Your sins are forgiven' (Luke 7:36-40, 47).

Now behold, two of them were travelling that same day [Resurrection Sunday] to a village called Emmaus, which was about seven miles from Jerusalem. And they talked together of all these things which had happened. So it was, while they conversed and reasoned, that Jesus Himself drew near and went with them. But their eyes were restrained, so that they did not know Him ... Then they drew near to the village where they were going, and He indicated that He would have gone farther. But they constrained Him, saying, 'Abide with us, for it is toward evening, and the day is far spent'. And He went in to stay with them. Now it came to pass, as He sat at the table with them, that He took bread, blessed and broke it, and gave it to them. Then their eyes were opened and they knew Him; and He vanished from their sight. And they said to one another, 'Did not our heart burn within us while He talked with us on the road, and while He opened the Scriptures to us?' (Luke 24:13-16, 28-32).

When God the Holy Spirit opens the eyes of our mind to see the glory of Jesus Christ and draws us to Him in faith, we begin a life of adoring His beauty, majesty and perfection, which will continue throughout eternity (Jude 24, 25; Rev. 4:11; 5:12, 13).

Verses two and three of Isaiah 53, however, focus on the natural and here predicted response of Israel to God's Servant when He did come, 700 years after the delivery of this divine prophecy. And by extension, of course, it has been true of all humankind ever since. Left to ourselves, human beings the world over, see 'no beauty that [they] should desire Him' (v. 2). 'In their case the god of this world has blinded the minds of the unbelievers, to keep them from seeing the light of the gospel of the glory of Christ, who is the image of God' (2 Cor. 4:4, ESV). What does that statement of the apostle Paul entail? In what way has Satan, through the fall, darkened the understanding of men and women? (Eph. 1:18; 4:18; Luke 24:45). The answer to that question is the subject of this chapter.

Satan has perverted our minds

> ² For He grew up before Him [Jehovah] like a young plant,
>   and like a root out of dry ground;
> He had no form or majesty that we should look at Him,
>   and no beauty that we should desire Him (Isa. 53:2).

To *pervert*, according to the Oxford Dictionary, is to 'lead astray (a person, or mind) from right opinion or conduct or especially religious belief'. So sin, in the first place, has radically affected the way the human mind perceives God and reality. The things of this world which are temporal, material and self-serving are seen as preferable by far to the things which are eternal, spiritual and God-pleasing. The worldly man believes that fun in the sun now is better than pie in the sky when you die, which is uncertain. That is who we are and how we think by nature, as fallen creatures. We cannot see further than our nose. Satan has perverted our ability to see spiritual realities and brought great harm to our souls.

The classic biblical story of the folly of judging persons or things purely by appearances is the anointing of David to be the king of Israel after Saul. God sent the prophet Samuel to the house of Jesse to carry out this task, saying, 'I have provided Myself a king among his sons' (1 Sam. 16:1). Jesse had eight sons and when the eldest, Eliab, was brought before him, Samuel looked at his strong, fine physical features and said, 'Surely the LORD's anointed is before Him. But the LORD said to Samuel, "Do not look at his appearance or at the height of his stature, because I have refused him. For the LORD does not see as man sees; for man looks at the outward appearance, but the LORD looks at the heart"' (vv. 6, 7). After Jesse had made seven of his sons pass before Samuel and all were rejected, he sent for David who was keeping the sheep. The Bible says, 'He was ruddy, with bright eyes, and good-looking. And the LORD said, "Arise, anoint him; for this is the one!"' (v. 12).

Samuel had to learn that God was not looking for a big man who would make an impressive king in the eyes of the people, but a good man, 'a man after His own heart', 'who will do all My will' (1 Sam. 13:14; Acts 13:22). We must not conclude from this story that God always rejects a good outward appearance, as if plain looks and a slight build are necessary requirements of God's call. After all, David was 'good-looking' (v. 12). Rather, external appearance neither qualifies nor disqualifies; it simply does not matter. Our understanding of God's calling to salvation or service will always be flawed by our fallen, finite human minds – God's choices are governed by free sovereign grace, for He can be glorified by many or by few; by the weak or by the strong; by learned men like Paul and Luke, or by uneducated fishermen like Peter, James and John.

This was the grave error committed by our Lord's generation. In spite of having clear, specific prophecies, they expected God's Messiah to be a resident of David's home town of Bethlehem and a prominent male descendant of David who would be a recognised heir to his throne. They pictured Messiah coming with regal splendour and military prowess to deliver them from Gentile oppression, and set up an everlasting kingdom of peace and righteousness on earth (Isa. 9:6-7; 11:1-10; Dan. 2:44-45; Micah 5:2-5; Luke 1:32-33; Acts 1:6-7).

Outwardly, however, the Servant of Jehovah did not fit this profile which the leaders and teachers of Israel had incorrectly put together, confusing elements of Messiah's first coming with those of His second coming. Although born in Bethlehem, the time He spent there was negligible. Jesus had grown up in obscurity and lowliness in Nazareth. Everybody knew Him as 'Jesus of Nazareth', even the demons and the angels (Matt. 21:10-11; Luke 18:37; Acts 2:22; Mark 1:24). Of course, if the Jews had dug deeper they would have found out that Jesus *had* been born in Bethlehem as predicted in Micah 5:2-5 (Matt. 2:1; Luke 2:4-7). Strengthening their belief that Jesus was not God's long-promised Messiah, was the commonly held misconception expressed by Nathaniel when Philip said to him, "'We have found Him of whom Moses in the law, and also the prophets, wrote – Jesus of Nazareth, the son of Joseph." And Nathaniel said to him, "Can anything good come out of Nazareth?" Philip said to him, "Come and see.'" (John 1:43-45).

Worldliness, which includes judging persons and things solely by outward appearance, is a grave sin that has damned many a soul to hell. It is essentially a sin of pride in our own rational powers. In the case of those who responded to our Lord with scepticism, they were deceived not only by His humble surroundings, but also His humble appearance. There was nothing in Christ's appearance that the carnal or worldly minded could be attracted by; everything was so different from what they pictured or anticipated. They expected a royal prince, but Jesus was just a peasant carpenter. They expected Messiah to be born of the nobility, and instead Jesus was seen as the illegitimate son of a peasant girl: 'Then they said to Him, "We were not born of fornication"' (John 8:41). They rightly assumed that Messiah could not be born out of wedlock, but wrongly assumed that He must of necessity have a human father. If they had only done their homework properly, they would have known that the Christ would come as a result of a *virginal conception:* 'Therefore the Lord Himself will give you a sign: Behold, the virgin shall conceive and bear a Son, and shall call His name Immanuel' (Isa. 7:14).

This is also how the Gospel writers, under the inspiration of the Holy Spirit, recorded the fulfilment of Isaiah's prophecy:

> Now the birth of Jesus Christ was as follows: After His mother Mary was betrothed [legally pledged to be married, mg. esv] to Joseph, before they came together, she was found with child of the Holy Spirit. Then Joseph her husband, being a just man, and not wanting to make her a public example, was minded to put her away secretly. But while he thought about these things, behold, an angel of the Lord appeared to him in a dream, saying, 'Joseph, son of David, do not be afraid to take to you Mary your wife, for that which is conceived in her is of the Holy Spirit. And she shall bring forth a Son, and you

shall call His name JESUS, for He will save His people from their sins.' Now all this was done that it might be fulfilled which was spoken by the Lord through the prophet, saying: 'Behold, a virgin shall be with child, and bear a Son and they shall call His name Immanuel', which is translated 'God with us' (Matt. 1:18-23; see also Luke 1:26-35).

Our Lord's natural appearance was very ordinary to everyone who saw and knew Him in Nazareth. When people walked into the carpenter's shop where He worked until He was thirty years old, there was nothing about His outward appearance to suggest that He would be the Saviour of the world. Even His brothers and sisters did not believe in Him, and misjudged Him (John 7:5; Mark 3:21). They did not become His followers until after His resurrection (Acts 1:14; 1 Cor. 15:7).

Little wonder, then, that at the beginning of Jesus' public ministry, when He entered the synagogue of Nazareth (where He would have worshipped every Sabbath since a child) and read the words from Isaiah 61:1-2, claiming their fulfilment in the ministry He was commencing, there was an uproar. According to Luke, 'Then all those in the synagogue, when they heard these things, were filled with wrath, and rose up and thrust Him out of the city; and they led Him to the brow of the hill on which their city was built, that they might throw Him down over the cliff. Then passing through the midst of them, He went His way.' The people who grew up with Jesus, and knew Him so well, wanted to kill Him when He claimed to be God's Christ and told them, 'No prophet is accepted in his own country' (4:16-30). And as our Lord continued His public ministry for the next three years, His rejection by the nation only increased, until He was finally put to death.

Let us not think that we are any better than they were; that if we had been eyewitnesses of Jesus we would have admired Him and become His disciples. By nature we all tend to place great faith in outward appearances, but our Lord in the wisdom of God did not give Himself to winning disciples in that way. We need God's help to believe in Christ, because we are more superficial than we think. Isaiah clearly predicted how Israel and the world would view the coming of the Servant to be God's 'salvation to the ends of the earth' (49:6). They will dismiss His life as being entirely unpromising; like a 'young plant' or 'a root' struggling in 'dry ground' to come to fruition. He will not inspire hope in them at all. How touching is the prophet's description of the scene in verse two: 'For He grew up before Him [God] like a young plant, and like a root out of dry ground; He had no form [physical impressiveness] or majesty [splendour of circumstances and clothes] that we should look at Him, and no beauty [nothing in His appearance] that we should desire Him.'

Satan has hardened our hearts or emotions

3a He was despised and rejected by men;
a man of sorrows, and acquainted with grief (Isa. 53:3a).

Jehovah's Servant will not only be misjudged as unattractive, but positively dismissed and shunned as unwanted. He will not be ignored, for none can ignore the Saviour. People will either be for or against Him (Matt. 12:30). Verse three is written in the past tense again, because although the event is predicted of the future, it is so certain that the event is regarded as having already occurred: 'He was despised and rejected by men; a man of sorrows, and acquainted with grief' (ESV). The margin has: 'He was despised and forsaken by men; a man of pains, and knowing sickness'.

Understood properly, these words show how reprehensible the response of human beings to Jesus Christ has been, and how it deserves divine condemnation. As J. Alec Motyer explains: 'The reappearance of *sorrows* in verse four indicates that Isaiah is not using *a man of sorrows* as the stereotyped language of lament, but is being realistic and descriptive. If verse three stood alone we would be left to think that the Servant was burdened with a morose temperament and a sickly body, but verses four and ten fill out the picture. The Servant was not an incessant sorrower and sufferer, but He was notably so, not by reason of His constitution, but because He took our sorrows and weaknesses as His own. *Familiar with* [acquainted with] means either "to know" and hence "with personal experience of", or is a homonym [parallel term] meaning "submissive to/humbled by", and either meaning suits. Both the experience and the willing acceptance of *suffering/sickness* (more in the sense of weakness than of illness) matches Isaiah's portrait of the Servant.'[1]

E.J. Young explains the phrase 'acquainted with grief/sickness' as follows: 'This statement is not to be understood in the sense that He is made known to others, or distinguished in the sight of others by His sicknesses. It means rather that He Himself has been made to know sicknesses, and so we may correctly translate "acquainted with sickness". It would be a serious mistake, however, to regard this phrase as implying that He was sickly in body and so fell prey to one disease after another. The word "sickness" is but a metaphor to describe sin. Isaiah had earlier set forth the sinful condition of Judah in terms of physical sickness, "... the whole head is sick, and the whole heart is faint. From the sole of the foot even unto the head there is no soundness in it; but wounds, and bruises, neither bound up, neither mollified with ointment" (Isa. 1:5b-6). That the word "sickness" is used in this sense here is clear from the fact that the deliverance to be accomplished is not from physical sorrows and sicknesses (at least not primarily) but rather from the source whence such sicknesses flow; namely, sin.'[2]

At first our Lord was regarded by the religious rulers of Israel as a nuisance not to be taken seriously. But as His miracles and teaching started drawing in the curious crowds, He became a serious threat to their prestige and power. Often what Jesus taught conflicted with what they had been teaching, as for instance in the Sermon on the Mount (Matt. 5:1–7:29). So they tried to find some sin or error to prove that He was not sent by God to be the King of Israel and the Saviour of the world (Matt. 12:9-14, 22:15-46; John 8:1-12). When this failed, His critics tried to frame Him. They accused Jesus of treason by proclaiming Himself to be the King of Israel, and demanded that Pilate, the Roman governor, try Him. And when even Pilate could find no fault with

---

1. J. Alec Motyer, *The Prophecy of Isaiah*, p. 428.
2. E.J. Young, *Isaiah Fifty-Three*, p. 40.

Jesus and sought to release Him, the priests and the Pharisees threatened the governor by saying, 'If you let this man go, you are not Caesar's friend. Whoever makes himself a king speaks against Caesar' (John 19:12). Unwilling to face potential punishment from Rome, Pilate brought Jesus before the people, saying, '"Behold your King!" But they cried out, "Away with Him, away with Him! Crucify Him!" Pilate said to them, "Shall I crucify your King?" The chief priests answered, "We have no king but Caesar!" So he delivered Him to them to be crucified. So they took Jesus and led Him away' (vv. 14-16).

We need to pause a little to ponder personally the pain of the contemptuous rejection which our dear Lord experienced when He came to save the world. We have all felt the pain and sorrow of rejection in our lifetime. But one sorrow or two does not make one 'a man of sorrows'; nor does an occasional experience of grief or weakness make one the 'acquaintance' (or familiar friend of it). Before the Servant of Jehovah had to bear the physical and spiritual sufferings of sin on the cross, demanded by the law as the just penalty of our sin (Ezek. 18:4; Rom. 6:23), He had to undergo the subtle, almost hidden, psychological pain of rejection. The need for acceptance, acknowledgment and love, is one of the basic needs of human personality. How much more deeply must His rejection by those He came to redeem, have been felt by the perfect, sensitive personality of our Lord Jesus Christ?

Quoting from an anonymous source, David Baron writes: 'How the Servant endured, with what fortitude and patience, with what faith in God and acquiescence in His will, is not brought into view, but simply the fact that sorrows came thick and heavy upon Him, like wind-driven rain beating on an unsheltered head, and that grief was present with Him as His close companion through life.' And the chief causes of His sorrows and grief were not personal ills, or physical pain, though these were great enough. It was *heart sorrow* and *grief of soul*. 'A noble nature, repelled in all its efforts to bless, is pained unspeakably more by that repulse than by the crowding in of merely personal ills, or by all the slings and arrows of adversity: and

His sorrow came, thus, because His brethren rejected the help He brought, repelled the Helper, and abode in their lost state.'[3]

If this sorrow of heart and grief of soul was felt by Jesus, it surely intensified as it grew to a climax in the last week of His life. That is only too apparent in our Lord's laments and tears as He approached Jerusalem. On the Sunday of His triumphal entrance into the city, Luke says:

> Now as He drew near, He saw the city and *wept over it,* saying, 'If you had known, even you, especially in this your day, the things that make for your peace! But now they are hidden from your eyes. For the days will come upon you when your enemies will build an embankment around you, surround you and close you in on every side, and level you, and your children within you, to the ground; and they will not leave in you one stone upon another, because you did not know the time of your visitation' (19:41-44, italics added).

On the following Tuesday, in His last public discourse in which He solemnly denounced the scribes and Pharisees, our Lord says:

Woe to you, scribes and Pharisees, hypocrites! Because you build the tombs of the prophets and adorn the monuments of the righteous, and say, 'If we had lived in the days of our fathers, we would not have been partakers with them in the blood of the prophets.' Therefore you are witnesses against yourselves that you are sons of those who murdered the prophets. Fill up, then, the measure of your fathers' guilt. Serpents, brood of vipers! How can you escape the condemnation of hell? Therefore, indeed, I send you prophets, wise men, and scribes: some of them you will kill and crucify, and some of them you will scourge in your synagogues and persecute from city to city, that on you may come all the righteous blood shed on the earth, from the blood of righteous

---

3. David Baron, *The Servant of Jehovah* (Marshall, Morgan and Scott, 1954), pp. 79-80.

Abel to the blood of Zechariah, son of Berechiah, whom you murdered between the temple and the altar. Assuredly, I say to you, all these things will come upon this generation. O Jerusalem, Jerusalem, the one who kills the prophets and stones those who are sent to her! How often I wanted to gather your children together, as a hen gathers her chicks under her wings, but you were not willing! See! Your house is left to you desolate; for I say to you, you shall see Me no more till you say, 'Blessed is He who comes in the name of the LORD!' (Matt. 23:29-39).

There is great solace here for every follower of the Lord Jesus Christ. It is very natural to want to be accepted and approved by our fellow human beings. We were created for community, and the second half of the Ten Commandments was given by God to protect and foster community in human society. Nobody likes being despised or rejected. It inflicts deep emotional pain and physical weakness/sickness that can make one feel that life is hardly worth living, and lead some even to commit suicide. Christians, however, have the supreme example of Christ, the Servant of Jehovah, who sought, first and foremost, the approval of God, even at the cost of the disapproval of men; who said repeatedly, 'My food is to do the will of Him who sent Me, and to finish His work' (John 4:34; see also 5:30; 6:38; 17:4; 19:30).

Many, the world over, are despised and rejected because they have become Christians. Take comfort from our blessed Lord and Saviour. Nobody has ever been as deeply rejected as He was, and nobody ever deserved to be accepted as much as He, God's greatest gift to humankind, deserved to be accepted and loved. But in spite of being despised and rejected by men, He found His strength and satisfaction in doing the will of God and being the Servant God wanted Him to be. As a result, Jesus triumphed. By His penal, substitutionary death on the cross, He won pardon and the gift of God's indwelling Spirit for all who by God's grace believe in Him. Here, truly, is balm for any kind of human rejection. 'If God is for us, who can be against us?' (Rom. 8:31). If Christ lives in us by His

Holy Spirit, 'we are more than conquerors through Him who loved us,' and can confidently say, 'I can do all things [that God requires of me] through Christ who strengthens me' (Rom. 8:37; Phil. 4:13).

But there is still something else to encourage and help us. Jehovah's Servant is presently also our great High Priest in heaven who intercedes for us that our 'faith should not fail' (Luke 22:31-34). So, because Christ is at the right hand of God, the throne of God is now not only a throne of glory, but also of grace. So the writer of Hebrews says, 'Seeing then that we have a great High Priest who has passed through the heavens, Jesus the Son of God, let us hold fast our confession [of faith in Him]. For we do not have a High Priest who cannot sympathise with our weaknesses, but was in all points tempted as we are, yet without sin' (4:14-15). He who reigns at the right hand of God, is the One who lived and died on earth. He has therefore carried with Him into heaven the benefits of His life and death: the sympathy which He gained by His life, and the salvation which He won by His death. He is therefore able to sympathise with us now because He suffered then, and He is able to save us now because He died then.

We have nothing to fear. We can count on our great High Priest. For if we do not seek help from a friend in time of need, it is usually for one of two reasons: either we say, 'He would not understand'; or we say, 'He could not help'. In other words, we question our friend's sympathy or ability. But our 'great High Priest who has passed through the heavens, Jesus the Son of God', has both. His temptations and sorrows on earth have given Him the deepest sympathy with us, while His sin-bearing death on the cross has given Him the greatest ability to save and keep us from falling. He feels for us in our weakness and can come speedily to our aid. No sin is so black that His blood cannot wash it white; no trial is so fierce that He cannot sympathise, and no burden so heavy that He cannot shoulder it with us. Having such a great High Priest, the writer of Hebrews says, 'Let us therefore come boldly to the throne of grace, that we may obtain mercy [for our failings] and find grace to help in time of need' (v. 16). What a glorious privilege God has given us! There is no need to wait for a summons, or apply for an audience. Our Lord bids us draw near. Let us ensure that we do so. Let us begin every day at 'the throne of grace'. Let us close every day there too. And in the midst of the daily round and all the trials of life, let us keep coming to 'obtain mercy and find grace to help' moment by moment.

> Behold the throne of grace,
> The promise calls me near;
> There Jesus shows a smiling face,
> And waits to answer prayer.
>
> That rich atoning blood,
> Which sprinkled round I see,
> Provides for those who come to God,
> An all-prevailing plea.
>
> My soul, ask what thou wilt,
> Thou canst not be too bold;
> Since His own blood for thee He spilt,
> What else can He withhold?
>
> Beyond thine utmost wants,
> His love and power can bless:
> To praying souls, He always grants
> More than they can express.
>
> Thine image, Lord, bestow,
> Thy presence and Thy love:
> I ask to serve Thee here below,
> And reign with Thee above.
>
> (John Newton, 1725-1807).

Satan has enslaved our wills

> [3b] And as one from whom men hide their faces
>   He was despised, and we esteemed Him not (Isa. 53:3b).

In characteristic Hebrew parallelism, the second half of verse 3 carries on and develops the first half. The first half, as we have seen, expresses the emotional effect that the Servant will have on men and women when He comes to the world. The second half expresses the effect that He will have on their wills. Jesus will be 'despised/scorned' and 'rejected/shunned' by humankind when they consider the 'sorrows/suffering' and 'grief/sickness' that He will become 'acquainted with/familiar with' on their behalf (as the prophet outlines in verses 4-9). The Servant's loving initiative to totally identify with and relieve man's spiritual sorrow and sickness will meet not only with hardness of heart, but with a wilful determination to have nothing to do with Him.

The human will is enslaved to the devil (John 8:44; Eph. 2:2; 1 John 5:19). At creation, Adam was free to obey God and do His will on the earth, but since the Fall all Adam's posterity is born in bondage to sin and Satan. Of course, we must understand that men and women are not victims held against their will. They willingly choose to disobey God's commandments because their desire is to please self rather than God. Thus our Lord said, 'And this is the condemnation, that the light has come into the world, and men loved darkness rather than light, because their deeds were evil. For everyone practising evil hates the light and does not come to the light, lest his deeds should be exposed' (John 3:19-20).

This is the picture that the prophet Isaiah is conveying in the second half of verse 3. The clause, 'And as one from whom men hide their faces He was despised', is not suggesting that the sufferings of the Servant are so repulsive that it is impossible to endure looking at Him; that the onlookers at Calvary will have to turn away their faces from the sight of Him. Some make this their interpretation and argue it from chapter 52:14, 'As many were astonished at You – His appearance was so marred, beyond human semblance, and His form beyond that of the children of mankind.' But I believe that just as chapter 52:14 is describing primarily the Saviour's spiritual sufferings, so chapter 53:3b is describing the spiritual response of men and women to His death on the cross. The spectators at Calvary did not cover their faces from Christ's physical sufferings. They looked Him in the face and taunted Him with mockery and abuse.

What, then, is Isaiah saying? He is saying that in wilful defiance men and women will cover their faces from the truth that the One they are rejecting is the Christ, the Son of the living God, dying on their behalf (vv. 4-6). How else could He cast out demons, heal the sick and raise the dead? How else could He teach with such authority and wisdom that His critics were silenced and the people convinced that He was the great Prophet that Moses predicted would come (Deut. 18:15-19; Luke 7:16; John 1:45; 7:40)? In rejecting such evidence, their wills were enslaved both to the deception of the devil and to their own evil desires. The messianic Servant was a threat to their religious prestige and privileges. At the trial of Jesus, even Pilate 'knew that the chief priests had handed Him over because of envy' (Mark 15:10). This was a terrible sin, as our Lord explained to His disciples on the eve of His crucifixion. He said, 'He who hates Me hates My Father also. If I had not done among them the works which no one else did, they would have no sin; but now they have seen and hated both Me and My Father. But this happened that the word might be fulfilled which is written in their law, "They hated Me without a cause"' (John 15:23-25; Psalm 69:4).

The indictment of the bondage of the human will to Satan in his hostility and rebellion against God, is continued in the last clause of verse 3: 'And we esteemed Him not.' J. Alec Motyer helpfully points out:

> *Esteemed* is an 'accounting' word, a reckoning up of value. When all that the human eye saw and the human mind apprehended was added up the result was zero. With this word, Isaiah completes a diagnosis of our human condition, which he has been unobtrusively pursuing throughout these three verses [Isa. 53:1-3]: to see the Servant and find *no beauty* in Him (v.2cd) reveals the bankruptcy of the human emotions; to be one with those who despise and then reject Him (v.3ac) exposes the misguidedness of the human will; to appraise Him and conclude that He is nothing condemns our minds as corrupted by, and participants in, our sinfulness. Thus every aspect of human nature is inadequate; every avenue along

which, by nature, we might arrive at the truth and respond to God is closed. Nothing but divine revelation can make the Servant known to us and draw us to Him.[4]

Evidence of divine revelation seen graciously at work even in the last hours of the Servant's life, is heartening and glorifying to God. Mathew tells us, 'Then two robbers were crucified with Him, one on the right and another on the left. And those who passed by blasphemed Him, wagging their heads and saying, "You who destroy the temple and build it in three days, save Yourself! If You are the Son of God, come down from the cross" … Even the robbers who were crucified with Him reviled Him with the same thing' (27:38-44). Luke, however, completes the story. After Jesus uttered the prayer, 'Father, forgive them, for they do not know what they do', Luke adds: 'Then one of the criminals who were hanged blasphemed Him, saying, "If You are the Christ, save Yourself and us." But the other, answering, rebuked him, saying, "Do you not even fear God, seeing you are under the same condemnation? And we indeed justly, for we receive the due reward of our deeds; but this Man has done nothing wrong." Then he said to Jesus, "Lord, remember me when You come into Your kingdom." And Jesus said to him, "Assuredly, I say to you, today you will be with Me in Paradise"' (23:34, 39-43).

One other account of divine revelation at the cross is the confession of the soldiers. Matthew says, 'Now when the centurion and those with him, who were guarding Jesus, saw the earthquake and the things that had happened, they feared greatly, saying, "truly this was the Son of God"' (27:54). These men were Gentile idolaters who had nailed Him to the cross, callously gambled for His garments, and hurled insults at Him while He hung there in agony. But then from noon till 3 p.m. 'there was darkness over all the land'; and when He died, 'the earth quaked, and the rocks were split' (vv. 45, 51). The English Standard Version translates this 'they feared greatly' as 'they were filled with awe' (v. 54).

John MacArthur comments: 'They sensed that those awesome natural phenomena had a supernatural origin, and their primary fear

---

4. J. Alec Motyer, *The Prophecy of Isaiah*, p. 429.

was not of those events themselves but of the divine power behind them. Their emotional fright soon turned to spiritual, reverential awe ... The declaration "Truly this was the Son of God!" became for them a profession of faith in Christ.'[5] Luke adds that by his confession the centurion 'glorified God' (23:47). Michael Green is of the same opinion: 'The man was a Gentile, and a Gentile with blood on his hands. But he was no longer far off. He had drawn near, and he was accepted.'[6] Some scholars maintain that, because the Greek has no definite article here, the confession of the soldiers should be rendered, 'Truly this was a son of God.' But in Greek grammar, proper nouns and titles without the article can still be definite. John 1:1 is a good example: 'and the Word was God' (i.e. the God, not a god). The centurion 'glorified' God, and as C.H. Spurgeon wisely points out: 'Every genuine revelation of God has this mark upon it, that it makes Him appear more glorious.'[7]

If we have believed the good news of Jesus Christ; if He is to us 'Chief among ten thousand' and 'altogether lovely' (Song 5:10, 16) it is not because we are more perceptive than those who do not believe. We once despised and rejected Him like everyone else. It is the Holy Spirit who has revealed the truth of the gospel to us and opened our eyes to the indescribable beauty of Jesus. Like Saul of Tarsus, before our conversion we prided ourselves in all our earthly attainments, religious or secular. But when the Holy Spirit removed the scales from our eyes, we could say with Paul the apostle 'But whatever gain I had, I *counted* as loss for the sake of Christ. Indeed, I *count* everything as loss because of the surpassing worth of knowing Christ Jesus my Lord. For His sake I have suffered the loss of all things and count them as rubbish, in order that I may gain Christ and be found in him, not having a righteousness of my own that comes from [keeping] the law, but that which comes through

5. John MacArthur, *Matthew* (Moody Press, 1989), pp. 279, 281.

6. Michael Green, *Matthew for Today* (Word Publishing, 1988), p. 280. See also R.C.H. Lenski, *The Interpretation of St. Matthew's Gospel* (Augsburg 1961), p.1133.

7. C.H. Spurgeon, quoted in John Blanchard, *Gathered Gold* (Evangelical Press, 1984), p. 267.

faith in Christ, the righteousness from God that depends on faith' (Phil. 3:7-9 ESV, italics added). Coming to faith in Christ by the power of the Holy Spirit changes forever the way we view, desire, and choose Christ above all things.

If, however, we see 'no beauty that we should desire Him'; and if we are hiding our faces from Him because to look at the Saviour of the world only makes us feel uncomfortable in our sins, that should not deter us from seeking mercy and forgiveness from Him. Indeed, two chapters further on, Isaiah urges us to do so: 'Seek the LORD while He may be found, call upon Him while He is near. Let the wicked forsake his way, and the unrighteous man his thoughts; let him return to the LORD, and He will have mercy upon him, and to our God, for He will abundantly pardon' (55:6-7). The Servant will not hold it against anyone who comes to trust in Him that they previously despised and rejected Him. After all, the 'we' in verses two and three are those who once did not desire or esteem Him, but now by the grace of God do. Cast yourself upon the mercy of Jesus who promised: 'The one who comes to Me I will by no means cast out' (John 6:37). Don't put it off until another day, that day may never come. Take Him at His word here and now.

7

The Fourth Servant Song IV:
The vicarious nature of His sufferings

53:4 Surely he has borne our griefs
    and carried our sorrows;
yet we esteemed him stricken,
    smitten by God, and afflicted.
⁵ But He was wounded for our transgressions;
    he was crushed for our iniquities;
upon him was the chastisement that brought us peace,
    and with his stripes we are healed.
⁶ All we like sheep have gone astray;
    we have turned – every one – to his own way;
and the LORD has laid on him
    the iniquity of us all.
          (Isa. 53:4-6, ESV).

The third stanza (53:4-6) is the centrepiece of the Fourth Servant Song, which has a kind of pyramid structure with God's sovereign purpose as its solid base. So if you look at the first (52:13-15) and the last stanzas (53:10-12), you will find that, generally speaking, the prophet Isaiah describes the Servant as God sees Him, calling Him 'My Servant', whose humiliation will lead to exaltation. Then in the second (53:1-3) and fourth stanzas (53:7-9), Isaiah describes the Servant as unbelievers will view Him, despised and rejected as a fake. In the third stanza, the prophet puts himself in the position of the believing people of God, and predicts how they, by grace, will ultimately understand the suffering and death of the Servant.

His vicarious sufferings are so pointedly described that the third stanza reads like history rather than prophecy. It is the pinnacle of what is probably the most crucial and amazing revelation in the Old Testament of Messiah's atoning work on the cross for sinners. Moreover, Isaiah writes as if we, who read or hear these words, and believe, were there at the cross, because by association we really were. It was the guilt and penalty of every believer's sin that required the suffering and death of Jesus at Calvary. In Rembrandt's painting *The Raising of Jesus*, he paints himself into the picture as one of the men crucifying God's beloved Son, conveying the complicity of all humanity. Not one of us can say, 'If I had been there, I would not have joined the chorus to have Him crucified!'

The Servant's sufferings were undeserved

> [4] Surely he has borne our griefs
>   and carried our sorrows;
> yet we esteemed him stricken,
>   smitten by God, and afflicted (Isa. 53:4, ESV).

In verse four we have a sharp contrast between what unbelievers will say is the cause of the Servant's suffering and death, and what the real cause is. For what the human eye completely misses can only be known by divine revelation; only by those to whom 'the arm of the Lord has been revealed' (v. 1). Right from the beginning of the world, men have instinctively believed what God in His word so clearly teaches; namely, that sorrow, sickness and death are God's curse upon human sin. That is why, when things go wrong, we self-righteously ask: 'Why has God allowed this to happen to me?' We believe, and rightly so, that God is sovereign and controls everything that happens in the world in such a way that justice is done; the wicked are eventually punished and the righteous rewarded.

Accordingly, when Jesus was crucified on Calvary, the people of Jerusalem believed that He was guilty of blasphemy, fraud and insurrection, and was now suffering His just deserts. That is how Isaiah sums up the opinion of those who view His execution: 'We esteemed Him stricken, smitten by God, and afflicted.' But because we are finite and fallen creatures, we are not infallible in our judgments of our fellow human beings. Some suffering is not deserved. When Job, in a matter of a few days, lost his ten children, his livestock and his good health, his friends, who were not prejudicial in their response, told him that it had to be because of some grave sin he had committed (Job 4:7-9). The same thing happened to David. When Absalom usurped his father's throne and David had to flee for his life from Jerusalem, Shimei cursed him, saying, 'Come out! Come out! You bloodthirsty man, you rogue! The LORD has brought upon you all the blood of the house of Saul, in whose place you have reigned; and the LORD has delivered the kingdom into the hands of Absalom your son. So now you are caught in your own evil, because you are a bloodthirsty man!' (2 Sam. 16:7-8).

In both cases, however, the accusers were wrong. The LORD could say to Satan, 'Have you considered My servant Job, that there is none like him on the earth, a blameless and upright man, who fears God and shuns evil?' (Job. 1:8). And Shimei was wrong about David. David was not guilty of shedding the blood of the house of Saul, and when David was restored to the throne, Shimei confessed the wrong he had done to David (2 Sam. 19:19). But never has anyone been more falsely accused of suffering for sin He never committed than Jesus. Pilate said to the Jewish priests, 'You take Him and crucify Him, for I find no fault in Him' (John 19:6). One of the thieves dying next to Jesus rebuked his partner in crime for blaspheming Jesus, saying, 'Do you not even fear God, seeing you are under the same condemnation? And we indeed justly, for we receive the due reward of our deeds; but this Man has done nothing wrong' (Luke 23:40-41).

Speaking of the cross, Paul says, 'He [God] made Him who knew no sin to be sin for us'; and Peter says, 'Christ also suffered once for sins, the just for the unjust' (2 Cor. 5:21; 1 Pet. 3:18). Unless unbelievers are given spiritual sight, they will completely misread the providential dealings of God with Jesus at Calvary. Yes, He was suffering there because of sins committed, but they were not for sins which *He* had committed (John 8:46; 1 John 3:5; Heb. 7:26-28). The sinless Servant was suffering in our place for our sins. This is the shocking revelation that came to Isaiah in verse four: 'Surely He has borne our griefs [sickness of soul] and carried our sorrows' [pains, physical and spiritual]. J. Alec Motyer comments, 'With neither co-operation nor understanding from us, the Servant took on Himself all that blights our lives. *Surely* is a conjunction emphasising the unexpected. Whatever people may have thought about the sorrow and sufferings they saw, the truth was dramatically different.'[1] The pains Jesus bore were *ours*. We were the guilty ones, and His griefs and sorrows were the just punishment due to our personal sins.

But as we pointed out at the beginning of this chapter, it is important to see the complicity of all humankind in the sufferings and death of the messianic Servant. We need to see ourselves, not as spectators only, but as guilty participants in what happened at Calvary. There is blood on our hands, for it was our sins that nailed Jesus to the cross. So before we can begin to see the cross as something done *for* us, we must see it as something done *by* us. It was the realisation of this fact that moved Horatius Bonar (1808-1889), called 'the prince of Scottish hymn-writers,' to write:

> I see the scourges tear His back,
> I see the piercing crown,
> And of that crowd who smite and mock,
> I feel that I am one.
>
> 'Twas I that shed the sacred blood,
> I nailed Him to the tree,
> I crucified the Christ of God,
> I joined the mockery.
>
> Of all that shouting multitude
> I feel that I am one;
> And in that din of voices rude
> I recognise my own.

---

1. J. Alec Motyer, *The Prophecy of Isaiah*, p. 430.

Yet not the less that blood avails,
To cleanse away my sin;
And not the less that cross prevails
To give me peace within.

His sufferings were penal and substitutionary

⁴ Surely he has borne our griefs
   and carried our sorrows ...
⁵ But he was wounded for our transgressions;
   he was crushed for our iniquities;
upon him was the chastisement that brought us peace,
   and with his stripes we are healed (Isa. 53:4-5, ESV).

The sufferings of the Servant which ended in His death were *penal*, because death is the penalty demanded by God for all who break His holy law (Ezek. 18:4; Rom. 5:12; 6:23). And they were *substitutionary*, because Jesus died in our place for our sins, and not for any of His own, for He was sinless (John 8:46; Heb. 4:15; 1 Pet. 2:24; 3:18; 1 John 3:5). In all three verses the Servant is presented as the sin-bearing substitute whom Jehovah has so graciously provided for His people (v. 8), to 'make many to be accounted righteous' (v. 11). These are the people Isaiah identifies himself with in verses four, five and six by using the first person plural pronouns *our, we* and *us*. The principle of penal, substitutionary suffering runs right through the third stanza of this fourth song. It piles on one expression after another as follows: 'He has borne our griefs and carried our sorrows ... He was wounded for our transgressions; He was crushed for our iniquities; upon Him was the chastisement that brought us peace, and with His stripes we are healed ... the LORD has laid on Him the iniquity of us all.'

The verbs Isaiah uses are also very significant. To 'bear' our griefs means 'to lift' them off us, and 'to carry' our sorrows means 'to shoulder' them as His own burden. To 'bear sin' in the Old Testament means to bear its penalty: 'They shall therefore keep My ordinance, lest they bear sin for it and die'; 'Whoever curses his God shall bear his sin. And whoever blasphemes the name of the LORD shall surely be put to death'; 'the children of Israel shall not come near the tabernacle of meeting, lest they bear sin and die' (Lev. 22:9; 24:15; Num. 18:22). Thus the New Testament speaks of Christ's death as a bearing of sin: 'So Christ was offered once to bear the sins of many'; 'Who Himself bore our sins in His own body on the tree' (Heb. 9:28; 1 Pet. 2:24).

The verbs in verse five are even more explicit. 'He was wounded' literally means 'to pierce' fatally (Job 26:13; Isa. 51:9). 'Crushed' (not merely 'bruised', as in KJV) is used variously of people 'trampled' into the dust, or 'broken' by the infliction of blows ending in death (Isa. 19:10; Lam. 3:34). Our Lord expressed a similar thought when at the Last Supper He broke the bread and said, 'Take, eat; this is My body which is broken for you; do this in remembrance of Me' (1 Cor. 11:24). E.J. Young says, 'The two words chosen, "pierced through" and "crushed" are among the strongest expressions found in the Hebrew language to denote a violent and a painful death. This cruel and painful death He underwent because He had taken our sins upon Himself to make an atonement for them.'[2] 'Chastisement' is better translated as 'punishment' (NIV), because what is in view here is not correction, but the execution of the death penalty demanded by God's law. Only in that way could peace with God be procured and our sin-sick souls 'healed' (Rom. 5:1; 2 Cor. 5:18-20).

The connection between the Servant's death and human sin is irrefutable:

> This is My blood of the new covenant which is shed for many for the remission of sins (Matt. 26:28).

> Thus it is written, and thus it was necessary for the Christ to suffer and to rise from the dead the third day, and that repentance and remission of sins should be preached in His name to all nations, beginning at Jerusalem (Luke 24:46-47).

> But God demonstrates His own love towards us, in that while we were still sinners, Christ died for us (Rom. 5:8).

---

2. E.J. Young, *Isaiah Fifty-Three*, p. 48.

For I delivered to you as of first importance what I also received: that Christ died for our sins in accordance with the Scriptures (1 Cor. 15:3, esv).

For He [God] made Him [Christ] who knew no sin to be sin for us, that we might become the righteousness of God in Him (2 Cor. 5:21).

Christ redeemed us from the curse of the law, by becoming a curse for us – for it is written, 'cursed is everyone who is hanged from a tree' (Gal. 3:13, esv).

You were ransomed from the futile ways inherited from your forefathers, not with perishable things such as silver and gold, but with the precious blood of Christ, like that of a lamb without blemish or spot ... He himself bore our sins in his body on the tree, that we might die to sin and live to right-eousness. By his wounds you have been healed ... For Christ also suffered once for sins, the righteous for the unrighteous, that he might bring us to God, being put to death in the flesh but made alive in the spirit (1 Pet. 1:18-19; 2:24; 3:18, esv).

The blood of Jesus Christ His Son cleanses us from all sin (1 John 1:7).

Yet in spite of the fact that the New Testament so unequivocally connects Christ's death with our sin, there are those who remain sceptical. 'Why should our forgiveness depend on Christ's death?' they ask. They think it is easy for God to forgive sins. After all, if we can forgive those who wrong us, surely God can just as easily forgive us when we wrong Him? But it is not as straightforward as that, and it is crucial to see why it is not. We can forgive sin with no difficulty at all, because we ourselves are guilty of sinning against others all the time. It would be hypocritical if we wanted those we have wronged to forgive us, when we are not willing to forgive those who have sinned against us. For God, however, it is quite different. In the first place, He is morally perfect or righteous, and so sin is infinitely more offensive to Him than it is to us. In the second place, and even more importantly, God is not just a private individual, nor is sin just a personal injury. On the contrary, God is Himself the *author* of the laws we break, as well as their *upholder.* God is the origin of good as well as the guarantee of its continuance. This is uniquely true of Him, and of no other.

Take love, for instance. Everybody agrees that love is better than hatred. But why do we believe that? Where does the moral value of love come from? What gives it virtue? Is it because love is part of human nature? Is it because we enjoy love more than we do hatred, or because we feel safer when love prevails in society rather than hatred? The answer is, 'No.' According to the Bible, love is better than hatred because 'God is love' (1 John 4:8). That is the root of it. It is God's moral character that guarantees moral values and makes them absolutes. We can overlook evil and it does not matter too much, but God is not like that. If God overlooks evil, it is as good as saying that evil does not matter; it is of no consequence. But as the upholder of the moral universe, that is something God cannot do. So with regard to the forgiveness of sin, God's seeming dilemma is this: How is *forgiveness* distinguished from moral *indifference?* If morality is to be preserved in the universe, it is absolutely necessary that God's righteousness should not only be done, but seen to be done. In the words of Romans chapter 3 it needs to be 'demonstrated' (vv. 25-26). God must in some way publicly dissociate Himself personally from all evil in the world. He must take a clear stand against it. Failure to do so would result in the undermining of all moral standards and values.

Seemingly, the obvious way for God to take a stand against evil is to judge and punish it as it deserves. The problem, of course, with that particular demonstration of God's righteousness is that the whole world would be condemned and justly destroyed. Is there an alternative? Is it possible for God's righteousness to be demonstrated in another way that would allow Him to forgive and acquit penitent sinners? The astonishing answer of the apostle Paul in Romans chapter 3 is that an alternative has indeed been found in Jesus Christ 'whom God set forth to be a propitiation by His blood [an appeasing sacrifice], through faith, to demonstrate His righteousness ... that He might be just and the justifier of the one who has faith in Jesus' (vv. 25-26).

Or as John Stott explains:

> The problem of forgiveness is constituted by the inevitable collision between divine perfection and human rebellion, between God as He is and us as we are ... For, although indeed 'God is love', yet we have to remember that His love is 'holy love,' love which yearns over sinners while at the same time refusing to condone their sin. How, then, could God express His holy love? – His love in forgiving sinners without compromising His holiness, and His holiness in judging sinners without frustrating His love? ... At the cross in holy love God through Christ paid the full penalty of our disobedience Himself. He bore the judgment we deserve in order to bring us the forgiveness we do not deserve. On the cross divine mercy and justice were equally expressed and eternally reconciled. God's holy love was satisfied.[3]

Now, if this costly substitution of Jesus was clearly predicted in these verses in Isaiah 53, it was also graphically illustrated by the great religious festival of the Jews at Passover that marked the beginning of Israel's national life and is described in Exodus chapter 12. A careful look at the passage will further strengthen our understanding of the fundamental principle of substitution if sinners are to be saved. The Egyptians had enslaved the children of Israel and were not prepared to let them leave the land. Their Jewish slaves were a very wealthy asset. So when Pharaoh would not relent after the first nine plagues had been sent upon the land, God determined that the last plague would be particularly devastating. All the firstborn children of every family in Egypt would be killed in a single night, as the angel of death passed through the land. No household would be exempt simply because they were Jews. Even the firstborn of all the animals would die. Jehovah said: 'Against all the gods of Egypt I will execute judgment' (v. 12), for the Israelites had been just as idolatrous as

---

3. John R.W. Stott, *The Cross of Christ* (IVP, 1986), pp. 88-89.

their Egyptian oppressors (Josh. 24:14-15). So God was as angry with them as He was with the Egyptians. How, then, could He be faithful to His promise to bless Abraham's descendants and yet pass this sentence of death upon them? If justice demanded that the Jews be punished for their sins too, then surely there was no alternative but to include them in this appalling holocaust.

God, however, had a plan. It was called 'the LORD's Passover' (v. 11). It is very significant that God did not pretend that the Israelites were innocent, and let them off simply because they were Jews. That would have been contrary to the truth. Nor did God issue some cheap, blanket decree of pardon, for that would make a mockery of His own righteousness. Instead, God made a provision which would avert His judgment when it fell, for any who had faith to appropriate it. God commanded the Israelites, saying, 'Every man shall take for himself a lamb ... a lamb for a household ... and they shall take some of the blood and put it on the two doorposts and on the lintel of the houses where they eat' (vv. 3, 7). But what difference would the blood of that slain lamb make? All the difference between life and death! For God went on to promise: 'The blood shall be a sign for you on the houses where you are. And when I see the blood, I will pass over you; and the plague shall not be on you to destroy you when I strike the land of Egypt' (v. 13). So the next morning, inside every Egyptian home there was a dead firstborn son, and inside every Jewish home there was a dead firstborn lamb.

What conclusion should the Jews draw from that? The obvious one, surely, was that the firstborn male lamb had died in the place of their firstborn son. That is why each family had to slay its own Passover lamb; each lamb substituted for that family's firstborn son, and bore the penalty of death for him. When the angel of death came through the land and saw the blood, it was a marker that in that home a death had already occurred whereby God's justice had been satisfied as far as that family was concerned. The blood of the lamb was not just an ethnic marker to distinguish the houses of the Jews from the houses of the Egyptians. Rather, it was a marker to identify the people who had put their trust in God's promise to accept the sacrifice of the Passover lamb as a substitute for their firstborn son. The blood was also smeared on the doorposts of their house for God to see: 'When He sees the blood on the lintel and on the two doorposts, the LORD will pass over the door and not allow the destroyer to come into your houses to strike you' (v. 23). The blood was put there, not to change the way they felt about their sin, but to change the way God felt about their sin. A death had occurred. God's justice had been satisfied by a costly substitution. An innocent substitute had to die in order for God to spare the firstborn son of each household marked by its shed blood.

This annual ritual was instituted as a sign, or type, pointing forward to its fulfilment in the penal, substitutionary death of God's Son, and the beginning of His new and redeemed community, the Christian Church. The New Testament writers clearly understood this, and so Paul could command the Corinthian church to be God's new redeemed community, because 'Christ, our Passover, was sacrificed for us' (1 Cor. 5:7). Moreover, Matthew, Mark and Luke, record the fact it was at a Passover supper the night before He died, that the Servant washed His disciples' feet and changed the Old Testament ritual into the Christian ordinance of the Lord's Supper (Matt. 26:17-25; Mark 14:12-21; Luke 22:7-18; see also John 13:1-30 and 1 Cor. 11:17-34). No longer would Christians be required to observe the Passover and sacrifice a lamb, for Jesus Himself was going to be sacrificed on behalf of His believing people. So in anticipation of the sacrifice of Himself on the cross the next day, the Saviour offered His disciples the bread and the wine, saying, 'This is My body which is given/broken for you' and 'this is My blood of the new covenant which is shed for many for the remission of sins' (Luke 22:19; 1 Cor. 11:24; Matt. 26:28). Not only that, but according to John's chronology of the crucifixion, Jesus was hanging on the cross at the precise time when the Passover lambs were being slaughtered (John 18:28; 19:14, 31).

The penal, substitutionary death of Jesus Christ on the cross of Calvary is the heart of the gospel and must and will for ever be the crowning theme of Christian praise. With no sympathy or help from us in our sin and rebellion, the Servant of Jehovah bore the punishment due to us, that we might have peace with God (v. 5).

O Christ, what burdens bowed Thy head!
　Our load was laid on Thee;
Thou stoodest in the sinner's stead,
　Didst bear all ill for me.
A victim led, Thy blood was shed,
　Now there's no load for me.

Jehovah bade His sword awake;
　O Christ, it woke 'gainst Thee;
Thy blood the flaming blade must slake;
　Thine heart its sheath must be;
All for my sake, my peace to make;
　Now sleeps that sword for me.

For me, Lord Jesus, Thou hast died,
　And I have died in Thee!
Thou'rt risen – my bands are all untied,
　And now Thou liv'st in me.
When purified, made white and tried,
　Thy glory then for me!

(Anne R. Cousin, 1824-1906)

His sufferings were the will and act of God

[6] All we like sheep have gone astray;
　we have turned – every one – to his own way;
and the LORD has laid on him
　the iniquity of us all (Isa. 53:6, ESV).

There is such a thing as noble suffering and death. We think of martyrs like Joan of Arc or victims like Ghandi who, one could argue, have added to the significance of their lives by the way they died. But when you consider the matter carefully, it is clear that you cannot speak of their sufferings and death as being an achievement or something that lies within the plan of God and which He is achieving. You cannot say that because they did not set out to die. Death came to them unsought and unwelcome, as it does to all of us.

Their death is seen as a tragedy. Any advantage for their cause, any advancement of their fame that arises from their death is really an accident of history, an ironic twist of fate. The death of any human being, as seen this side of the grave, is a cruel anti-climax. It is the final exit.

But that is not how Isaiah in vv. 4-6 sees the death of Jehovah's Servant. He will not be the victim of unforeseen and unfortunate circumstances. His death will not be a cruel anti-climax, but the successful accomplishment of God's eternal plan of redemption for the world. The messianic Servant will not be the victim of sin and death, but God's victor over sin and death. His death will not be the end of His life's work, but only its beginning. If He is going to be 'wounded' and 'crushed' and 'punished' and 'scourged', it is because 'the LORD has laid on Him the iniquity of us all.' This astounding fact is more fully stated in verse 10: 'Yet it was the will of the LORD to crush Him; He has put Him to grief.' Octavius Winslow sums it up well when he says, 'Who delivered up Jesus to die? Not Judas, for money; not Pilate, for fear; not the Jews for envy; – but the Father, for love!'[4]

Although our Lord was put to death by lawless and wicked men, He did not die as a martyr. On the contrary, He went to the cross voluntarily, even deliberately. Right from the beginning of His public ministry He knew that this was His Father's will for Him; that He was 'the Lamb of God who takes away the sin of the world' (John 1:29). He said, 'as Moses lifted up the serpent in the wilderness, even so must the Son of Man be lifted up, that whoever believes in Him should not perish but have eternal life'; and 'I am the living bread which came down from heaven. If anyone eats of this bread, he will live forever; and the bread that I shall give is My flesh, which I shall give for the life of the world ... Whoever eats My flesh and drinks My blood has eternal life, and I will raise him up at the last day'; and again, 'I am the good shepherd. The good shepherd

---

4. Octavius Winslow, quoted by John Murray, *Romans* (Marshall, Morgan and Scott, 1960), vol. 1, p. 324, from Winslow's *No Condemnation in Christ Jesus*, 1857, p. 358.

gives His life for the sheep' (John 3:14-15; 6:51, 54; 10:11; see also Matt. 16:21; 17:22-23; 20:18-19).

If it was not the will of God for the Son to die a penal, substitutionary death for sinners, Jesus could have avoided going to the cross. He did not have to go up to Jerusalem. He knew it was dangerous, but He insisted on going. He did not have to choose Judas to be one of His disciples. He knew that Judas was a traitor, but He still made him one of the twelve. He did not have to expose Himself to the risk of easy arrest, yet He went outside the city to pray in the garden of Gethsemane. Most of all, He did not have to stay on the cross. When the chief priests, with the scribes and elders, mocked Him, saying, 'He saved others, Himself He cannot save. If He is the King of Israel, let Him now come down from the cross, and we will believe in Him' (Matt. 27:41-42), why did He not come down? The answer is the answer He gave Peter when the apostle tried to defend Him in Gethsemane: 'Put your sword into its sheath. Shall I not drink the cup which My Father has given Me?' (John 18:11). Matthew adds, 'Or do you think that I cannot now pray to My Father, and He will provide Me with more than twelve legions of angels?' (26:53).

If ever a death needed an explanation, the death of Christ on the cross does. The divine explanation given 700 years before the Servant of Jehovah died is found here in Isaiah 53:6, 'All we like sheep have gone astray; we have turned – every one – to his own way, and the LORD has laid on Him the iniquity of us all.' It was an act of God determined by the will of God 'from the foundation of the world' (Rev. 13:8). God the Father planned and willed it, not just in the sense that He looked on and allowed it to happen, but that He actually made it to happen (Acts 2:22-24). Of course, in the minds of those who cynically reject what the Scripture says, the very idea that God would punish the innocent for the guilty, borders on blasphemy! To attribute such a miscarriage of justice to God, they contend, is preposterous!

It sounds like a strong argument, but it has a serious flaw. It overlooks the divine nature of Jesus. The mystery of the incarnation is unfathomable! We cannot explain it; we can only formulate it, and the Athanasian Creed does it well. 'Our Lord Jesus Christ, the Son of God, is God and man, ... perfect God, and perfect man, ... who although He be God and man: yet He is not two, but one Christ; one not by conversion of the Godhead into flesh: but by taking of the manhood into God.' So when we look at Jesus on the cross, we are not looking at a third party as far as God is concerned. There are not three parties involved at the cross, only two: God and us. Jesus was God on the cross! God was not punishing somebody else, He was bearing the punishment in Himself. This is the Plaintiff, the Person who has been injured, who is absorbing the penalty of sin in Himself, rather than pressing charges against us.

Thus Paul can say, 'God was in Christ reconciling the world to Himself' (2 Cor. 5:19). That is why Jesus, God incarnate, shrank from the cross the night before He died: an observation that otherwise should strike us as most surprising. For many Christian martyrs have gone to their deaths rejoicing. Our Lord, however, was 'exceedingly sorrowful and deeply distressed,' and 'His sweat became like great drops of blood' as He prayed, saying, 'Father, if it is Your will, remove this cup from Me; nevertheless not My will, but Yours be done' (Matt. 26:37-38, Luke 22:44, 42). Was the Servant less courageous than some of His followers who would later die for Him? Absolutely not! The reason for His distress was that His death would be a different death to ours. His death would be a death no Christian would have to die, for the mysterious unity of the Father and the Son in the Godhead somehow made it possible for God to be forsaken by God, so that believers might never be forsaken by Him.

No one can get their mind around that! It is incomprehensible! It is a mystery that forever will remain a mystery. The cross almost by its very shape speaks of paradox and contradiction. For here, in order to save us in such a way as to satisfy His law, God through Christ substituted Himself for us. Here divine love satisfied divine justice by divine self-sacrifice. Here, now in His grace, God treats sinners as His sons, because then, in His justice, He treated His Son as a sinner. It is an astonishing claim, and it is absolutely unique to Christianity. There is not one of us who would have dared to interpret the cross in such an unthinkable and scandalous way (1 Cor. 1:21-25), if the prophet Isaiah had not spoken with the authority of God and told us: 'He was wounded for our transgressions; He was crushed for our iniquities ... the LORD has laid on Him the iniquity of us all.' Among all the gods of all the religions in the world, there is not one who has vicarious wounds but God in Christ alone.

Before we conclude our study of verses 4-6 and its revelation of the penal, substitutionary death of the Servant of Jehovah, there are some important issues to clarify. First of all, when Scripture says, 'The LORD laid on Him the iniquity of us all', and 'He [God] made Him who knew no sin to be sin for us' (Isa. 53:6; 2 Cor. 5:21), it is not suggesting that the Son of God was made personally sinful with all our sin, but rather that He assumed the guilt and penalty of our sins. What was transferred to Jesus was not the *moral character* of our sin, but its *legal consequence.* He voluntarily accepted liability for our sins. He lived without sin and died without sin as our innocent substitute.

Secondly, we must not caricature the roles of God the Father and God the Son at Calvary. We must not set them over against each other in such a way as to imply that the Son was extracting from the Father a pardon He was reluctant to bestow, or that the Father compelled the Son to be our sin-bearing substitute. Both God and Christ, the Father and the Son, were willingly and lovingly acting together in the divine initiative to save sinners. Neither Jesus alone as man nor the Father alone as God could have secured our salvation. Only God in Christ could have reconciled guilty sinners to Himself.

Thirdly, Isaiah means us to understand that we have not only sinned in *general,* but also in a *particular* sense. That is what the prophet means by the words: 'We have turned – everyone – to his own way.' Our way is not only distinct from God's way, but unique to ourselves. Spurgeon is helpful here:

> There is a distinctive sinfulness about every individual. Each of us has some special aggravation. While genuine repentance naturally associates us with other penitents, it also produces a kind of loneliness. 'We have turned, everyone, to his own way', is a confession that each one has sinned uniquely, or

sinned with an intensity that could not be perceived in others. This confession is unreserved. There is not a word to detract from its force, not a syllable of excuse. The confession gives up all claims of self-righteousness. It is the declaration of the consciously guilty; guilty with aggravations, guilty without excuse. We stand with our weapons of rebellion broken in pieces and cry, 'All we like sheep have gone astray; we have turned, everyone, to his own way.' Yet there are no hopelessly distressing moans with this confession, because the next sentence makes it almost a song: 'The LORD has laid on Him the iniquity of us all.' This phrase is the most grievous in our text; yet it overflows with comfort. Isn't it amazing that where misery was concentrated, mercy reigned. Where sorrow reached a climax, weary souls find rest. The Saviour bruised is the healer of bruised hearts. The lowest repentance gives way to assured confidence by gazing at Christ on the cross.[5]

Fourthly, the penal, substitutionary death of Christ does not automatically absolve sinners of the guilt and penalty of their sins. It is a truth that must not only be accepted intellectually but also spiritually by faith. That is to say, by a personal commitment of our life, body and soul, to Christ whose death was the only way by which God's holy love could be satisfied and yet rebellious human beings could be saved. None of us, however, find this easy to do, for nothing in the world cuts us down to size like the 'stumbling block' of 'Christ crucified' (1 Cor. 1:23). All of us, by nature, have inflated views of our own respectability. We cannot bear to acknowledge either the heinousness of our sin or our utter indebtedness to the cross. We prefer to call our sins 'weaknesses' or 'shortcomings', which we can make amends for by telling God we are sorry, and trying to appease Him with a few good works.

That is the path to doom. We cannot trust in ourselves and in Christ crucified simultaneously. If we could save ourselves, there would have been no need for Christ to die on the cross for us. We

---

5. C.H. Spurgeon, *Morning and Evening* (Thomas Nelson, 1994), April 3, evening.

need to be humbled before the cross as hell-deserving sinners, and hear, as it were, the Son of God saying: 'I am here because of *you*. It is *your* sin I am bearing, *your* curse I am suffering, *your* debt I am paying, *your* God-forsaken death I am dying.' Come to Jesus as a helpless, penitent sinner like that, and trust Him to put you in the right with God. You can rely on His precious promise: 'Come to Me, all you who labour [under a guilty conscience] and are heavy laden [with the burden of sin], and I will give you rest' (Matt. 11:28).

> See how the patient Jesus stands,
>   Insulted in His lowest case!
> Sinners have bound the Almighty's hands,
>   And spit in their Creator's face.
>
> With thorns His temples gor'd and gash'd
>   Send streams of blood from every part;
> His back's with knotted scourges lash'd,
>   But sharper scourges tear His heart.
>
> Nailed naked to the accursed wood
>   Exposed to earth and heaven above,
> A spectacle of wounds and blood,
>   A prodigy of injured love!
>
> Hark! How His doleful cries affright
>   Affected angels, while they view;
> His friends forsook Him in the night,
>   And now His God forsakes Him too!
>
> Behold that pale, that languid face,
>   That drooping head, those languid eyes!
> Behold in sorrow and disgrace
>   Our conquering Hero hangs, and dies!
>
> Ye that assume His sacred name,
>   Now tell me, what can all this mean?
> What was it bruised God's harmless Lamb,
>   What was it pierced His soul but sin?

Blush, Christian, blush: let shame abound:
If sin affects thee not with woe,
Whatever life is in thee found,
The life of Christ thou dost not know.

(Joseph Hart, 1712-1768)

8

The Fourth Servant Song V:
The majestic silence of His submission

53:7 He was oppressed, and he was afflicted,
  yet he opened not his mouth;
like a lamb that is led to the slaughter,
  and like a sheep that before its shearers is silent,
so he opened not his mouth.
      (Isa. 53:7, ESV).

Verse seven continues the story of the Servant of Jehovah from the beginning of His life (vv. 1-3) to the point where He was led out to die for the sins of His people (vv. 4-6, 12a). The LORD is going to lay on Him 'the iniquity of us all', and as a result He will be fatally pierced for our transgressions, crushed for our iniquities and punished so that we might have peace with God. The question that the prophet Isaiah now wants to deal with is: 'How did the Servant go to His vicarious death?' Verse seven emphasises the voluntary, silent submissiveness of Christ to the affliction of both divine justice and human injustice. The words of the second line, 'He opened not His mouth', are repeated in the fifth line to emphasise the majestic self-restraint with which the Servant accepted His penal, substitutionary death. There was no self-defence, no complaint, no angry denunciation of His accusers or judges. Rather, the meekness and quiet strength that were always evident in His public ministry were even more apparent in His three trials and on the cross.

This wonderful display of silent submissiveness is further stressed in the two similes that Isaiah uses when he compares Jesus to a *lamb* led to the slaughter and to a *sheep* silent before its shearers. Motyer brings out the meaning as follows: 'Animals go with blind compliance whatever the destination. The Servant goes with knowing submission to what awaits Him. The lamb here is led to an impending experience; the sheep is undergoing an actual experience; the Servant maintains His self-imposed silence both as He goes and as He endures.'[1] His death was no evidence of weakness, but the manifestation of deliberate, unwavering self-submission to the will of God. He willingly laid down His life for His sheep (John 10:11, 14, 17-18). To quote Motyer again, 'The Servant's tongue and mind were alike disciplined to say an unequivocal 'yes' to injustice and to a death He did not deserve.'[2]

The opening clause of verse seven also has a significant bearing on the silent, patient submissiveness of Jehovah's Servant in the face of mistreatment: 'He was oppressed, and He was afflicted, yet He opened not His mouth.' The word 'oppressed' is used in the sense of severe mistreatment (Isa. 3:5; 58:3). In Exodus 1:11 the word 'taskmasters' comes from the same root: 'Therefore they set taskmasters over them [their Jewish slaves] to afflict them with their burdens.' It could equally be translated, 'He was treated harshly (or severely).' That is surely the conclusion anyone would come to witnessing the spitting in the face, the slapping, the scourging, the mocking, and the piercing with thorns and nails that Jesus endured that day (Matt. 26:57-68; 27:26-43).

Isaiah, however, does not stop there, but adds the words: 'and He was afflicted'. Actually, it is the same verb as Isaiah used in verse 4d, only here in verse 7a it reappears as a participle in a reflexive form which literally reads: 'and for His part kept submitting to affliction'. The New English Bible renders the clause as 'He submitted to be struck down.' E.J. Young gives this fuller paraphrase of verse 7ab: 'He was afflicted, and while He was afflicted He

---

1. J. Alec Motyer, *The Prophecy of Isaiah*, p. 433.

2. *Ibid*, p. 432.

Himself suffered voluntarily and did not open His mouth.'[3] This is the beautiful, Christ-honouring emphasis of verse 7: the majestic, clear-headed, voluntary, silent submissiveness with which the divine–human Servant approached and accepted the sufferings of His vicarious death.

Of course, we are not to understand our Lord's silence in an absolute sense. He did utter some brief and crucial words at His trials before Caiaphas and Pilate, as well as from the cross. They were very few, however, and were uttered solely to honour the Father who had sent Him and comfort the people He had given Him. They were not spoken in angry retaliation to the cruel insults hurled at Him by His enemies, or in complaint of His mistreatment, or in self-defence of His innocence.

Caiaphas and Pilate and Herod were experienced judges who were all too familiar with the protests and complaints that came from men about to die for their crimes. The calm silence of Jesus, therefore, unnerved His judges when they began to examine Him and could find no fault in Him. They even chided Him for not answering His accusers. Caiaphas, the high priest, rebuked Jesus, 'saying, "Do you answer nothing? What is it these men testify against You?" But He kept silent and answered nothing' (Mark 14:60-61). When God's Servant was taken to Pilate, Matthew says, 'And while He was being accused by the chief priests and elders, He answered nothing. Then Pilate said to Him, "Do you not hear how many things they testify against You?" And He answered him not one word, so that the governor marvelled greatly' (27:12-14). That is what the prophet Isaiah is predicting in verse seven when He says, 'He opened not His mouth'; and we can now turn our thoughts to the chief lessons to be learned from the Servant's silence.

He was silent in obeying His Father's will

Verse four says, 'Surely He has borne our griefs and carried our sorrows, yet we esteemed Him stricken, smitten by God and afflicted.' Erroneously, humankind will attribute the Servant's sufferings to His own sins. But as the prophet goes on to point out in verses

---

3. E.J. Young, *Isaiah Fifty-Three*, p. 59.

five and six: 'He was pierced for our transgressions, crushed for our iniquities', punished to bring us 'peace', scourged so that we might be 'healed', for 'the LORD has laid on Him the iniquity of us all.' Our Lord, who had deeply meditated on the Old Testament Scriptures all His life, knew that the whole process of His ill-treatment and execution were ordained of God and must happen for Scripture to be fulfilled (Matt. 16:21; 17:22-23; 20:18-19; 26:51-54). Verses 9-10 clearly state that 'although He had done no violence, and there was no deceit in His mouth, yet it was the will of the LORD to crush Him; He has put Him to grief' [or, 'and caused Him to suffer']. Caiaphas and Pilate and the Roman soldiers were only the instruments God used to verbally and physically afflict His only begotten and beloved Son.

The suffering Servant, the night before He died, was profoundly aware of the cup of suffering that Jehovah was about to give Him. Thus, He prayed in the garden of Gethsemane, 'O My Father, if it is possible, let this cup pass from Me; nevertheless, not as I will, but as You will' (Matt. 26:39). He was submissive, even when He asked if there could possibly be another way consistent with the Father's purpose for Him to save the world. Was the cross truly the only way? After praying first on His knees and then twice prostrate with His face on the ground, there was no voice from heaven (Luke 22:41; Matt. 26:39). Scripture was clear: He must suffer physical and spiritual death on the cross, if salvation is to be procured for the world. God's righteousness demanded it. Our law-breaking required it.

Speaking of this ordeal in Gethsemane, the writer of Hebrews says, 'So also Christ ... in the days of His flesh, when He had offered up prayers and supplications, with vehement cries and tears to Him who was able to save Him from death, and was heard because of His godly fear, though He was a Son, yet He learned obedience by the things which He suffered. And having been perfected, He became the author of eternal salvation to all who obey Him' (5:5, 7-9). We must not misunderstand this. He never needed correction. His obedience was always complete. What He learned, as the divine–human Servant, was the cost of obedience; the cost of being our sin-bearing substitute, enduring our hell so that we might be spared to enter His heaven.

In Gethsemane, the Saviour's obedience was unwavering. Thus, when Peter lashed out with the sword to rescue Him from arrest, Jesus stopped him, saying, 'Put your sword into the sheath. Shall I not drink the cup which My Father has given Me?' (John 18:11). At unspeakable cost Christ drank the cup of suffering, that we might drink from the 'cup of salvation' (Ps. 116:13).

> Death and the curse were in our cup.
>   O Christ, 'twas full for Thee!
> But Thou hast drained the last drop,
>   'Tis empty now for me.
> That bitter cup, love drank it up,
>   Now blessing's draught for me.
>
>   (Anne R. Cousin)

What unparalleled obedience! Our Lord looked beyond the mistreatment and suffering that would have distracted any other human being, and saw the sovereign hand of God working out His plan of salvation for the world. We tend to be very selective in accepting what we think is God's will for our lives. We readily and gladly accept God's will when good things happen to us, but we are not so accepting when it involves pain and loss. The truth is that 'all things work together for good to those who love God, to those who are the called according to His purpose' (Rom. 8:28). All things are under God's control. Even Satan had to ask God for permission to afflict Job, and when he did, God said to Satan, 'Behold, he is in your hand, but spare his life.' Job was quite right, then, when he rebuked his wife for urging him to 'curse God and die', saying, '"You speak as one of the foolish women speak. Shall we indeed accept good from God and shall we not accept adversity?" In all this Job did not sin with his lips' (Job 2:1-10).

That is how every believer should accept the lot God has apportioned him or her, and no one has exemplified it as perfectly as our Lord Jesus Christ in Gethsemane and on the cross. We become complainers about the circumstances of our life precisely when we see them somehow as independent of God and not as the instruments that He is using to accomplish His good and perfect plan for us. The Son of God, however, never stumbled in unbelief. Before the world was made, He agreed with the other members of the Trinity to be the One who would bear the punishment of the sins of the people the Godhead planned to save from a fallen humanity doomed to eternal death. This was the purpose of His incarnation. And as the appointed time approached, He notified His disciples three times of His impending sufferings and death (Matt. 16:21; 17:22-23; 20:18-19). It is the supreme example in Scripture of willing and total submission to the will of God no matter what the cost. 'Like a lamb that is led to the slaughter, and like a sheep that before its shearers is silent, so He opened not His mouth.' Our tendency to complain and become bitter will only diminish as we follow His example and learn obedience by quietly and meekly submitting to the will of God for our lives.

He was silent in bearing His people's sin

Again, the majesty of the silence of Jesus, the Son of God, continues to amaze us. We can understand His total, quiet submission to His Father whose love for Him is eternally and altogether wise and strong and true. God the Father merits that quiet and trusting submission from God the Son, but such cannot be said for those for whom He suffered and died on the cross. Who could find fault with Jesus if He had complained that the people He had come to redeem were not worth dying for? They saw no beauty in Him to desire Him (v. 2). They despised and rejected Him as of no account (v. 3), though He preached the truth and healed the sick as no one else did before or since His coming to earth. The majority wrote Him off as 'a man of sorrows and acquainted with grief' (v. 3b); that is to say, as someone in whose company you would not want to spend any time.

Moreover, as God incarnate and therefore all-knowing, the Servant of Jehovah knew how spiritually weak and inconsistent many of His followers would be. He knew in the hours before His crucifixion that of the Twelve, Judas would betray Him, Peter would deny Him, and the rest would forsake Him; this after being with Him for three years, hearing His marvellous teaching and seeing His mighty works. He saw all the disobedience, lukewarmness, disunity, heresy and backsliding that would plague His church throughout the age. Knowing all this, and a lot more besides, our Lord would have been justified if He had expressed feelings of disappointment to those disciples who still lingered at the cross (John 19:25-27), but He opened not His mouth. He uttered not one word of castigation against His people; not a word of regret or reproof of their disloyalty and ingratitude for His enormous sacrifice at Calvary. How utterly and wonderfully different our Saviour is compared to us, who naturally complain and express displeasure when we have to clean up or fix the mess which other people make.

It was the majestic silence of divine love; love to the uttermost for unlovely human beings so that they, 'through His poverty, might become rich' (2 Cor. 8:9). As J.I. Packer explains:

> On the cross Jesus lost all the good that He had before. All sense of the Father's presence and love, all sense of physical, mental and spiritual well-being, all enjoyment of God and of created things, all ease and solace of friendship were taken from Him. In their place was nothing but loneliness, pain, a killing sense of human malice and callousness, and a horror of great spiritual darkness. The physical pain, though great (for crucifixion remains the cruelest form of judicial execution that the world has ever known), was yet only a small part of the story; Jesus' chief sufferings were mental and spiritual. What was packed into less than four hundred minutes was an eternity of agony – agony such that each minute was an eternity in itself, as mental sufferers know that individual minutes can be.[4]

We must always live within sight of the cross of our Lord Jesus Christ, pondering how God in His grace treats sinners as His sons,

---

4. J.I. Packer, *Knowing God Devotional Journal* (IVP, 2004), p. 109.

because there in His justice, He treated His Son as a sinner. It is mysterious and incomprehensible, defying every human analogy or theological definition. But its claims upon a Christian's heart are irresistible. Thus the apostle can say, 'The love of Christ constrains us, because we judge thus: that if One died for all, then all died; and He died for all, that those who live should live no longer for themselves, but for Him who died for them and rose again' (2 Cor. 5:14-15). It is the same verb used by Luke of people 'gripped by fever' or 'seized' by a powerful emotion like fear (Luke 4:38; 8:37). There is an irresistible logic about the love of Christ revealed at Calvary. Because of what He suffered there for us, it is inconceivable that, as His people, we should now live for ourselves. To quote Paul again, 'You were bought at a price; therefore glorify God in your body and your spirit, which are God's' (1 Cor. 6:20).

The life of Count Nicolaus von Zinzendorf is a fine example of this. He was born in 1700 into the Austrian nobility. After graduating in law from the University of Wittenberg, he was sent off (like every eighteenth-century nobleman) to complete his education by touring the great cities of Europe. In Dusseldorf he visited the art gallery and was arrested by the masterly painting of Jesus Christ by Domenico Fetti, portraying the Saviour as Pilate presented Him to the crowd after His scourging – clothed in purple, bound with ropes, and crowned with thorns. It is entitled *Ecce Homo,* the Latin for 'Behold the Man!' Zinzendorf stood before it transfixed by the words above and below the painting which seemed to be directly addressed to him:

> This I did for you;
> What are you doing for Me?

It was the major turning point in this young aristocrat's life. According to A.J. Lewis, 'There and then the young Count asked the Crucified to draw him into "the fellowship of His sufferings" and to open up a life of service to him.'[5] At the age of twenty-two he purchased an estate at Berthelsdorf where he started a Christian

---

5. A.J. Lewis, *Zinzendorf, the Ecumenical Pioneer* (SCM, 1962), pp. 28, 29.

community called *Herrnhut* for religious refugees from Moravia, which grew into the Moravian Church. His other great concern was worldwide evangelisation. From 1727 to 1760, the year of Zinzendorf's death, he had 226 missionaries from Herrnhut serving in Greenland, North America, South America, the West Indies and South Africa. During the eighteenth-century the Moravian Church did more for worldwide evangelism than all the other Protestant churches put together.[6]

At the same time, the silence of the Lamb of God being led to the slaughter can be a great encouragement to anyone who is not yet a Christian. You may still be bowed down with a sense of how vile a sinner you are, and are hesitant to come to Jesus Christ for the forgiveness of your sins. You truly feel that He would not accept anyone so sinful. Here is hope for you. If you will be emboldened like the penitent thief on the cross next to Jesus, to throw yourself upon His mercy, He will not turn you away. Though this thief at first mocked the King of the Jews with his companion in crime on the other side of Christ, he, by the grace of God, had a change of heart. He was touched by the silence and humility with which Jesus was accepting the wrong being done to Him, especially with His prayer, 'Father, forgive them, for they do not know what they do' (Luke 23:34). So in faith he turned to the Saviour and said, '"Lord, remember me when you come into Your kingdom." And Jesus said to him, "Assuredly, I say to you, today you will be with Me in Paradise"' (Luke 23:42-43).

Take heart if you feel too sinful to come to Christ for pardon and eternal life. Do not let that stop you. As James Durham reasons:

> What may not the believer expect from God, when He spared not His own Son for him? And what may he expect from Christ, who spared not Himself for his sake? And who is the good Shepherd, that laid down His life for the sheep, and held His tongue, and quarrelled not with those who smote Him? Will He quarrel with a poor sinner coming to Him, and pleading for the benefit of satisfaction [i.e. Christ's satisfaction of the law's demands]? No, certainly ... He will not

---

6. A.J. Lewis, *ibid*, p. 80.

upbraid you, nor cast up your former miscarriages [failures];
He will not say reproachfully to you, 'Where were you so long
playing the prodigal?' He is better content with your recovery,
than ever He was discontent or ill-pleased with all the wrong
you did unto Him.[7]

Come to the Saviour while there is still time for Him to accept you.
The day is coming when the Servant who came to 'give His life as
a ransom for many', will change roles and 'be Judge of the living
and the dead' (Mark 10:45; Acts 10:42; 17:30-31). When that time
comes, the day of grace will be over. He will open His mouth for all
to hear, and say to 'those who do not know God' and 'do not obey the
gospel', 'Depart from Me, you cursed into the everlasting fire prepared for the devil and his angels' (2 Thess. 1:7-8; Matt. 25:31-46).
But now, in this age of grace, the Son of God will not open His
mouth to utter one word of condemnation and rejection to the vilest
sinner who comes to Him in penitence and faith. He will not give
him or her a dressing down, or ask them why they have left it so late.
Cry for mercy now, for the promise still stands: 'Whoever calls on
the name of the LORD shall be saved' (Acts 2:21; Joel 2:32).

He was silent in suffering human injustice

The death of Jehovah's Servant was a shocking, blatant miscarriage
of human justice perpetrated through three separate and consecutive
trials. He was tried first by Caiaphas, the Jewish high priest, and
the Sanhedrin, the highest religious court in the land, bound by
Old Testament law. This was the most unjust of the three trials, for
what happened there was more a plot than a trial. Those present had
only one aim, the death of Jesus (Mark 14:1-2). Here is the story as
Mark records it:

> And they led Jesus to the high priest. And all the chief priests
> and the elders and the scribes came together ... Now the chief
> priests and the whole council were seeking testimony against
> Jesus to put him to death, but they found none. For many

---

7. James Durham, *Christ Crucified*, p. 305.

bore false witness against him, but their testimony did not agree. And some stood up and bore false witness against him, saying, 'We heard him say, "I will destroy this temple that is made with hands, and in three days I will build another, not made with hands."' Yet even about this their testimony did not agree. And the high priest stood up in the midst and asked Jesus, 'Have you no answer to make? What is it that these men testify against you?' But he remained silent and made no answer (14:53; 55-61a, ESV).

Our Lord could easily have refuted this testimony of His accusers, for neither had quoted Him correctly, and both had completely misunderstood His words. The Son of God did not say, 'I will destroy this temple that is made with hands', nor was He referring to the physical temple of Jerusalem from which He had just driven out the moneychangers who had turned the temple into 'a house of merchandise' (John 2:13-16). On that occasion, the Jewish religious leaders questioned His actions, demanding, 'What sign do You show to us, since You do these things?' Whereupon, Jesus answered them saying, "Destroy this temple, and in three days I will raise it up." Then the Jews said, "It has taken forty-six years to build this temple, and will You raise it up in three days?" But He was speaking of His body. Therefore, when He had risen from the dead, His disciples remembered that He had said this to them; and they believed the Scripture and the word which Jesus had said' (vv. 18-22). On another occasion our Lord repeated His offer of this sign (Matt. 12:38-42).

Caiaphas and the Sanhedrin, however, knew very well that Jesus was referring to His resurrection as the final and ultimate sign of His divine messiahship. That is why they took every precaution they could to ensure that His body remained in the tomb. According to Matthew:

On the next day, which followed the Day of Preparation, the chief priests and Pharisees gathered together to Pilate, saying, 'Sir, we remember while He was still alive, how that deceiver said, "After three days I will rise." Therefore command that the tomb be made secure until the third day, lest His disciples come by night and steal Him away, and say to the people, "He has risen from the dead." So the last deception will be worse than the first.' Pilate said to them, 'You have a guard; go your way, make it as secure as you know how.' So they went and made the tomb secure, sealing the stone and setting the guard (Matt. 27:62-66).

But, of course, all their efforts were futile. No one can stay the hand of God and prevent Scripture from being fulfilled (Ps. 16:10-11; Matt. 16:21; 17:22-23; 20:17-19). Nonetheless, they refused to accept the irrefutable sign of Christ's resurrection, a miracle without parallel! 'Fast bound in sin and nature's night', they came up with an implausible explanation which could not account for the whereabouts of His body. Again, it is Matthew who fills us in with this information:

> Now while they [the women] were going [to tell His disciples that Jesus was risen from the dead], behold, some of the guard came into the city and reported to the chief priests all the things that had happened. When they had assembled with the elders and taken counsel, they gave a large sum of money to the soldiers, saying, 'Tell them, "His disciples came at night and stole Him away while we slept." And if this comes to the governor's ears, we will appease him and make you secure.' So they took the money and did as they were instructed; and this saying is commonly reported among the Jews until this day (28:11-15).

In a beautiful way, Frederick S. Leahy draws out the significance of our Lord's riddle:

> 'Destroy this temple, and in three days I will raise it up, and His silence before His judges and accusers. He says, 'God does not unfold His mysteries to the wicked. The members of that Sanhedrin were not seekers after truth: they were murderers at heart ... Christ will take His riddle with Him to

the grave. The meaning will become apparent in due course. He will not cast His pearls before swine, rather He will leave it to His judges to execute their high office before God. In this He did justice to them and at the same time condemned them ... In that ecclesiastical court Satan was tempting Christ with His own riddle, twisted though it was. By a single word He might have freed Himself from His enemies. But our silent Priest continued majestically to His death. O blessed silence that lay at the heart of our redemption!

The Sanhedrin finally concluded its proceedings to its own satisfaction. This Holy Temple, the subject of the riddle, could now be broken down, to be raised in glory. Just as the first temple was erected without sound of hammer, or any iron tool (1 Kings 6:7), so this Temple of Christ's body will be restored in a silence that nothing can profane.[8]

Coming back to the trial before Caiaphas, we read:

Again the high priest asked Him, saying to Him, 'Are you the Christ, the Son of the Blessed?' Jesus said, 'I am. And you will see the Son of Man sitting at the right hand of the Power, and coming with the clouds of heaven.' Then the high priest tore his clothes and said, 'What further need do we have of witnesses? You have heard the blasphemy! What do you think?' And they all condemned Him to be deserving of death. Then some began to spit on Him, and to blindfold Him, and to beat Him, and say to Him, 'Prophesy!' And the officers struck Him with the palms of their hands (Mark 14:61-65) ... Immediately, in the morning [about six o'clock] the chief priests held a consultation with the elders and scribes and the whole council [the Sanhedrin]; and they bound Jesus, led Him away, and delivered Him to Pilate (Mark 15:1).

---

8. Frederick S. Leahy, *The Cross He Bore* (Banner of Truth, 1996), pp. 26, 27, 29.

The Roman governor was the only one in Judea and Galilee who had the authority to impose capital punishment on criminal offenders (John 18:31); and John's Gospel gives us the fullest account of this trial:

> Then Pilate entered the Praetorium again [the official residence of the Roman governor in Jerusalem, having gone out to hear what accusation Caiaphas was bringing against Christ], called Jesus, and said to Him, 'Are You the King of the Jews?' Jesus answered him, 'Are you speaking for yourself on this, or did others tell you about Me?' [Are you personally interested to know, or just repeating what Caiaphas has told you?] Pilate answered, 'Am I a Jew? Your own nation and the chief priests have delivered You to me. What have You done?' Jesus answered, 'My kingdom is not of this world. If My kingdom were of this world, My servants would fight, so that I should not be delivered to the Jews; but now My kingdom is not from here' [Christ's kingdom is a spiritual kingdom made up not of soldiers, but of disciples who seek to know and live by God's truth]. Pilate therefore said to Him, 'Are you a king then?' [or 'You are a king, then!' (NIV)] Jesus answered, 'You say rightly that I am a king. For this cause I was born, and for this cause I have come into the world, that I should bear witness to the truth. Everyone who is of the truth hears My voice.' Pilate said to Him, 'What is truth?' [Pilate dismisses the claim of Jesus to be the source of truth, for there is no such thing as truth as far as Pilate is concerned]. And when he had said this, he went out again to the Jews, and said to them, 'I find no fault in Him at all' (John 18:33-38).

At this point in the proceedings, Luke tells us how Pilate decided to send Jesus to be tried by Herod Antipas the Tetrarch, who had beheaded John the Baptist (Matt. 14:1-12; Luke 9:7-9). Luke says:

> Then Pilate said to the chief priests and the crowd, 'I find no fault in this Man.' But they were the more fierce, saying, 'He stirs up the people, teaching throughout all Judea, beginning

from Galilee to this place.' When Pilate heard of Galilee, he asked if the Man were a Galilean. And as soon as he knew that He belonged to Herod's jurisdiction, he sent Him to Herod, who was also in Jerusalem at that time. Now when Herod saw Jesus, he was exceedingly glad; for he had desired for a long time to see Him, because he had heard many things about Him, and he hoped to see some miracle done by Him. Then he questioned Him with many words, but He answered him nothing. And the chief priests and scribes stood and vehemently accused Him. Then Herod, with his men of war, treated Him with contempt and mocked Him, arrayed Him in a gorgeous robe, and sent Him back to Pilate. That very day Pilate and Herod became friends with each other, for previously they had been at enmity with each other (23:4-12).

Pilate was clearly unwilling to handle the case. He could see that the Jews were determined to have him put Jesus to death, and yet he also saw that the prisoner had done nothing that Roman justice could regard as meriting the death penalty. So it suited him to send Jesus to Herod. The tetrarch was delighted. First, because Pilate had generously acknowledged his jurisdiction over the matter, and secondly, it would be entertaining to have a close look at this much talked about figure, and see Him perform a miracle or two. The interview, however, must have disappointed Herod. He received no answer to his many questions and no miracle. He is the only person in the Gospels to whom our Lord said nothing, for Herod was a trifler, not a sincere seeker. Not surprisingly, Herod's curiosity turned to contempt. He joined his soldiers in mocking the Son of God. Although he did not find Jesus guilty, he did not release Him, as he could well have done, and as Pilate probably hoped he would do. The mockery showed that Herod had no interest in seeing justice done. Our Lord was sent back to Pilate who had no option but to take up the case again.

Then Pilate, when he had called together the chief priests, the rulers, and the people, said to them, 'You have brought this Man to me, as one who misleads the people. And indeed,

165

having examined Him in your presence, I have found no fault in this Man concerning those things of which you accuse Him; no, neither did Herod, for I sent you back to him, and indeed nothing deserving of death has been done by Him. I will chastise Him and release Him' (for it was necessary for him to release one of them at the feast). And they all cried out at once saying, 'Away with this Man, and release to us Barabbas' – who had been thrown into prison for a certain rebellion made in the city, and for murder. Pilate, therefore, wishing to release Jesus, again called out to them. But they shouted, saying, 'Crucify Him, crucify Him!' Then he said to them the third time, 'Why, what evil has He done? I have found no reason for death in Him. I will therefore chastise Him and let Him go.' But they were insistent, demanding with loud voices that He be crucified. And the voices of these men and of the chief priests prevailed. So Pilate gave sentence that it should be as they requested. And he released to them the one they requested, who for rebellion and murder had been thrown into prison; but he delivered Jesus to their will (Luke 23:13-25).

We cannot miss the emphasis that in this second trial before Pilate Luke lays the chief blame for Jesus' death on the Jewish chief priests and their followers. Three times Pilate proposes to release Jesus, and three times the Jews shout him down. But Luke is not being anti-Semitic and indicting the nation as a whole. He is simply highlighting a specific group. Michael Wilcock, therefore, strikes the right balance when he says:

Nevertheless all are guilty, not only the Jews. Frivolous Herod and feeble Pilate are guilty too, and so is treacherous Judas. And so is Peter. And so are the rest of the disciples. All are sucked into the vortex of Satan's cosmic plan for the destruction of the Son of God. We may be in the most literal sense, eternally grateful to God that the fate to which they all helped to send Jesus was in fact the cross which God Himself had planned as the means of our redemption. But that is no excuse ... As Peter says afterwards, in words reported by Luke in Acts 2:23, Jesus was 'delivered up according to the plan and foreknowledge of God', but even so He was 'crucified and killed by the hands of lawless men.' The two plans converge at Calvary. But the difference between them is all-important, and men must choose on which side they will be: either beneficiaries of the plan by which God brought Jesus to the cross, or accomplices in the plan by which Satan brought Him there.[9]

So, although the death of the Servant of Jehovah was a terrible perpetration of human injustice, it was also His own deliberate choice to carry out Jehovah's plan. He was not caught in a web of events beyond His control. In His own words, 'Therefore My Father loves Me, because I lay down My life that I may take it again. No one takes it from Me, but I lay it down of Myself. I have power to lay it down, and I have power to take it again. This command I have received from My Father' (John 10:17-18). The Servant's death was not a capitulation to His enemies, but a silent, willing submission to God's command. He was not overcome. He chose not to resist. The only time He spoke to His judges was to affirm His messiahship and His kingship (Matt. 26:64; John 18:37). To have remained silent here would have been to deny His deity.

One more lesson to learn from the Servant's silent submission to unjust treatment remains: as His servants, we too must be willing to suffer for righteousness' sake. For God is glorified and His kingdom is commended to unbelievers by such suffering. That is how God worked at Calvary and still works. It is an amazing thing that God took the worst injustice ever done to a human being to bring about the greatest good to humankind. Thus Peter says:

> For this is commendable, if because of conscience toward God one endures grief, suffering wrongfully. For what credit is it if, when you are beaten for your faults, you take it

---

9. Michael Wilcock, *The Message of Luke* (IVP, 1979), p. 196.

patiently? But when you do good and suffer for it, if you take it patiently, this is commendable before God. For to this you were called, because Christ also suffered for us, leaving us an example, that you should follow His steps: 'Who committed no sin, nor was deceit found in His mouth'; who, when He was reviled, did not revile in return; when He suffered, He did not threaten, but committed Himself to Him who judges righteously (1 Pet. 2:19-23).

Our Lord expected His followers to suffer for Him: 'Blessed are those who are persecuted for righteousness' sake, for theirs is the kingdom of heaven. Blessed are you when they revile and persecute you, and say all kinds of evil against you falsely for My sake. Rejoice and be exceedingly glad, for great is your reward in heaven, for so they persecuted the prophets who were before you'; and again, 'Then they will deliver you up to tribulation and kill you, and you will be hated by all nations for My name's sake' (Matt. 5:10-12; 24:9). As we read the book of Acts and the Epistles, we see that Jesus' prediction was amply fulfilled. Indeed, the 2,000 years of the church's existence has been marked by wide-scale persecution and martyrdom.

As we sit in what is still at this time the security and freedom of our Western churches, there are millions of law-abiding Christians, especially in Muslim and Marxist countries, who are being restricted and persecuted in various ways because of devotion to Jesus Christ. Unfortunately, in the West, the toleration of Christianity is not so much now due to the democratic principle of freedom to worship according to individual conscience, but to the church's willingness to compromise with the world and its deteriorating moral values. The church is being more and more ignored. By and large nobody opposes it any longer, because really there is nothing to oppose.

If, however, we Christians were to compromise less, we would surely suffer more. If we were to faithfully proclaim the gospel of salvation by grace alone, through faith alone, in Christ alone, then the cross would again become a stumbling block to the proud. If we were to maintain the high moral standards of the New Testament – of honesty and integrity, of chastity before marriage and fidelity in it, then there certainly would be public indignation and denunciation of the church. If we were once more to talk plainly about the alternatives of heaven and hell, then the world's animosity towards the church would seriously increase. This should not surprise us, nor should it intimidate us. On the contrary, the example and triumph of the Servant of Jehovah should encourage us to live, to suffer and even to die 'for His sake'. For us too, it will not be in vain (Matt. 5:10-12; 2 Tim. 2:12; 1 Pet. 4:12-14).

9

The Fourth Servant Song VI:
His penal death and honourable burial

53:8 By oppression and judgment he was taken away;
  and as for his generation, who considered
that he was cut off out of the land of the living,
  stricken for the transgression of my people?
⁹ And they made his grave with the wicked
  and with a rich man in his death,
although he had done no violence,
  and there was no deceit in his mouth.
        (Isa. 53:8-9, ESV).

Up to this point in the Servant Songs, the prophet Isaiah, under the inspiration of the Holy Spirit, has predicted the sufferings of Messiah/Christ, but not His vicarious death. He has described the Servant of Jehovah as 'One deeply despised, abhorred by the nation, the Servant of rulers' (49:7, ESV); as One who said, 'I was not rebellious, nor did I turn away. I gave My back to those who struck Me, and My cheeks to those who plucked out the beard; I did not hide My face from shame and spitting' (50:6). Then in the fourth song, the Servant's suffering is portrayed as being so severe that 'His appearance was ... marred beyond human semblance, and His form beyond that of the children of mankind' (52:14, ESV). Most astonishingly, Isaiah has also made it known that 'He was wounded for our transgressions ... crushed for our iniquities', punished to procure our 'peace' and scourged so that we

171

may be 'healed', because 'the LORD has laid on Him the iniquity of us all' (53:5-6, ESV).

However, the Servant's death which could indeed be inferred from some of these expressions, is now explicitly stated in verses eight and nine when Isaiah speaks of Jesus being 'cut off out of the land of the living', and having 'a grave with ... a rich man in His death'. In the New Testament, therefore, as we have seen, the apostles unequivocally present the death of God's Servant as both *penal* (He bore the penalty of sin) and *substitutionary* (the penalty He bore was for our sin, and not for His own, for He was sinless).

He was taken by lawless hands and put to death

That is how the apostle Peter describes what happened on Good Friday (Acts 2:23). It is a perfect interpretation, under the Holy Spirit, of Isaiah's words: 'By oppression and judgment He was taken away ... cut off out of the land of the living' (v. 8ab). The Hebrew word translated 'oppression', literally means 'restraint', which suits the context better, and the preposition 'by' is best taken with it to give the meaning 'without restraint.'[1] Again, the word translated 'judgment' is a versatile word that can also be rendered as 'justice' or 'due process' (Num. 27:21; Deut. 1:17). Verse 8a, then, literally reads, 'Without restraint [with all restraints and protections removed] and without justice [without a proper trial] He was taken away'. The last phrase means 'taken out to die' (Prov. 24:11; Ezek. 33:4), as confirmed by the explanatory clause that follows: 'He was cut off out of the land of the living.' In other words, the Servant 'was the victim of a judicial murder.'[2]

Only in its fulfilment 700 years later could the full import of verse 8a be understood. Our Lord's arraignment was the greatest travesty of justice ever witnessed on earth. It began with Judas, one of the Twelve, who had seen the marvellous miracles and heard the inspired teaching of Jesus for three years, and yet without any restraint, led a crowd from the chief priests with swords and clubs, to arrest his Master in the secluded spot of Gethsemane. By prior arrangement,

---

1. See J. Alec Motyer, p. 433; also E.J. Young, *Isaiah Fifty-Three*, p. 61.
2. Allan A. MacRae, *The Gospel of Isaiah* (Moody, 1977), p. 140.

Judas identified Christ with a kiss of feigned affection which was a treacherous act on the part of one who had been treated as a trusted friend (Matt. 26:47-50; see also Ps. 41:9 and John 13:18, 21).

The Jewish religious leaders, in turn, had no scruples about bribing Judas with 'thirty pieces of silver' to do the dastardly deed, nor to carry out the arrest in a clandestine manner to avoid the risk of a public outcry (Matt. 26:3-5). 'Then Jesus said to the chief priests, captains of the temple, and the elders who had come to Him, "Have you come out, as against a robber, with swords and clubs? When I was with you daily in the temple, you did not try to seize Me. But this is your hour, and the power of darkness"' (Luke 22:52-53). Clearly, our Lord saw His arrest as part of God's sovereign timetable. The 'hour' of which He spoke was the hour in which the prince of darkness was given leave to do his worst, and he did it through the leaders of Judaism. But because God, as always, was in total control of the situation, it was also the hour appointed for His Servant's atoning sacrifice for the sins of the world. Christ was well aware when His 'hour' had 'not yet come' and equally aware when it had come (John 2:4; 7:30; 8:20; 12:23; 13:1; 16:32; 17:1). This hour was predestined and prophesied. Thus, Jesus also said at His arrest: 'But all this has taken place that the Scriptures of the prophets might be fulfilled' (Matt. 26:56, ESV). God's eternal plan is always on schedule.

Worse was still to come. From the outset, the Sanhedrin had no intention of giving the Son of God a fair trial. And so the Prisoner was taken to Annas, a former high priest, to give Caiaphas, the current high priest, time to assemble the Sanhedrin (Israel's supreme Council) and recruit false witnesses (John 18:13; Matt. 26:54). No other kind of witness would enable them to obtain the death sentence they wanted (Matt. 26:3-5). Infuriated and frustrated, Annas was unable to bring a charge against Jesus, and sent Him to Caiaphas (John 18:19-24). The gathering of the Sanhedrin at Caiaphas' palace, however, was illegal. To quote Leon Morris, 'It was not lawful to conduct a trial on a capital charge at night. It was not even lawful to give the verdict at night after a trial had been held during the day. But the Jewish hierarchy was in a hurry, so they rushed Jesus into an examination immediately after His arrest, night-time though it was.'[3]

The next illegality had to do with their unscrupulous use of false witnesses. John MacArthur explains: 'The Council was empowered to act only as a judge and jury in a legal proceeding. They could not instigate charges, but could only adjudicate cases that were brought before them. But because they as yet had no formal charge against Jesus, they were forced to illegally act also as prosecutor in order to carry out their predetermined plan to convict and execute Him.'[4] Consequently, Matthew says, 'The chief priests and the whole Council kept trying to obtain false testimony against Jesus, in order that they might put Him to death; and they did not find it, even though many false witnesses came forward' (Matt. 26:59-60, NASB). As could be expected, their testimonies were grossly inconsistent with each other (Mark 14:55-59). This so-called trial was a travesty of justice! The use of false witnesses did not seem to bother the consciences of these custodians of God's law. What hypocrites!

The next injustice perpetrated against the Servant of Jehovah was to force Him into incriminating Himself. Utterly exasperated that no charge could be brought against Jesus, Caiaphas gambled on a last resort. He applied what was called the Oath of Testimony: 'I adjure You by the living God that You tell us if You are the Christ, the Son of God' (Matt. 26:63). This was a question under oath to which the accused was legally bound to reply, but it was illegal for it to be administered in a capital case. The accused was never required to incriminate himself. The fact that Caiaphas administered this oath was an admission that the court had so far failed to fabricate a charge against Jesus. If He said 'No', He would walk out of that trial a free man. If He said 'Yes' He would sign His own death warrant. His reply was affirmative: 'It is as you said. Nevertheless, I say to you, hereafter you will see the Son of Man sitting at the right hand of Power, and coming on the clouds of heaven' (Matt. 26:64; see also Mark 14:62).

---

3. Leon Morris, *Luke* (IVP, 1974), p. 317.

4. John MacArthur, *Matthew 24–28* (Moody, 1989), p. 205.

Our Lord was echoing words from Psalm 110 and Daniel 7 affirming His messiahship. He unabashedly claimed to be 'David's Lord' whom Jehovah would vindicate by seating Him at His right hand and making Him 'a priest forever according to the order of Melchizedek' (Ps. 110:1-4). He also claimed to be 'the Son of Man' who will return on the clouds of heaven to judge the world and set up 'an everlasting dominion' (Dan. 7:13-14). In other words, after Jesus' death there would be a complete reversal of order. The old priesthood of Judaism with its temple would be destroyed and replaced by a new High Priest with 'a royal priesthood', and a new temple 'not made with hands', the 'temple of His body', the church (Heb. 9:11; John 2:18-21; 1 Cor. 3:16; Heb. 7:11-28; 1 Pet. 2:9). Caiaphas understood none of this, but he had heard all he wanted to hear. His stratagem had worked. If Jesus' claims to messiahship and kingship were false (which, of course, they were not), He could now be deemed worthy of death for blasphemy by the Sanhedrin. In a mock show of horror and outrage, Caiaphas tore his robes and cried out, "He has spoken blasphemy! What further need do we have of witnesses? Look, now you have heard His blasphemy! What do you think?" They answered and said, "He is deserving of death"' (Matt. 26:65-66).

The verdict of guilty and the sentence of death were unjust because untrue. They were not based on a careful consideration of the Prisoner's character, teaching and miracles. Earlier on in His public ministry, when members of the Sanhedrin discounted Jesus' claims to deity and took up stones to stone Him, He had chided them, saying, "'Many good works I have shown you from My Father. For which of these works do you stone Me?" The Jews answered Him, saying, "For a good work we do not stone You, but for blasphemy, and because You, being a Man, make Yourself God." Jesus answered them ... "If I do not do the works of My Father, do not believe Me; but if I do, though you do not believe Me, believe the works, that you may know and believe that the Father is in Me, and I in Him." Therefore they sought again to seize Him, but He escaped out of their hand' (John 10:31-33, 37-39). They had closed their minds and hearts to the truth, and no amount of evidence would open their eyes to it. Unbelief and prejudice blinded them to the truth. It was an unjust verdict and sentence.

The next injustice was their unconscionable treatment of the Prisoner, which revealed their animosity towards Him: 'Then they spat in His face and beat Him; and others struck Him with the palms of their hands, saying, "Prophesy to us, Christ! Who is the one who struck You?"' (Matt. 26:67-68). This was the supreme court of Israel, sworn to uphold the law, and yet no sooner had they passed the death sentence, when they threw all restraint aside and indulged in the most unholy revelry of verbally and physically abusing the innocent and sinless God–man. In seeking to degrade Him, they succeeded only in degrading themselves.

But their unrestrained injustice towards Jesus Christ did not stop there. Although the Jewish religious leaders had already reached a verdict about His guilt and punishment, they still had two problems to overcome. First, they had to legitimatise the trial in the eyes of the people. The trials before Annas and Caiaphas were contrary to rabbinical law, because, as we have already pointed out, they were conducted during the night and away from the temple council room where the public could attend. So to give their death sentence an air of legitimacy, the Sanhedrin proceeded to hold an early morning meeting in which the essentials of the night meeting were publicly repeated and confirmed. But even then, they still came short of what was required, for a verdict of condemnation could not be given until after the trial.[5]

All three of the synoptic gospels tell us of this day meeting, but Luke's account is more detailed (Matt. 27:1; Mark 15:1). Luke says, 'As soon as it was day, the elders of the people [the Sanhedrin], both chief priests and scribes, came together and led Him into their council [their official meeting chamber in the temple], saying, "If You are the Christ, tell us." But He said to them, "If I tell you, you will by no means believe. And if I do ask you, you will by no means answer Me or let Me go. Hereafter the Son of Man will sit on the right hand of the power of God." Then they all said, "Are You then the Son of God?" And He said to them, "You rightly say that I am."

---

5. Mishnah, *Sanhedrin* 4:1.

And they said, "What further testimony do we need? For we have heard it ourselves from His own mouth'" (22:66-71).

Because the Jews as a subject nation were not allowed to administer the death penalty themselves (though they had no hesitation over stoning Stephen to death, Acts 7:54-60), the second problem the Sanhedrin had to overcome was to convince the Roman governor to execute Jesus that same day, because Passover and the Sabbath, both holy days, would begin at 6:00 pm Friday. After careful consultation, they settled on the charge of treason: 'Then the whole multitude of them [the Sanhedrin and the people who had attended the early morning session] arose and led Him to Pilate. And they began to accuse Him, saying, "We found this fellow perverting the nation [sedition], and forbidding to pay taxes to Caesar, saying that He Himself is Christ, a king'" (Luke 23:1-2). All three charges were serious and, if true, merited the death penalty. Pilate knew that they were lying, because if the Servant had been guilty of any one of these charges, he would already have known of it and summarily executed Him. Instead of inciting insurrection, our Lord had publicly declared that the Jews should 'render to Caesar the things that are Caesar's' (Matt. 22:21).

Indeed, the Gospels say, 'He knew that for envy they had delivered Him' (Matt. 27:18; Mark 15:10). So four times Pilate declared the Prisoner's innocence, and tried hard to avoid condemning Jesus to death (Luke 23:4, 14, 15, 22; *cf.* John 18:38; 19:4, 6). But in the end, he gave in to the Council's demands, afraid that another riot by the Jews would ruin his political career (Mark 15:15). In a great miscarriage of justice, Pilate had Christ 'scourged', and then 'delivered to be crucified'. But not before allowing his soldiers first to mock and ill-treat Him. Matthew says, 'Then he released Barabbas to them; and when he had scourged Jesus, he delivered Him to be crucified. Then the soldiers of the governor took Jesus into the Praetorium and gathered the whole garrison around Him. And they stripped Him and put a scarlet robe on Him. When they had twisted a crown of thorns, they put it on His head, and a reed in His right hand. And they bowed the knee before Him and mocked Him, saying, "Hail, King of the Jews!" Then they spat on Him, and took the reed and struck Him on the head. And when they had mocked Him, they took the robe off Him, put His own clothes on Him, and led Him away to be crucified' (Matt. 27:26-31).

But Pilate's efforts to save his career eventually failed. In AD 36 he brutally quelled Samaritan unrest and was ordered back to Rome, banished to Gaul (France), where tradition says that he eventually committed suicide. The Jewish nation also paid a severe price for instigating the unjust execution of their Messiah by the Romans. When, earlier on, the Sanhedrin worried that Jesus would win the hearts of the people, and a popular tumult be stirred up by messianic expectations, 'and the Romans will come and take away both our place [probably the temple] and nation', Caiaphas gave them this assurance: 'You know nothing at all, nor do you consider that it is expedient for us that one man should die for the people, and not that the whole nation should perish' (John 11:48-50). For the Jews, however, it did not work out that way. Forty years later the Romans destroyed the temple and dispersed the nation throughout the empire. God's purpose, on the other hand, triumphed! His Son, the Servant, died 'not for that nation only, but also that He would gather together in one the children of God who were scattered abroad' (John 11:51-52). Caiaphas, unwittingly, prophesied the salvation of Jewish and Gentile believers through Christ, and their gathering into one worldwide body, the Christian church.

What an amazing amount of detail regarding the trial and execution of Jesus was forecast by the prophet Isaiah's short but terse prediction: 'Without restraint and justice He was taken away.' How indebted we are to God the Holy Spirit for so fully revealing the fulfilment of verse 8a through the Gospel writers.

He was stricken for the transgression of My people

If Jesus was unjustly put to death, why did He submit to it? After all, the Servant of the LORD is said in verse one to be 'the Arm of the LORD'. Although He was 'a man of sorrows and acquainted with grief', Jesus was also the very embodiment of the almighty power of God. Indeed, that divine power was momentarily displayed in the garden at His arrest. When the soldiers arrived, Jesus said to them: "'Whom are you seeking?" They answered Him, "Jesus of Nazareth" ... Then when He said to them, "I am He", they drew back and fell to the ground"' (John 18:4-6). At that moment Jesus could have evaded arrest. And by that same power He could have continued evading arrest indefinitely. Earlier on in His ministry He had said to His disciples, 'I lay down My life that I may take it again. No one takes it from Me, but I lay it down of Myself. I have power to lay it down, and I have power to take it again' (John 10:17-18). Why then did Jesus, of His own accord, lay down His life? In that same passage we have the answer to that question: I lay down My life for the sheep ... And I give them eternal life, and they shall never perish; neither shall anyone snatch them out of My hand' (John 10:15, 28). Jesus laid down His life for the benefit of His sheep, to save them from perishing in hell and give them eternal life instead.

So the death of Jesus was not an accident. It was not simply the result of a miscarriage of justice. From time to time, innocent men and women are unjustly condemned and put to death. This explanation, however, does not fit in the case of Christ's death. What caused Jesus to die was the sin of those He came to save, for Isaiah goes on to say, 'And as for His generation, who considered that He was cut off out of the land of the living, for the transgression of My people to whom the stroke was due?' (v. 8b, NASB). The Hebrew word translated 'generation' does not mean 'descendants' as the New International Version renders it. It literally means 'contemporaries', those of His own generation, as we say. The contemporaries of Jesus did not give serious consideration to the reason for His death. They hurriedly concluded that He was being smitten by God for His own sins (vv. 4, 9b). They did not stop to consider that He had no sin of His own; that He was sinless, as He claimed. How could they? For what could only be known by divine revelation was that Jesus was cut off out of the land of the living, for the transgression of My people to whom the stroke was due.'

It is God who is speaking, and He says in effect: 'My people (the people I want to save) have rebelled against My rule. They have gone their own way and transgressed My laws. The terrible stroke of My judgment should have fallen on them, but in order to spare them it has fallen on My Servant. He has redeemed them by bearing the stroke due to them.' It could be no other way. The innocent must suffer for the guilty, if God is to be a just Judge and His holy law is to be honoured and its just demands satisfied. The Servant acted as our substitute. He took our place at the cross and completely satisfied the punishment justly demanded by God for breaking His commandments. To quote yet another verse from Anne R. Cousin's fitting hymn:

> Jehovah lifted up His rod;
>   O Christ, it fell on Thee!
> Thou wast sore stricken of Thy God;
>   There's not one stroke for me.

That is the gospel, pure and unadulterated. There are many who claim to preach the gospel and yet in reality do not preach it at all. For they do not preach this great doctrine of grace: namely, the penal, substitutionary death of Christ for the sins of His people. It is quite common in our day to hear people speak of the death of Christ and not give any explanation of the true nature of His death. But it is not enough to say that Christ died because He loved us, or that He died to save sinners. What must be preached (if the gospel is to be preached faithfully) is that Christ died for sinners, in their place and stead to satisfy the penal demands of God's law. That is the heart of the gospel. And that is the truth which Isaiah was constrained by God to proclaim. Would to God that believers were fired up with this glorious truth today! May the Spirit of God raise up preachers who will proclaim, not some bare modicum of Christian truth, but the fullness of the gospel of grace. For men and women will not repent of sin and come to Christ, unless first they come to know what sin is, and the price Christ has paid to redeem them from it. The answer to the world's need is not to be found in some watered-down version of the gospel, but in the penal, substitutionary death of Christ upon the cross for the sins of those who will put their trust in Him.

He was assigned a grave with the wicked

Isaiah moves sequentially from the revelation of the Servant's sufferings and death to the facts of His burial. Verse nine is a strange and wonderful verse, full of mystery in its wording and meaning. The first half needs to be translated carefully. The Hebrew does not specify who is behind the action taken, but scholars suggest that it is best to take the verb ('He made', KJV) as impersonal and to translate it by a passive.[6] For the prophet is not talking about something God's Servant did. The Servant is dead. Literally, then, the Hebrew for the first line reads: 'He [the pronoun is singular, not 'they' as in the ESV] was assigned a grave with the wicked.'

The enemies of God's Servant were determined that He should be executed as a criminal and given a dishonourable burial. It is significant, therefore, that Jesus was taken outside the city of Jerusalem to be put to death as a criminal. He was regarded as unclean and had to die in an unclean place. Not only that, Jesus was hanged from a cross of wood. The law of Moses required that the body of an executed criminal should hang on a tree until sunset (Deut. 21:22, 23). Those punished in this manner were not accursed of God because they were hanged on a tree, but hanged on a tree because they had sinned grievously and were accursed. That is also how the apostle Paul saw its meaning when he said, 'Christ redeemed us from the curse of the law by becoming a curse for us – for it is written, "Cursed is everyone who is hanged on a tree"' (Gal. 3:13). Jesus was treated as if He were a sinner, because He bore the punishment of our wrongdoing. As Surety for God's people, the Son 'suffered outside the gate' and endured *before* death the pains of hell which sinners experience *after* death (Heb. 13:12). 'He was numbered with the transgressors', being crucified between two of them who had shed innocent blood in the act of robbery (Isa. 53:12; Matt. 27:38).

It was intended, of course, that the final humiliation our Lord's enemies could heap upon Him was a dishonourable burial assigned with the 'wicked' (plural, literally 'the wicked ones'). It was usual for a man to be buried 'with his fathers', which for Jesus would have been in Galilee. To be denied such a burial and have one's corpse

6. See E.J. Young, *Isaiah Fifty-Three*, p. 67; and John L. Mackay, *Isaiah*, p. 355.

thrown into the common pit used for the remains of paupers and criminals, was a cause for shame (1 Kings. 13:22; Jer. 26:23). The Jewish historian Josephus writes, 'He that blasphemeth God let him be stoned, and let him hang upon a tree all that day, and let him be buried in an ignominious and obscure manner.'[7]

The sovereignty of God in His honourable burial

The second line or clause in verse nine also needs careful examination: 'and with a rich [singular] man in His death.' To begin with, should the first word be translated as 'and' indicating a parallel link, or as 'but' signifying a contrast? If it should be 'and', then the parallelism between the two lines is synonymous, conveying the sense that the Servant was buried with criminals and with a wicked rich man. The fulfilment of this prophecy in the New Testament, however, shows that the 'rich man' spoken of in line two was actually a good man, even a disciple of Jesus (John 19:18; Luke 23:50-51; Matt. 27:57). Moreover, the adjective 'rich' in itself does not have evil connotations. Abraham, Isaac, Jacob, Joseph, Job and David were both rich and godly men (cf. Prov. 10:22; 14:24).

It is clear, then, that we are to regard the parallelism between lines one and two as *antithetical* and not *synonymous*, and to translate the first word in line two as declaring a contrast: 'but with a rich man in His death.' The contrast introduces what E.J. Young terms, 'a turn in the Servant's fortunes. It was intended that He should die and be buried as a criminal. But whereas man proposes, it is God who disposes. As a matter of fact, after His violent death, He was ... buried in a tomb intended for a rich man. Thus, in a certain sense, His exaltation and glorification began with His death.'[8] After the Servant cried, 'It is finished', and gave up His spirit because He had accomplished His redemptive work (John 19:30), Jehovah said in effect, 'Stop! That is enough! The time of His humiliation is over. I will allow no more indignities to be perpetrated upon Him.'

The honourable burial of our Lord in a rich man's tomb is an amazing example of the providence of God over human affairs. God

---

7. Josephus, *Antiquities*, iv.viii.6

8. E.J. Young, *Isaiah Fifty-Three*, p. 68.

is the Sovereign Ruler over all creation, and He accomplishes His purposes either directly through miracles (creation, the flood, the plagues in Egypt, etc.) or indirectly through providence (Joseph's appointment as prime minister of Egypt, the hanging of Haman on the gallows he had prepared for Mordecai, the crucifixion of Christ, etc.). In providence, what humans mean for evil, God in His overruling power uses to bring about His good will (Gen. 50:20; Acts 2:23). His hand may be hidden, but His rule is absolute.

Jewish law forbade the body of an executed Jewish person to be left hanging all night. It had to be buried by sundown, when the Jewish day ended (Deut. 21:22f). It was 'about the ninth hour' or 3:00 pm that Jesus died (Matt. 27:46-50). It was, therefore, imperative that our Lord be buried immediately before 6:00 pm in order not to profane the Sabbath, and also for Him to be buried for thirty-six hours and 'be raised the third day' (Matt. 27:62-63). But who was going to bury Him? None of His family or His disciples owned a property and a tomb in Jerusalem, since they all came from Galilee. God, however, had His man ready and waiting to perform the sacred duty, Joseph of Arimathea. He has not appeared in the Gospels before this moment, 'being a disciple of Jesus, but secretly, for fear of the Jews'. Although he was a member of the Sanhedrin, he now came out of his shell and refused to give his consent to the execution of the Saviour (Matt. 27:57; Mark 15:43; Luke 23:50-51; John 19:38). Moreover, having paid little honour to Jesus during the three years of His public ministry, Joseph now saw that the chance to bury God's Servant fittingly would be his last opportunity to openly and appropriately show his true convictions.

The location of Arimathea is not known. But because Joseph had a newly-hewn tomb outside Jerusalem, he had evidently left his home town and come to live in the capital (Matt. 27:60). He was also a man of piety who was 'waiting for the kingdom of God' and must have become a 'disciple' by listening to Christ's constant preaching of the kingdom of God (Mark 15:43; 1:14-15; Matt. 13). In all of this the hand of God was preparing Joseph for the most courageous and important act of his life – his 'bold' request to the governor for permission to bury the body of Jesus (Mark 15:43). His request was daring because it amounted to a confession of his commitment to the condemned and crucified Jesus, for which he was now prepared to face the hostility of his colleagues in the synagogue, forfeit his seat in the Sanhedrin, and jeopardise his economic, social, and family welfare. He was not going to pass up this last opportunity to express his love for Jesus and give Him a proper Jewish burial and a splendid tomb. It was a costly gift to make, since it was close to the city, and the Law forbade the use of the tomb by anyone else again if the person buried there was executed on a criminal charge.

Pilate was surprised that Jesus was already dead, since crucified men often lived two or three days before dying. But when he was assured by the centurion who had superintended the execution that Jesus was dead, he granted Joseph's request (Mark 15:44-45). With servants to assist him, he took the body of Jesus down from the cross and carried it to the nearby tomb with the 'linen cloth' he had bought beforehand (John 19:41; Mark 15:46). Nicodemus, a prominent Pharisee (see John 3:1) and almost certainly a member of the Sanhedrin as well, must have been an ally in this plan, for he met Joseph at the tomb: 'And Nicodemus, who at first came to Jesus by night, also came, bringing a mixture of myrrh and aloes, about a hundred pounds [an expensive gift]. They then took the body of Jesus, and bound it in strips of linen with the spices, as the custom of the Jews is to bury' (John 19:39-40). After that, Matthew says, 'And he rolled a large stone against the door of the tomb, and departed' (27:60). Seeing this was an exceptionally fine tomb, it probably had a disc-shaped stone, about three feet in diameter, placed in a groove which sloped toward the opening so it could easily be rolled into place to close the tomb. To roll the stone up the incline would require the strength of several men.

Neither Joseph nor Nicodemus were aware that they were fulfilling prophecy. What they did, they did for personal, devotional reasons. It seemed only right that this innocent Man, who was a Prophet the likes of whom Israel had never seen before, and whom these two had come to believe was the promised Messiah, should have an honourable burial. But it was exactly what God had predicted through the prophet Isaiah: 'He was assigned a grave with ... a rich man in His death, because He had done no violence, nor was any deceit in His mouth' (v. 9c). The reason why the Servant of Jehovah will be given an honourable burial after His dishonourable death, is to be found in His perfect innocence. He wronged nobody by His deeds, and He deceived nobody by His words. Why, then, did Jehovah allow His Servant to go through all that unjust suffering and death? For the reason already given in verse eight: 'He was cut off out of the land of the living, for the transgression of My people to whom the stroke was due' (NASB). In the words of J. Alec Motyer, 'Together *violence* and *deceit* [v. 9] embrace the total guiltlessness of the Servant; in neither outward behaviour nor inner person, in neither deed nor word, could a charge be justly levelled ... succinctly, He is accorded that moral majesty essential in a true substitute for sinners.'[9]

How wonderful of God! The crucifixion of Jesus which had caused the disciples to flee for their lives, had the opposite effect on these two secret disciples. For now, when they had nothing at all to gain by confessing their allegiance to Christ (He was dead!), they came right out into the open. Today is also an opportunity for us to confess our faith in Jesus Christ, God's Servant and our Sin-bearer (2 Cor. 6:1-2). It is not, however, a commitment we can make in our own strength, but only in the strength which the Holy Spirit supplies as He opens our spiritual eyes to see what the Saviour did for us at Calvary, and draws us to Him in faith. May God help us to experience something of what John Bunyan expresses he felt when in his mind and heart he was drawn in faith to Christ crucified:

> Thus far did I come laden with my sin;
> Nor could ought ease the grief that I was in
> Till I came hither: What a place is this!
> Must here be the beginning of my bliss?
> Must here the burden fall from off my back?
> Must here the strings that bound it to me crack?
> Blest Cross! blest Sepulchre! blest rather be
> The Man that there was put to shame for me.[10]

---

9. J. Alec Motyer, *The Prophecy of Isaiah*, p. 436.
10. John Bunyan, *The Pilgrim's Progress* (Lutterworth Press, 1944), p. 46.

10

The Fourth Servant Song VII:
The will of the Lord shall prosper in His hand

53:10 Yet it was the will of the Lord to crush him;
 he has put him to grief;
when his soul makes an offering for guilt,
 he shall see his offspring; he shall prolong his days;
the will of the Lord shall prosper in his hand.
 ¹¹ Out of the anguish of his soul he shall see and be satisfied;
by his knowledge shall the righteous one, my servant,
 make many to be accounted righteous,
and he shall bear their iniquities.
     (Isa. 53:10-11, esv).

The main lines of thought that flow throughout the fourth song (52:13–53:12) converge in the fullness of truth with which the poem ends in the fifth stanza (53:10-12). The physical suffering of the Servant that begins in the first stanza with the disfigurement of His appearance, continues in the next nine verses with word after word giving descriptions of His actual afflictions: *stricken, smitten, afflicted, pierced, crushed, punishment, wounds, cut off, grave.* But in verses ten and eleven it is revealed that the Servant's chief sufferings are not *physical*, but *spiritual*; they are not those inflicted by men on His body, but those inflicted by God on His soul. So Isaiah says, 'Yet it was the will of the Lord to crush Him; He has put Him to grief; when You make His *soul* [see mg.]

an offering for guilt [or sin, NKJV] ... out of the anguish of His *soul* He shall see and be satisfied' (italics added).

Again, the revelation of the Servant's humiliation followed by His exaltation, hinted at in chapter 52:15, is fully stated in chapter 53:10-12. The wickedness and injustice of men in their ill-treatment of Jehovah's Servant will not determine His ultimate destiny. Nor is it God's will that He will simply have a lasting legacy cherished by later generations. Rather, the amazing truth predicted in these last three verses is that by the Servant's 'offering for sin' (NKJV), the 'will' or 'pleasure of the LORD' is going to 'prosper'; He will rise again from the dead to see His numerous offspring; and He will 'make many to be accounted ... righteous' before God, 'for He shall bear their iniquities' (NKJV). Although afflicted for the sins of others, Jehovah's Servant will be divinely vindicated and receive a great reward (or 'spoil').

That, in general terms, is the closing theme of the fifth stanza of the fourth song. In this chapter, however, we will look in particular at verses 10-11.

The Servant's chief suffering will be inflicted by Jehovah

The terrible physical suffering and verbal abuse which the Servant of Jehovah will have to endure in His trials and crucifixion will not be solely the afflictions wicked men will be permitted to heap upon Him as an expression of their hostility to God. What the prophet Isaiah is repeating in verses ten to eleven is that they were sufferings foreordained by the will of the LORD Himself. God in His almighty sovereignty and infinite love and wisdom, will make the voluntary, unrestrained cruelties of wicked men inflicted upon His innocent Son subservient to His predetermined plan to redeem the world. It is a great mystery that defies all explanation, but it was revealed to the prophet Isaiah 700 years beforehand: 'Although He had done no violence, and there was no deceit in His mouth, yet it was the will ['purpose' or 'pleasure'; cf. 44:28] of the LORD to crush Him [lit. 'break into pieces', often used in a metaphorical sense of a 'broken heart'; cf. Ps. 51:17]; He has put Him to grief' [lit. 'suffering' or 'weakness'] (vv. 9-10).

God, who has 'no pleasure in the death of the wicked', was 'pleased ... to bruise' His righteous Servant (Ezek. 33:11; v. 10, NKJV). This does not mean that Jehovah found pleasure in looking upon the physical and emotional pain that the Son of God was subjected to by men who 'hated [Him] without a cause' (Ps. 69:4; John 15:25). Of course not! Verse ten means that God the Father was pleased to accept His suffering as part of the penalty of death demanded by the Law in order for the sins of men and women to be forgiven (Ezek. 18:4; Rom. 6:23). Nor does the sovereign purpose of God absolve from responsibility those who put Jesus to death. It simply means that His human enemies were not in control of the situation. Unknowingly, but culpably, they were being used to carry out God's great plan of redemption designed and decreed before the world began (Acts 2:22-24; Rev. 13:8).

But no amount of physical and emotional suffering on its own, whether endured by an individual for himself, or even by a nation (like the Jewish holocaust) can ever atone for sin, not even one sin. The penalty of sin is death for the whole of our human being, body and soul. The death of the physical body is simply the doorway into the eternal, spiritual death of the body and soul in hell, a terrible place of everlasting torment and endless destruction (Luke 16:19-31; Mark 9:48). It is also called 'the second death' (Rev. 20:11-15).

The chief suffering of Jesus, then, in paying the penalty incurred by human sin, was spiritual, not physical. Here is how Frederick S. Leahy puts it:

> At times one may wonder at the almost matter-of-fact way in which the evangelists [Matthew, Mark, Luke and John] describe the crucifixion of the Saviour. They do not dwell, as many have done since, on the horrors of this form of death; the emphasis is not on the physical aspect of Christ's sufferings. Great as the physical agony of Christ undoubtedly was, it is unlikely that on the cross He suffered more in this sense than did those crucified with Him. His physical agony was as nothing in comparison to His spiritual suffering. That is why

the Gospels direct our attention to what the Lord endured as our sin-bearer.[1]

Significantly, the Servant of Jehovah gave no audible expression to the physical pain He endured when He was scourged and nailed to the cross, but He did give audible expression to His spiritual anguish when at the end He cried, 'My God, My God, why have You forsaken Me?' (Matt. 27:46; Ps. 22:1). This was not a cry of despair or of loneliness, but of *real dereliction* in which Jesus sought to inform every onlooker present and future that on the cross an actual and dreadful separation between His soul and the Father had taken place. It was the penalty due to our sin; the just separation of the immortal soul of a sinner from his or her Creator, who is 'of purer eyes than to behold evil, and cannot look on wickedness' (Hab. 1:13).

So the reason why our Lord quoted Psalm 22:1 was because it is the only verse in Scripture which specifically describes and predicts the awful spiritual darkness and God-forsakenness which Messiah must suffer in order to save His people from the just punishment of their sins. Psalm 22 is a messianic psalm, and so the Servant quoted verse 1 because He believed He was fulfilling it on the cross. Moreover, His cry was in the form of a question ('Why have You forsaken Me?'), not because He did not know its answer, but only because the text He was quoting was in the form of a question. This spiritual aspect of the suffering of the Servant is what Isaiah is predicting in verse ten line three: 'When You make His soul an offering for sin' (NKJV). We must never lose sight of this, for as Calvin explains:

> Nothing had been done if Christ had only endured corporeal [bodily] death. In order to interpose between us and God's anger, and satisfy His righteous judgment, it was necessary that He should feel the weight of divine vengeance. Whence also it was necessary ... that not only was the body of Christ given up as the price of redemption, but that there was a greater and

---

1. Frederick S. Leahy, *The Cross He Bore*, p. 69.

more excellent price – that He bore in His soul the tortures of condemned and ruined man ... had not His soul shared in the punishment, He would have been a Redeemer of bodies only.[2]

In the garden of Gethsemane, just a few hours before His ordeal on the cross, our Lord's anticipation of this spiritual agony at the hand of His Father was so great that His mind nearly broke under the prospect of it. Taking Peter, James and John with Him to a more secluded spot, Matthew says, 'He began to be sorrowful and deeply distressed. Then He said to them, "My soul is exceedingly sorrowful, even to death. Stay here and watch with Me." He went a little farther and fell on His face, and prayed, saying, "O My Father, if it is possible, let this cup pass from Me; nevertheless, not as I will, but as You will"' (27:36-44). Three times Jesus prayed that prayer in a slightly different form. Luke, however, gives us some additional information regarding that scene, when he says, 'Then an angel appeared to Him from heaven, strengthening Him. And being in agony, He prayed more earnestly. And His sweat became like great drops of blood falling down to the ground' (Luke 22:43-44).

No human being or even angel will ever be able to fathom the depth of the agony the Son of God experienced when He was forsaken by Jehovah God for our sins. Who can understand how God can be forsaken by God? How dreadful the anticipation of it must have been! To quote Professor John Murray: 'Our Lord was now looking into the abyss that He was to swallow up in Himself. The recoil of His whole soul was inevitable. If He had not recoiled from the incomparable ordeal, it would be unnatural in the deepest sense. We must reckon with the enormity of His agony and the reality of His human nature. Here was the unrelieved, unmitigated judgment of God against sin. It filled Him with horror and dread.'[3] And it is exactly what the prophet predicted when he said that Jehovah would make His Servant's soul 'an offering for sin'.

---

2. John Calvin, *Institutes of the Christian Religion*, II.xvi.10 and 12.

3. John Murray, *Collected Writings* (Banner of Truth, 1982), vol. two, p. 155.

The satisfying results of His vicarious suffering

Verse ten, 'When You make His soul [mg.] an offering for guilt [or sin], He shall see His offspring; He shall prolong His days; the will of the LORD shall prosper in His hand.' The conjunction 'when', at the beginning of the third line of verse ten is not used here to introduce a situation where the event is in doubt, meaning 'If' (NASB), but to emphasise an event where the timing is indefinite. The event will most certainly take place, even though the precise timing is not specified. The next word, 'LORD' in the rendering of the New International Version is an interpretative addition ('and though the LORD makes'). It is more accurate to translate the Hebrew, 'When You make' (ESV, NKJV) rather than 'If He would render Himself' (NASB). The Servant is not making the sacrifice, for He is the sacrifice. It is Jehovah who is making the soul of His Servant 'an offering for guilt'.

The guilt or sin offering was one of the basic Levitical sacrifices (see Lev. 5:14–6:7; 7:1-6). It was required when one deprived another (whether God or man) of his rightful due. And as J. Alec Motyer points out: 'The distinctive testimony of the guilt offering is satisfaction. Thus, in the present verse the death of the Servant satisfied both the needs of sinful people before God and the "needs"/requirements of God in relation to His broken law and offended holiness.'[4]

The Servant's willing obedience to be made a guilt offering for 'the sin of many' (v. 12e) will result in the glorious victory of the resurrection and the satisfying success of an ever-growing number of believing followers: 'When You make His soul an offering for sin, He shall see His seed' (NKJV). While not explicitly stating that Jehovah will raise His servant from the grave, His resurrection is clearly implied not only because the Servant will personally 'see His seed/offspring' after His death and burial, but also because 'He shall prolong His days.' This too, in the context, must refer to the satisfaction and enjoyment of life after death in spite of His soul being given as a sin offering and His being 'cut off out of the land of the living' (v. 8c).

---

4. J. Alec Motyer, *The Prophecy of Isaiah*, p. 439.

Again, in the context, the 'seed' referred to will not be a line of physical descendants, for the Servant had no children before He died. The reference is rather to a spiritual seed, whose guilt the Servant has removed by His atoning death. The prophecy recalls God's promise to Abraham in Genesis 22:15-18 of a seed as numerous 'as the stars of the heaven and as the sand which is on the seashore', and in which 'all the nations of the earth shall be blessed'. And as the apostle Paul explains in Galatians 3, 'Know then that it is those of faith who are the sons of Abraham. And the Scripture, foreseeing that God would justify the Gentiles by faith, preached the gospel beforehand to Abraham, saying, "In you shall all the nations be blessed." So then, those who are of faith are blessed along with Abraham, the man of faith' (vv. 7-9 ESV). The verbs 'to justify' and 'to bless' are used as equivalents in verse eight; and the means by which Jew and Gentile would inherit the blessing of justification would be 'faith'. Thus Paul affirms that the true children of Abraham are not his posterity by *physical* descent, but his *spiritual* progeny, Jews and Gentiles who share his faith as believers in the Christ (see also Rom. 2:28-29).

This is even more explicitly stated at the end of Galatians 3, 'For you are all sons of God through faith in Christ Jesus ... There is neither Jew nor Greek, there is neither slave nor free, there is neither male nor female; for you are all one in Christ Jesus [there is no distinction of race, rank or of gender, for we are all equally the spiritual fruit of Messiah]. And if you are Christ's, then you are Abraham's seed, and heirs according to the promise' [we take our place in the noble, historical succession of redeemed believers from Adam till the end of time]. The humiliation and death of Christ was the effective means God used 'in bringing many sons to glory', and the chief 'joy that was set before Him', for the sake of which He 'endured the cross, despising the shame, and is seated at the right hand of the throne of God' (Heb. 2:10; 12:2).

The second satisfying result of the Servant's vicarious suffering, which we have already mentioned, will be His glorious victory over death: 'He shall prolong His days.' Although 'He poured out His soul to death' (v. 12c), and 'He was cut off out of the land of the living' (v. 8c), and buried, the Servant shall enjoy life after death. How is it possible? The answer to this question is that Jehovah not only decreed that His Servant should die for the forgiveness of our sins, but also be 'raised for our justification', to sit at the right hand of God Almighty 'as our great High Priest' and 'save to the uttermost those who come to God through Him, since He ever lives to make intercession for them' (Rom. 4:25; Heb. 4:14; 7:25). Like all the seeming paradoxes in the Old Testament, this paradox of Messiah's resurrection is clarified in its fulfilment in the New Testament. So, Paul can say, 'Christ died for our sins in accordance with the Scriptures, that He was buried, that He was raised on the third day in accordance with the Scriptures' (1 Cor. 15:3-4).

The clearest Old Testament prediction of the messianic Servant's resurrection is found in Psalm 16:8-11. Here is how the apostle Peter made use of it in his sermon to the people of Jerusalem on the day of Pentecost:

> Men of Israel, hear these words: Jesus of Nazareth ... being delivered by the determined counsel and foreknowledge of God, you have taken by lawless hands, have crucified, and put to death [God used evil men to accomplish His purpose of making His Servant an offering for sin, yet without violating their will or removing their culpability for doing so]; whom God raised up, having loosed the pains of death, because it was not possible that He should be held by it [because God promised to raise Him from the dead]. For David says concerning Him: 'I foresaw the LORD always before my face, for He is at my right hand, that I may not be shaken [at the prospect of death]; therefore my heart rejoiced, and my tongue was glad; moreover my flesh will also rest in hope, because You [God] will not leave my soul in Hades [a bodiless state]. Nor will You allow Your Holy One [a messianic title; cf. Mark 1:24; John 6:69] to see corruption [decay]. You have made known to me the ways of life; You will make me full of joy in Your presence.' Men and brethren, let me speak freely to you of the patriarch David, that he is both dead

and buried, and his tomb is with us to this day. Therefore, being a prophet, and knowing that God had sworn with an oath to him that of the fruit of his body, according to the flesh, He would raise up the Christ to sit on his throne, he [David], foreseeing this, spoke concerning the resurrection of the Christ, that His soul was not left in Hades, nor did His flesh see corruption. This Jesus God has raised up, of which we are all witnesses (Acts 2:22-32).

Thirdly, the Servant shall be satisfied with the knowledge that through His penal, substitutionary suffering and death, 'the pleasure/will of the LORD shall prosper in His hand' (v. 10e). And if we want to know more particularly what this pleasure or will of the LORD is, we will find the answer in the commission entrusted to Jehovah's perfect Servant as set forth in the whole of the four Servant Songs. In brief they are these: He shall establish a just order in the earth (42:4b); He shall be given as a covenant to the people, as a light to the Gentiles, to open blind eyes, to bring out prisoners from the prison (42:6-7); He shall be God's salvation to the ends of the earth (49:6e); He will obediently bear the suffering due to our sin when Jehovah makes His soul an offering for sin (50:6; 53:4-10); He shall justify (declare righteous) many, for He shall bear their iniquities (53:11).

Again, to this we must add the testimony of the New Testament. In Ephesians chapter 1 Paul says, 'In Him [Jesus Christ] we have redemption through His blood, the forgiveness of sins, according to the riches of His grace ... according to His good pleasure which He purposed in Himself ... in whom also we have obtained an inheritance, being predestined according to the purpose of Him who works all things according to the counsel of His will, that we who first trusted in Christ should be to the praise of His glory' (vv. 7-12).

In Colossians chapter 1, Paul expresses it like this: 'For it pleased the Father that in Him [Jesus Christ] all the fullness should dwell, and by Him to reconcile all things to Himself, by Him, whether things on earth or things in heaven, having made peace through the blood of His cross. And you, who once were alienated and enemies in your mind by wicked works, yet now He has reconciled in the body of His flesh through death, to present you holy, and blameless and irreproachable in His sight' (vv. 19-22). Both these passages indicate how the will and pleasure of Jehovah for things in heaven and on earth will be successfully and satisfactorily carried out through the atonement of the blood of Christ's cross.

The fact of the Servant's satisfaction with His saving work is concluded in verse 11a, 'As a result of the anguish of His soul, He will see it [the results] and be satisfied' (NASB). The New International Version has, 'After the suffering of His soul, He will see the light [of life] and be satisfied.' But the main Hebrew text (the Masoretic Text) does not have 'the light of life'. It is found in the Septuagint (the Greek translation of the Hebrew Old Testament), and is most probably an early interpretation of verse 11a rather than the original reading. John L. Mackay is correct when he says, 'the verb [see] is to be heard as echoing the previous verse, where the Servant was said to "see His seed". 'The thought of the Servant's conscious awareness of all those for whom He has procured life is now reinforced with the statement that "He will be satisfied" with all that His suffering has achieved.'[5]

As the Servant of Jehovah, our Lord Jesus Christ, looks at God's saving plan and measures the price He had to pay to redeem damned humankind; how does He feel about it? The answer is: 'satisfied'! He is satisfied not to the limited and finite degree that a human being or even an angel would be satisfied, but to the measure of His infinite, divine capacity which is so vast that nothing short of a seed as numerous as the stars of the heaven and as the sand which is on the seashore could satisfy it. F.B. Meyer says, 'Great as the harvest of sin has been, we believe that the saved shall vastly outnumber the lost. Nothing less will satisfy Christ ... The curse gone from nature. Grace abounding much more where sin and death reigned. Man lifted nearer God than he could have been had he dwelt for ever in an unsullied paradise. The kingdoms of the world, and of all other worlds, become the kingdoms of our God and of His Christ ... We shall see the satisfactory termination of the mystery of evil. And if Christ is satisfied, we shall be. On this let us rest.'[6]

5. John L. Mackay, *Isaiah*, vol. 2, p. 362.

6. F.B. Meyer, *Christ in Isaiah*, pp. 149-151.

The design of Christ's offering for sin

> [11bcd] By his knowledge shall the righteous one, my servant,
>   make many to be accounted righteous,
> and he shall bear their iniquities (Isa. 53:11bcd, ESV).

According to J. Alec Motyer, 'Isaiah 53:11 is one of the fullest statements of atonement theology ever penned. (i) The Servant knows the needs to be met and what must be done. (ii) As "that righteous One, My Servant" He is both fully acceptable to the God our sins have offended and has been appointed by Him to the task. (iii) As righteous, He is free from every contagion of our sin. (iv) He identified Himself personally with our sin and need. (v) The emphatic pronoun "He" [shall bear their iniquities] underlines His personal commitment to this role. (vi) He accomplishes the task fully. Negatively, in the bearing of iniquity; positively, in the provision of righteousness.'[7]

With that summary in mind, let us proceed with examining the meaning of the words of v.11bcd, and then draw from them some important conclusions. The Hebrew word translated 'by His knowledge' could be a subjective possessive meaning the knowledge which the Servant possesses, or it could be an objective possessive meaning the knowledge that others come to possess of the Servant. E.J. Young rightly notes, 'If the phrase is speaking of the knowledge which the Servant Himself possesses, then the thought is that by means of this knowledge the Servant carries on His work of justification. Such a conception, however, appears to be quite foreign to the context. The justification of the many is accomplished, according to this verse, not by means of the knowledge which the Servant has, but by means of His bearing their iniquities. Hence, it is more in keeping with the context, and it is perfectly grammatical to translate "by the knowledge of Him", or "by knowing Him" ... This knowledge is not only intellectual apprehension of who He is and what He has done – although it certainly includes that – but it is also the practical appropriation of all His benefits ... It involves faith, trust, intellectual apprehension and belief. It is that intimate, experiential

7. J. Alec Motyer, *The Prophecy of Isaiah*, p. 442.

relationship which we have in mind when we speak of one person's knowing another ... and the expression rightly reminds me of the New Testament phrase "justification by faith". It is by or through knowing Him that the Servant justifies many.'[8]

The next clause ('make many to be accounted righteous') emphasises the righteousness of the Servant in Jehovah's eyes, because His obedience has been perfect throughout His life of service and suffering on earth. Moreover, because He has borne their iniquities and secured their pardon, the Servant is in a position to extend His righteousness to them; 'to make many to be accounted righteous'. It is a glorious and blessed exchange! The 'many' receive the righteousness of the Servant, and He receives their iniquities. And if we ask: Who are the many? The answer from this fourth song is that they are a vast multitude drawn by the Servant from the 'many nations' He will 'sprinkle' clean (52:15) with His blood, when Jehovah shall 'make His soul an offering for sin' (53:10), and the 'many' whom He 'shall justify' (53:11). This key concept of the 'many' is crucial to our understanding of the extent or efficacy of the atonement of Christ. It occurs at least 10 times in the New Testament (Matt. 8:11; 26:28; Mark 10:45; Luke 2:34; Rom. 4:17; 5:15, 19; 8:29; 12:5; Heb. 9:28). It is a precise company of Jews and Gentiles (Isa. 49:5-6), *numerous* but not *all-inclusive*.

In the light of the above, then, there are two important conclusions to be drawn from verses ten and eleven: First, negatively, *It was not God's will to make Jesus, His Servant, an offering for everybody's sin.* There is no such thing as universal atonement, because hell is not empty. In the Old Testament we read: 'The wicked shall be turned into hell, and all the nations that forget God' (Ps. 9:17); 'And many of those who sleep in the dust of the earth shall awake, some to everlasting life, some to shame and everlasting contempt' (Dan. 12:2). Again, in the New Testament we read: 'When the Son of Man comes ... He will sit on the throne of His glory. All the nations will be gathered before Him, and He will separate them one from another, as a shepherd divides his sheep from the goats. And He will set the sheep on His right hand, but the goats on the

---

8. E.J. Young, *Isaiah Fifty-Three*, p. 74.

:ft. Then the King will say to those on His right hand, "Come, you
lessed of My Father, inherit the kingdom prepared for you from
he foundation of the world ...Then He will also say to those on
he left hand, "Depart from Me, you cursed, into everlasting fire
repared for the devil and his angels'" (Matt. 25:31-34, 41; see also
: Thess. 1:6-10; Rev. 20:11-15).

How, then, are we to explain those references in the New
Testament where Christ's death is declared to be for the 'world'
John 3:16; 4:42; 1 John 2:1-2)? Because the Bible is God's word
nd cannot contradict itself, it is only logical to understand the word
world' in these verses as referring to the fact that Jesus died to save
ll mankind without *distinction* as to race, class or gender. It does not
efer to all mankind without *exception*. Moreover, it was necessary
o keep emphasising this, because most Jews instinctively thought
and still do) that God's Messiah will be the Saviour of Jews only.
t was also necessary to stress the fact that there is no limit to the
cope of Christ's offering for sin. Because of the infinite worth of
he divine–human Servant who suffered on the cross, there is infinite
irtue to save any number of sinners who come to Him for the
orgiveness of their sins. Christ's invitation to sinners for salvation
s universal. It is addressed to 'whoever believes in Him' and comes
vith the assurance that 'whoever calls on the name of the LORD shall
e saved' (John 3:16; Acts 2:21; see also Matt. 11:28-29). Those who
re condemned are those who refuse to believe (John 3:16-20).

The second important conclusion to be drawn from verses ten
nd eleven is that, positively, *it was God's will that Christ's death make
ertain the salvation of a great company of people that no one can number.*
n a true sense God desires all men to be saved, just as in a true sense
-Ie desires all men to be as holy as He is (Ezek. 33:11; 1 Tim. 2:3-6;
! Pet. 3:9; Lev. 19:2; 1 Pet. 1:16). But God who is all-wise and
ıll-loving in His sovereignty does not always decree that which
-Ie prescribes. For although He prescribes the remedy of Christ's
ıtoning work on the cross for every sinner, it is part of the mystery of
-His eternal purpose that He does not apply Christ's atoning work to
ıll sinners, but only to those who by His grace believe. It is therefore
:he *design* that God had in making His Servant an offering for the

199

sin of many that is being emphasised in Isaiah 53, and not the *worth* of His sacrifice. By its infinite worth it is *sufficient* for any number of sinners who will receive Jesus Christ as their Saviour, but by divine design it is *efficient* only for 'the many' who will believe in Him. Put another way, the design of Christ's atonement was *particular* and *definite* rather than *general* and *vague*. God's word never speaks of Jesus suffering on the cross simply to make salvation *possible* for everybody, but *certain* for nobody.

In the inscrutable wisdom of the Godhead, it was determined that choosing to save a numerous but not all-inclusive company of undeserving sinners would magnify the grace and justice of God in a far greater way than any other plan could. So, in the counsel of the Trinity, before the world was made, there was perfect unity within the Godhead with regard to the plan of salvation. The Father in unsolicited, unmerited love will choose in eternity past an untold number of helpless, fallen human beings to be His Son's bride (John 17:1, 2, 6; 1 Cor. 1:26-29; Eph. 1:3-6; 1 Thess. 1:4). The work of the Son will be to redeem them by becoming a man and dying as a sin offering to remove their guilt and impute His righteousness to them (Isa. 53:10-11; Mark 10:45; John 1:29; 6:51; 2 Cor. 5:18, 21; Gal. 3:13-14; Heb. 2:14-18; Rev. 13:8). The work of the Holy Spirit will be to convict of sin those whom the Father has chosen and the Son has redeemed; to draw them to Christ in repentance and faith, and progressively transform them into the image of their Redeemer (John 6:65; 16:7-11; Acts 10:42-48; 1 Cor. 3:15-18).

Do you realise, Christian, what a delight you are to your Saviour? True, there is remaining sin in every believer (Rom. 7:18-25; Eph. 4:17-24), but our gracious Lord sees the travail of His soul and is satisfied with its end results. Right now, today, He is enjoying the sheer pleasure of making many sinners to be accounted right-eous in God's sight. Just as at creation He looked at everything He had made and 'saw that it was very good' (Gen. 1:31; John 1:1-3; Col. 1:16); so after Calvary, when He saw His 'new creation', He was satisfied with what He saw (2 Cor. 5:17). Things may look bleak at times, but Jesus, God's almighty Servant and Redeemer, is the One in whose hand the will of God will prosper. The completion of the church, His bride, is guaranteed (Eph. 5:25-27; Rev. 21:1-2). His offering for sin is a remedy that evil cannot reverse. Nothing will ever rob Christ of His hard-won right to 'justify many'.

If, after reading and thinking about verses ten and eleven, there is, in your heart, the least desire to be numbered among the 'many to be accounted righteous', then come to Jesus in faith. He has given us this assurance: 'all that the Father gives Me will come to Me, and the one who comes to Me I will by no means cast out' (John 6:37). Come to Him in believing prayer and He will make Himself known to you. And as you put your trust in the efficacy of His 'offering for sin', it will become efficacious for you. Your sins will be charged to Christ, and His righteousness credited to you.

For your encouragement, here is how the Holy Spirit drew Charles Simeon (1759-1836), a famous evangelical Anglican minister, to Christ. Upon beginning his studies at King's College, Cambridge, he discovered that attendance at Holy Communion was compulsory:

> On being informed that I must, the thought rushed into my mind that Satan himself was as fit to attend as I; and that if I must attend, I must prepare for my attendance there ... My distress of mind continued for about three months, and well might it have continued for years, since my sins were more in number than the hairs on my head ... But in Passion Week, as I was reading Bishop Wilson on the Lord's Supper, I met with an expression to this effect – 'That the Jews knew what they did, when they transferred their sin to the head of their offering.' The thought came into my mind: What, may I transfer all my guilt to another? Has God provided an Offering for me, that I may lay my sins on His head? Then, God willing, I will not bear them on my own soul one moment longer. Accordingly I sought to lay my sins upon the sacred head of Jesus ... and on the Sunday morning, Easter day, April 4, I awoke early with those words upon my heart and lips: 'Jesus Christ is risen today! Hallelujah! Hallelujah!'

From that hour peace flowed in rich abundance into my soul; and at the Lord's Table in our Chapel, I had the sweetest access to God through my blessed Saviour.[9]

---

9. Quoted by Handley Moule in his biography of *Charles Simeon* (IVP, 1965), pp. 25, 26.

11

The Fourth Servant Song VIII:
Exalted as Victor and Intercessor for His people

53:12 Therefore I will divide him a portion with the many,
    and he shall divide the spoil [booty] with the strong,
because he poured out his soul to death
    and was numbered with the transgressors;
yet he bore the sin of many,
    and makes intercession for the transgressors.
        (Isa. 53:12, ESV).

It is impossible to mistake the almighty, majestic Person speaking in verse twelve. It is Jehovah Himself. And it is fitting that as He introduced His Servant in the opening words of the fourth song as Someone who 'will be high and lifted up and greatly exalted' (52:13, NASB), so in these closing words, Jehovah should re-emphasise His supreme exaltation in spite of a cruel and humiliating death. We have watched, as chapter 53 has unfolded, how the Servant will be 'despised and rejected by men' as One 'esteemed ... smitten by God, and afflicted. But He was wounded for our transgressions, He was crushed for our iniquities', for in reality 'the LORD has laid on Him the iniquity of us all', and 'He was cut off from the land of the living', and given 'a grave with the wicked'.

That, however, is not to be the final word on the Servant's divinely-appointed career. Because 'it was the will of the LORD to crush Him' and 'make his soul an offering for sin, he shall see his offspring;

he shall prolong his days; the will of the LORD shall prosper in his hand. Out of the anguish of his soul he shall see and be satisfied; by his knowledge shall the righteous one, my servant, make many to be accounted righteous, and he shall bear their iniquities' (vv. 10-11, ESV). In other words, because the Servant will perfectly satisfy the penalty demanded by the Law for the sins of Jehovah's people (v. 8d), He will be raised from the grave to enjoy the fruit of the travail of His soul for eternity. It remains for us now to see in verse twelve how greatly Jehovah shall exalt and reward His Servant for His willing, humble and perfect obedience to the penal, substitutionary death assigned to Him. None could ever deserve more or better than Jesus Christ. If He were without due recognition or reward, heaven would surely be charged with failing to value faithful, God-honouring service.

But what reward should the Servant have? What could compensate the Son of God for being 'emptied' of His divine privileges, in order to take 'the form of a servant' and be 'made in the likeness of men' (Phil. 2:7, NASB)? It involved unparalleled self-sacrifice all the way to the cross, which called for a laying aside of His divine glory behind the veil of His flesh; a voluntary restraint of divine power and wisdom; an acceptance of hardship, isolation, ill-treatment, malice and misunderstanding; and a death that involved not just extreme physical agony, but ultimately the damnation of hell itself. What reward could be adequate?

The answer lies in verse twelve. And to understand properly what this reward would be, we must, of course, carefully ascertain the meaning of its key words. The first is the word translated 'great' in line one: 'Therefore I will divide Him a portion with the great' (NKJV, NASB, NIV). The Hebrew word can mean 'great', but its basic meaning is 'many' (ESV). Which meaning we choose entirely depends on the context, and the context of Isaiah 53 demands that it be translated as 'many', for two reasons. In the first place, the word translated 'great' in verse 12a, as Henri Blocher points out, 'is one which keeps recurring throughout the fourth song ... In all other instances, including those immediately before and after this occurrence, it is rendered "many." Many were astonished at the Servant [52:14];

He will sprinkle many nations [52:15]; He will make many to be accounted righteous [53:11]; He bore the sin of many [53:12e]. Such repetition is surely not without significance; consistency demands that the word be translated "many" throughout the entire passage, and therefore in verse 12a also: "I will divide Him a portion with the many." The "many" are the multitude of those who will benefit from the Servant's work.'[1]

In the second place, the context of chapter 53 and the whole of the New Testament militates against translating the Hebrew word as 'great', for it takes away from the supreme glory of the messianic Servant. As John L. Mackay argues, 'This makes the Servant one among the many victorious conquerors that earth has seen. While being reckoned as a prince among princes is a significant advance on a pauper's grave His enemies would have accorded Him (cf. 53:9), it fails to bring out the unique status of the Servant and His achievement. The translation offered ["Therefore I will allot to Him the many, and He will divide the strong as booty"] is a grammatically well-grounded rendering of the text, and brings the song to a resounding climax. The resurrected Servant is here alone on the victor's podium, not lined up among a crowd in the hall of fame.'[2]

Surely no one can read this amazing fourth song and come to the conclusion that after rising from the dead and making many to be accounted righteous, the Servant's reward will be no more than to have a portion with 'the great'. The unanimous testimony of Scripture is that Jesus Christ is incomparable! No other great leader on earth has risen from the grave and become the sole heir of an everlasting and universal kingdom ('He shall sprinkle many nations'). Our Lord says of Himself, 'I am He who lives, and was dead, and behold, I am alive for evermore. Amen. And I have the keys of Hades and of Death' [of everything, the living and the dead; Rev. 1:18].

The second line of verse twelve has a similar weakness in the traditional translation, because it portrays the Servant dividing the

---

1. Henri Blocher, *Songs of the Servant*, p. 66.
2. John L. Mackay, *Isaiah*, vol. 2, p. 364.

spoil with the strong: 'Therefore I will divide Him a portion with the great, and He shall divide the spoil with the strong.' The word translated 'divide' is literally 'to allocate', and when it is translated as such, line two can only make sense if the Hebrew words are translated: 'and the strong He will allocate as spoil.' John L. Mackay suggests, 'It is possible to see in "strong" a reflection of the "kings" of 52:15 who were rendered speechless when they realized what the Servant had done [in gaining everlasting dominion by sprinkling many nations with the shedding of His blood]. Now they are vanquished and treated as spoil to be disposed of as He wishes.'[3]

The Hebrew of the first two lines, then, is an exclamatory statement calling attention to a profound reversal of the Servant's position. By His 'offering for sin', the Servant has received as His own people 'the many' whom He died to save, and become the King of kings before whom all kings 'shall shut their mouths' (52:15), having become spoil for His disposal. It is important to notice that though He is 'allocated' the many, the 'strong' are not given to the Servant by some other power, but are His 'spoil' by right of conquest. Jesus Christ is victor over Satan, sin, death and hell (Rev. 20:7-15).

The Servant will be given many devotees

Jesus Christ, the suffering Servant, will not die in vain. 'When the LORD makes His soul an offering for sin, He shall see His seed.' This was the plan devised and agreed upon by the Triune God in eternity past: 'I will declare the decree: The LORD said to Me, "You are My Son; today I have begotten You. Ask of Me, and I will give You the nations for Your inheritance, and the ends of the earth for Your possession"' (Ps. 2:7-8). The giving of a people from the nations by the Father to the Son was decreed in eternity past when their names were 'written before the foundation of the world in the book of life of the Lamb that was slain' (Rev. 13:8, ESV; see also Eph. 1:4). And now here in Isaiah 53:12, Jehovah says, 'Therefore [because His righteous Servant has borne their iniquities and made many to be accounted righteous] I will allocate to Him the many.' It was determined before the world began.

---

3. John L. Mackay, *Isaiah*, vol. 2, p. 364

This is a precious truth repeated several times in the New Testament, and nowhere more particularly than in the prayer Jesus prayed the night before He died. It is stated eight times in John 17. In verse two He prays, 'You have *given* Him [the Son] authority over all flesh, that He should give eternal life to as many as You have *given* Him.' Then we have it stated twice in verse six: 'I have manifested Your name to the men whom You have *given* Me out of the world. They were Yours, You *gave* them to Me' out of a world of fallen, sinful human beings. And then it occurs four more times in verses 9, 11, 12 and 24: 'I do not pray for the world but for those You have *given* Me, for they are Yours ... Holy Father, keep through Your name those whom You have *given* Me ... those whom You *gave* Me I have kept ... Father, I desire that they also whom You gave Me may be with Me where I am' (italics added).

But this prayer is not the only occasion on which our Lord Jesus refers to His followers as those who have been given to Him by God the Father. Earlier on in His ministry Jesus said, 'All that the Father gives Me will come to Me, and the one who comes to Me I will by no means cast out ... This is the will of the Father who sent Me, that of all He has given Me I should lose nothing, but should raise it up at the last day' (John 6:37, 39). Again, in John 10:27-29, our Lord says, 'My sheep hear My voice, and I know them, and they follow Me. And I give them eternal life, and they shall never perish; neither shall anyone snatch them out of My hand. My Father, who has given them to Me, is greater than all; and no one is able to snatch them out of My Father's hand.' Elsewhere, in Hebrews 2:13, the writer quotes a prophecy from Isaiah 8:18 and applies it to Jesus Christ: 'Here am I and the children whom God has given Me.' Unless we grasp this truth that all believers in the one true God are His predetermined gift to His Son, the messianic Servant, we do not fully understand the plan of salvation or the message of the gospel.

How many are 'the many'? We are prone to think, to our loss of morale, that they will not be very many. But the Father does not bestow paltry gifts. Jehovah will not give His Servant a meagre or modest reward for the enormous suffering He will have to endure to pay the penalty of sin. That is not the meaning being conveyed in verse 12a. Rather, the opposite is true! The term 'many' is used here and in other similar passages to designate the truth that although the final number of the saved will be very many indeed, it will not include every human being (Matt. 8:11-12; 26:28; Mark 10:45; Rom. 8:29; Heb. 9:28). More positively, when the apostle John is given a vision of the redeemed in heaven, he says, 'I looked, and behold, a great multitude which no one could number, of all nations, tribes, peoples, and tongues, standing before the throne and before the Lamb, clothed with white robes, with palm branches in their hands, and crying out with a loud voice, saying, "Salvation belongs to our God who sits on the throne, and the Lamb"' [Christ, the Servant; Rev. 7:9-10; cf. Isa. 53:7; John 1:29]. The 'many' are also the countless spiritual descendants from all the nations of the earth that God promised Abraham (Gen. 15:5-6; 22:15-18; Gal. 3:26-29).

The Servant will vanquish the strong

Verse twelve says not only that Jehovah 'will allocate to Him the many', but also that the Servant as victor 'will allocate [or dispose of] the strong as spoil'. Spoil is plunder taken or destroyed in war. It is a military analogy that runs right through the Bible which sees history, especially biblical history, as a prolonged spiritual conflict. It began with Satan and many of the angelic host who rebelled against God. Being cast out of heaven, they are carrying on the war on earth, attempting to thwart God's purpose for creating the earth and the human race (Rev. 12:7-12). Thus, Satan is called 'the ruler of this world' and the 'god of this age', and it is said that 'the whole world lies under the sway of the wicked one' (John 12:31; 2 Cor. 4:4; 1 John 5:19).

The apostle Paul therefore urges us to 'fight the good fight of faith' and 'endure hardship as a good soldier of Jesus Christ' (1 Tim. 6:12; 2 Tim. 2:3). More specifically, he says, 'My brethren, be strong in the Lord and in the power of His might. Put on the whole armour of God, that you may be able to stand against the wiles of the devil. For we do not wrestle against flesh and blood, but against principalities [rulers], against powers [the authorities], against the rulers of the darkness of this age, against spiritual hosts of wickedness in the heavenly places' (Eph. 6:10-12). Against our powerful foes, we are not alone! We have a champion, for the writer of Hebrews says that 'in bringing many sons to glory', it was fitting for God the Father to 'make the captain of their salvation perfect through sufferings' AV). The term 'captain' can also be translated as 'Prince' or 'author' Acts 5:31; Heb. 5:9; 12:2). In its basic meaning it refers to someone who is a leader or originator of a movement.

This is how God's people are consistently portrayed in the Bible, and the glorious truth that we are being told in Isaiah 53:12b is that he victorious outcome of the war with Satan and his hosts has been predetermined by God: 'the strong He will allocate as spoil'. The decisive battle will be fought and won, not at Armageddon when he Son of God comes as King of kings and Lord of lords to *reign*, but at Calvary when He comes as the Servant of God to *suffer* for he sins of the world. In between the first coming of Jesus that will spell Satan's *defeat* and the second coming that will seal his *doom*, there will occur the 'mopping up' operations.

The devil will then be somewhat in the position that the Axis forces (Germany and Italy) were in during the Second World War. The Normandy landings by the Allied forces in June,1944 and the battle of Caen to which they led proved utterly decisive for the outcome of the war. There was no denying that the critical battle had been won. The Axis forces could look forward to nothing but final defeat. But the war went on. They refused to accept defeat until they were completely routed. Sometimes moments of significant success attended their continuing struggle, but nothing could alter the fact that they were doomed to destruction. The ultimate Victory Day would dawn, as it did in 1945. That is how it will be with Satan.

Looking back to Calvary, the apostle Paul describes our Lord's decisive victory in these astonishing words: 'God ... raised Him from the dead. And you, who were dead in your trespasses ... God made alive together with Him, having forgiven us all our trespasses, by cancelling the record of debt that stood against us with its legal demands. This He set aside, nailing it to the cross. He disarmed the rulers and authorities [mg. demonic] and put them to open shame, by triumphing over them in Him' (Col. 2:12-15, ESV).

There could be no meaningful, God-glorifying victory ove the devil without the cross. Of course, God could have destroyed Satan and Adam and Eve right after the Fall, and be done with them all. But it would have been a hollow victory because God' plan for humankind and creation would have been thwarted (an impossibility for God). Rather, true victory over evil could only be achieved if God's original plan were salvaged in conjunction with the destruction of Satan and all his rebel armies. This is what the Servant's single offering for sin did.

Because the penalty of our sin was paid in full by Christ on the cross, God can justly forgive sinners who by His grace turn to Him in repentance and faith, 'cancelling the record of debt that stood against us with its legal demands ... nailing it to the cross'. That being the case, the record of our debt has been wiped clean. Every single entry has been deleted and now nothing remains to hinder our fellowship with God. We have been reconciled and restored to favour with God. His plan for humankind and creation can be achieved even *beyond what was originally intended.*

But the cross meant not only the cancellation of the record of sin's debt, but also the conquest of the powers of evil. The victory is pictured here by Paul in terms of a Roman triumphal military procession. At the head of the parade came the victorious general, followed by his regiments in their best uniform. At the back came the prisoners of war, stripped and forlorn. Shamed, and exposed before the cheering crowds in Rome, no one was left in doubt that their enemy had been roundly defeated. That is the message every Christian should draw from the cross, for there 'He [God] disarmed the rulers and author- ities and put them to open shame, by triumphing over them in Him [Christ]. Indeed, as J. Philip Arthur says, 'While the devil retains a certain limited freedom of movement, he is already a defeated foe People who enjoy God's forgiveness should not be flippant about the evil one. They should certainly pay him a healthy respect, but equally they should not react towards him with slavish fear.'[4]

There is an incident in the Gospels in which our Lord Jesus pro- claims and pictures His conquest of Satan (Matt. 12:22-30; see also

---

4. J. Philip Arthur, *Christ All-Sufficient* (Evangelical Press, 2007), p. 364.

Mark 3:20-27; Luke 11:14-22). When the Pharisees dismissed His healing of a demon-possessed man as a work done by the power of 'Beelzebub, the ruler of the demons', He countered by saying, 'Every kingdom divided against itself will not stand. And if Satan casts out Satan, he is divided against himself. How then will his kingdom stand? ... But if I cast out demons by the Spirit of God, surely the kingdom of God has come upon you. Or else how can one enter a strong man's house and plunder his goods, unless he first binds the strong man? And then he will plunder his house.' Luke has, 'When a strong man, fully armed, guards his own palace, his goods are safe; but when one stronger than he attacks him and overcomes him, he takes away his armour in which he trusted and divides his spoil' (vv. 21-22, ESV).

Although Jesus is speaking specifically of the casting out of a demon, He is only using it as an example of what is true when He delivers anyone from any kind of demonic oppression, for it was Satan who brought sin and sickness and death into the world. In every case there has to be a spiritual coup or palace revolution. Anyone who needs to be saved, in whatever sense, is being kept under guard in the palace of Satan, the 'strong man'. Only the 'One stronger than he' can pull off the successful spiritual coup we call salvation. But we must never think he will not put up a fight. When our Lord cast out evil spirits, they did not always leave the person peacefully, but sometimes flung them to the ground (Luke 4:35).

In the light of this New Testament teaching, how then do we understand Isaiah 53:12b: 'And the strong He will allocate as spoil'? The 'strong' obviously refers to Satan and all his rebel followers, angelic as well as human. These will be treated by the Servant as 'spoil' to be allocated at the end of the age to 'the lake of fire and brimstone where ... they will be tormented day and night forever and ever' (Rev. 20:10; see also 12-15). But not all of the spoil will be destroyed. As the war wages on, much of the 'strong man's' goods are being plundered by the 'stronger than he' for the fellowship and service of Jehovah. Thus it is written, '"They shall be Mine," says the LORD of hosts [of the armies of heaven], "on the day that I make them My jewels [mg. literally *special treasure*]. And I will spare them as a man spares his own son who serves him." Then you shall again discern between the righteous and the wicked, between one who serves God and one who does not serve Him' (Mal. 3:17-18; see also Dan. 12:1-3 and Matt. 18:24-30).

Last but not least, even the universe which Satan usurped at the Fall, will be reclaimed by the Servant/Christ, cleansed by fire to remove the curse of sin, and transformed into 'new heavens and a new earth in which righteousness dwells' (2 Pet. 3:10-13; Rev. 21:1; 22:3; Isa. 65:17-19). Satan is a defeated and doomed foe, but he is not by any means dead. Until Jesus Christ returns, we are told to 'Be sober, be vigilant; because your adversary the devil walks about like a roaring lion, seeking whom he may devour. Resist him, steadfast in the faith, knowing that the same sufferings are experienced by your brotherhood in the world.' Again, in Revelation 12 we are warned that 'the devil has come down to you in great wrath, because he knows that his time is short!' (v. 12, ESV).

But we are not to lose heart. To quote Michael Green, 'The ultimate outcome is not in doubt. Satan will be defeated and abolished. Eternity will not be disfigured by the self-seeking, deceit, hatred and accusations of the Adversary, but God will be all in all and the redeemed will be for ever satisfied with their Lord, who has turned Paradise lost into Paradise regained.'[5] Indeed, Jesus, Jehovah's Servant, will give His redeemed people far more than we ever lost in the Fall.

The Servant's rewards are due to His sin-bearing death

The next three lines of verse 12 give us the reason why Jehovah has allocated 'the many' as the Servant's portion and why 'the strong' will be spoil, to be treated as He wishes. It is 'because He poured out His soul to death and was numbered with the transgressors; yet He bore the sin of many.' The Hebrew word translated 'because' is the strongest expression of cause and result Isaiah could have used. To quote Joseph A. Alexander, 'This phrase does not simply mean *because*, but expresses more distinctly the idea of reward or

---

5. Michael Green, *I Believe in Satan's Downfall* (Eerdmans, 1981), p. 219.

compensation.'[6] It could be rendered 'for the very reason that He poured out His soul to death'. His rewards are exactly what the Servant's unique death merited.

Firstly, He laid down His life of His own free will: 'because He poured out His soul [or life, NIV] to death.' Although He was without sin and therefore death had no claim or power over Him (Rom. 6:2), the Son of God and the Son of Man willingly and unreservedly exposed Himself to death. The word 'poured' means literally to 'empty to the last drop'.[7] It calls to mind both our Lord's words in John 10:17-18, 'Therefore My Father loves Me, because I lay down My life that I might take it again. No one takes it from Me, but I lay it down of Myself'; and Paul's words in Philippians 2:7-8, 'But emptied Himself ... becoming obedient to the point of death, even death on a cross' (NASB).

Secondly, the Servant of Jehovah personally identified Himself with the spiritual rebels whom He came to save by His death. Verse 12d literally reads, 'And let Himself be numbered with the transgressors.' The word *transgressors* is a participle, meaning those living in a state of rebellion. In other words, He was content not only to suffer the loss of His life, but also the rightful outcome of His record of perfect obedience to the will of God and be reckoned among the rebels who are defying the authority of Jehovah. But to say that Jesus was content to let Himself be numbered with those in rebellion against God is still putting it too mildly. Hebrews 12:2 captures the true spirit of that epic moment by speaking of Jesus as 'the author and finisher of our faith, who for the joy that was set before Him endured the cross, despising [or scorning] the shame.' Lesser beings would have categorically refused the shame of being unjustly identified with law-breakers, but not Jesus. He scorned the shame, and joyfully took His place with us for the greater glory of God and the good of humankind.

Thirdly, verse 12e says that the messianic Servant was rewarded and greatly exalted because although He was absolutely sinless and righteous (v. 9cd), 'yet He Himself bore the sin of many'. He acted

---

6. Joseph A. Alexander, *Isaiah* (Kregel, 1992), vol. 2, p. 307.

7. David Baron, *The Servant of Jehovah*, p. 138.

as their substitute when He lifted the guilt of their sin off their shoulders and bore the punishment it deserved in His own body and soul on the cross. The 'many' had sinned in rebelling against the authority and commandments of God, but God's humble and righteous Servant took the guilt of their sin upon Himself in order that He might 'make many to be accounted righteous' (v. 11). As Paul explains in 2 Corinthians 5:20-21, 'We implore you on Christ's behalf, be reconciled to God. For He made Him who knew no sin to be sin for us, that we might become the righteousness of God in Him.'

It is a most glorious and blessed exchange for 'the many'. And it is little wonder that in the Gospels God the Father says to His Servant, 'This is My beloved Son in whom I am well pleased' (Matt. 3:17; 17:5); or that Jesus said, 'Therefore My Father loves Me, because I lay down My life [for the sheep] that I may take it again' (John 10:17). The Son of God had to love sinners utterly, to exchange the virtue of His sinless life on earth for the guilt of the sinful lives of the many. The world has never seen, nor ever will see such a magnanimous and incredibly generous Victor. All human conquerors become hardened by their bloody and cruel exploits. But instead of spilling the blood of His ungodly enemies, our merciful and gracious Conqueror allowed His own blood to be 'shed for many for the remission of [their] sins' (Matt. 26:28).

Here is good news for sinners of every kind. To quote Paul Tournier, 'The guilt that men are never able to efface, in spite of sacrifices, penance, remorse and vain regrets, God Himself wipes away; and men are at once freed from their past and transformed.'[8] The cross is not some fanciful religious idea. The cross is the power of God to save sinners. Christ is actively saving guilty rebels today. His cross is a power that Satan and sin cannot withstand. Nothing will ever stop Christ from receiving the rewards of His hard-fought victory. The Father will allocate to Him every one of 'the many' He has promised His Son. And the Son will destroy all His impenitent enemies in the lake of fire and brimstone. Who else would willingly bear your guilt and punishment? Who else can love and keep you so

8. Paul Tournier, *Guilt & Grace* (Harper & Row, 1962), p. 184.

utterly and eternally? You can be freed from your past. But Christ is the only One who can do that for you or anyone else.

The Servant will intercede for the transgressors

Verse 12f, 'And makes intercession for the transgressors.' E.J. Young says, 'We may bring out the thought by saying that "He makes" – for the verb should be translated by the present and not by the past – a meritorious and prevailing intercession. Thus the chapter closes with a statement of priestly activity upon the part of the Servant. In the midst of His suffering, He makes intercession. Even while others regarded Him as a transgressor, He, the great High Priest, was praying for those who were the real transgressors.'[9] Its beginning, of course, was the prayer our Lord prayed on the cross: 'Father, forgive them, for they do not know what they do' (Luke 23:34). But Christ's continuous and effectual high priestly intercession for the transgressors is referred to in several places in the New Testament where we are given some insight into the nature of His prayers.

To begin with, Jesus prays for the conversion of transgressors living in a state of rebellion against God. Peter says, 'Him God has exalted to His right hand to be Prince and Saviour, to give repentance to Israel and forgiveness of sins' (Acts 5:31). Having paid the penalty of sin and been exalted to the seat of supreme authority, the Servant is active in dispensing the gifts of repentance and faith to all 'the many' for whom He died. He prays for the Father to send the Holy Spirit to give men and women the desire and the ability to turn from their sin in repentance, and believe in Him for salvation.

Our great High Priest acts as mediator and 'makes intercession'. As J. Alec Motyer, again, explains, 'The base meaning of ["makes intercession"] is "to cause to reach", and hence to "cause someone's plea to reach someone's ears" (to intercede) or to "introduce someone into someone's presence" (to mediate). The Servant is thus a go-between, interposing between two parties, not as a barrier but as a bridge. In verse six, the LORD put His Servant in between, using Him as a means of disposing of that (our iniquity) which alienated

9. E.J. Young, *Isaiah Fifty-Three*, p. 76.

Him from us. Here the Servant comes voluntarily to stand with us so that when He had borne our sin He might bring us to God.'[10]

This is the gospel in a nutshell, the good news that Christians bring to the world. On earth the Servant, Jesus the Christ, 'bore the sin of many'. In heaven He intercedes and mediates for us, causing our plea to reach the ears of the Father, and His satisfaction for our sins to bring us to God. Here are some significant verses that support this wonderful work of our Saviour:

> I have manifested Your name to the men whom You have given Me out of the world ... I pray for them. I do not pray for the world but for those whom You have given Me, for they are Yours ... Now I am no longer in the world, but these are in the world, and I come to You. Holy Father, keep through Your name those whom You have given Me, that they may be one as We are ... keep them from the evil one ... Sanctify them by Your truth. Your word is truth (John 17:6-17).

> And the Lord said, 'Simon, Simon! Indeed, Satan has asked for you, that he may sift you as wheat. But I have prayed for you, that your faith should not fail; and when you have returned to Me, strengthen your brethren (Luke 22:31-32).

> Who shall bring a charge against God's elect? It is God who justifies. Who is he who condemns? It is Christ who died, and furthermore is also risen, who is even at the right hand of God, who also makes intercession for us (Rom. 8:33-34).

> Because Jesus lives forever, He has a permanent priesthood. Therefore he is able to save completely those who come to God through him, because he always lives to intercede for them (Heb. 7:24-25, NIV).

> If anyone sins, we have an Advocate with the Father, Jesus Christ the righteous. And He Himself is the propitiation for our sins, and not for ours only but also for the whole world (1 John 2:1-2).

---

10. J. Alec Motyer, *The Prophecy of Isaiah*, p. 443.

This amazing fact should fill every believer with hope and excitement. 'Because He poured out His soul to death … and He bore the sin of many', we have an Advocate before God the Father who can plead for our sins to be forgiven. The old proverb, 'He who is his own lawyer has a fool for a client' is never more true than when we all have to stand before the bar of God's judgment. Time is limited and uncertain. The Bible says, 'Now is the favourable time; behold, now is the day of salvation'; and again, 'Seek the LORD while He may be found, call upon Him while He is near' (2 Cor. 6:2, ESV; Isa. 55:6). The only reason why this godless world continues is because our great High Priest is still making intercession for transgressors to be saved. As Peter says, 'The Lord is not slack concerning His promise [to return and judge the world], as some count slackness, but is longsuffering towards us, not willing that any should perish but that all should come to repentance' (2 Pet. 3:9). Don't presume on God's mercy. His patience is not unlimited. Call upon Jesus now to represent you on Judgment Day.

That brings us to the end of our meditation on these glorious Servant Songs in Isaiah. Nowhere else in the Old Testament is the suffering and exaltation of Christ as God's sin-bearing Servant more gloriously and fully portrayed. We are humbled that the Son of God, who is 'very God of very God', should take our flesh (apart from our sinful nature) and voluntarily restrain His divine powers so that He might 'give His life a ransom for many'. If His Father is well pleased with His Son's perfect life and saving work, how much more should you and I be?

Let me close then with these appealing words from a tract by John Mason (1646-1694):

Invitation to sinners

Have you sins, or have you none? If you have, whither should you go, but to the Lamb of God, which taketh away the sins of the world? Have you souls, or have you none? If you have, where should you go, but to the Saviour of souls? Is there a life to come, or is there not? If there is, where would you go but to Him, who only hath the words of eternal life? Is there a wrath to come, or is there not? If there is, where should you go but to Him, who only can deliver from the wrath to come?

And will the Saviour not receive you? If He yielded Himself into the hands of them that sought His life, will He hide Himself from the hearts of them that seek His mercy? If He was willing to be taken by the hand of violence, is He not more willing to be taken by the hands of faith? He that died for your sins, will He cast you off for your infirmities? O come, come, come! I charge you, come. I beseech you, come. Come, and He will give you life. Come, and He will give you rest. Come, and He will receive you. Knock, and He will open to you. Look to Him, and He will save you.

Did ever any come to Jesus for a cure, and go away without it? You would find something in yourself, but you find nothing but what you have reason to be ashamed of; but let not that hinder, but further your coming. Come as you are; come poor, come needy, come naked, come empty, come wretched, only come, only believe. His heart is free, His arms are open; 'tis His joy and His crown to receive you. If you are willing, He never was otherwise.

Grace
Publications

Grace Publications Trust

Grace Publication Trust is a not for profit organisation that exists to glorify God by making the truth of God's Word (as declared in the Baptist Confessions of 1689 and 1966) clear and understandable, so that:

- Christians will be helped to preach Christ
- Christians will know Christ better and delight in him more
- Christians will be equipped to live for Christ
- Seekers will come to know Christ

From its beginning in the late 1970s the Trust has published simplified and modernised versions of important Christian books written earlier, for example by some of the Reformers and Puritans. These books have helped introduce the riches of the past to a new generation and have proved particularly useful in parts of Asia and Africa where English is widely spoken as a second language. These books are now appearing in editions co-published with Christian Focus as *Grace Essentials*.

More details of the Trust's work can be found on the web site at: *www.gracepublications.co.uk*.

ISAIAH
BY THE DAY

A New Devotional Translation

Alec Motyer

Isaiah by the Day
A New Devotional Translation
ALEC MOTYER

These daily devotionals are birthed from a lifetime of study on the prophecy of Isaiah. Day by day you will be provided with passages from Isaiah and an opportunity to explore the passage further. Take time to acquaint yourself with these passages from God's Word and treasure them in your heart.

Dr Alec Motyer (1924-2016) was a well-known Bible expositor and from an early age had a love for studying God's Word. He was principal of Trinity College, Bristol and wrote many widely appreciated commentaries and other books.

ISBN: 978-1-84550-654-4

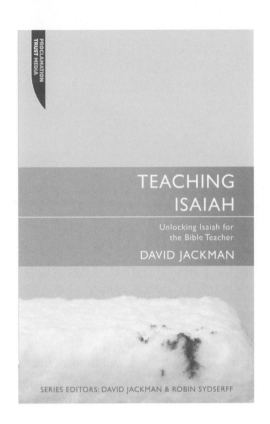

Teaching Isaiah
Unlocking Isaiah for the Bible Teacher
DAVID JACKMAN

This is not another commentary but a useful resource, which will help the pastor/ preacher, a small group leader or a youth worker communicate a message of grace when speaking from the book of Isaiah. It will give you help in planning and executing a lesson in particular with background, structure, key points and application.

Teaching Isaiah is part of the 'Teaching the Bible' series and is published in conjunction with Proclamation Trust Media whose aim is to encourage ministry that seeks above all to expound the Bible as God's Word for today.

ISBN: 978-1-84550-565-3

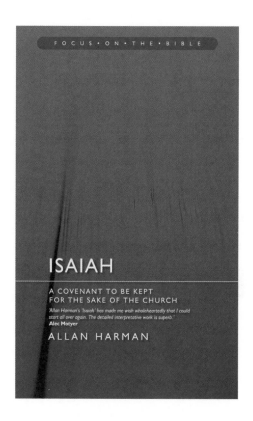

Isaiah

A Covenant to be Kept for the Sake of the Church

ALLAN HARMAN

This is a key Old Testament book, as well as charting a key change in the life of God's people it provides some of the most important prophecies fulfilled only in the life of Jesus of Nazareth. Its lessons for the contemporary church are particularly apt.

Too often modern commentaries become a discussion between commentators rather than an exploration of what the text has to say to contemporary readers. Allan Harman's methods follow those of Leon Morris and Allan McRae in that he devotes most of his energy to discovering what God is saying through his prophet, rather than what we are saying amongst ourselves.

ISBN: 978-1-84550-053-5

Christian Focus Publications

Our mission statement –

STAYING FAITHFUL
In dependence upon God we seek to impact the world through
literature faithful to His infallible Word, the Bible. Our aim is to
ensure that the Lord Jesus Christ is presented as the only hope
to obtain forgiveness of sin, live a useful life and look forward to
heaven with Him.

Our books are published in four imprints:

CHRISTIAN
FOCUS

Popular works including biographies, commentaries, basic doctrine
and Christian living.

CHRISTIAN
HERITAGE

Books representing some of the
best material from the rich heritage
of the church.

MENTOR

Books written at a level suitable
for Bible College and seminary
students, pastors, and other serious readers. The imprint includes
commentaries, doctrinal studies,
examination of current issues and
church history.

CF4•K

Children's books for quality Bible
teaching and for all age groups: Sunday
school curriculum, puzzle and activity
books; personal and family devotional
titles, biographies and inspirational sto-
ries – because you are never too young
to know Jesus!

Christian Focus Publications Ltd,
Geanies House, Fearn, Ross-shire,
IV20 1TW, Scotland, United Kingdom.
www.christianfocus.com